LIGHT MUSIC IN BRITAIN SINCE 1870: A SURVEY

In memory of
Jennie

Light Music in Britain since 1870:
A Survey

Geoffrey Self

Ashgate

Aldershot • Burlington USA • Singapore • Sydney

Published by
Ashgate Publishing Limited
Gower House
Croft Road
Aldershot
Hants GU11 3HR
England

Ashgate Publishing Company
131 Main Street
Burlington, VT 05401-5600 USA

Ashgate website: http://www.ashgate.com

British Library Cataloguing-in-Publication data

Self, Geoffrey
    Light music in Britain since 1870: A survey
    1. Music – Great Britain – 19th century – History and
    criticism 2. Music – Great Britain – 20th century – History
    and criticism 3. Music and society – Great Britain – History
    – 19th century 4. Music and society – Great Britain –
    History – 20th century
    I. Title
    781.6'4'0941'0904

Library of Congress Cataloging-in-Publication data

Self, Geoffrey.
    Light music in Britain since 1870: A survey / Geoffrey Self.
        p. cm.
    Includes bibliographical references and index.
    ISBN 1-85928-337-3 (alk. paper)
        1. Music – Great Britain – 19th century – History and criticism. 2. Music – Great
    Britain – 20th century – History and criticism. I. Title.

ML285.S45 2000
80'.941'09034—dc21

00-038572

ISBN 1 85928 337 3

Printed on acid-free paper

Typeset in Times by Manton Typesetters, Louth, Lincolnshire, UK and printed and bound in Great Britain by TJ International, Padstow, Cornwall.

Contents

Because, unlike serious work, light music lacks musical content, it acts as a series of vials, often charmingly shaped and coloured, for the distillations of memory. The first few bars of it remove the stopper; we find ourselves reliving, not remembering, but magically recapturing, some exact moments of our past.

J.B. Priestley, *Margin Released*, 1962

Common tunes that make you choke and blow your nose,
Vulgar tunes that bring the laugh that brings the groan –
I can rip your very heartstrings out with those.

Rudyard Kipling, *The Song of the Banjo*

Play, orchestra play,
Play something light and sweet and gay,
For we must have music
We must have music
To drive our fears away.

Noël Coward, *Tonight at Eight-Thirty*, 1935

Preface

In about one hundred years between roughly 1870 and 1970, some of the most entertaining music of the time originated in Britain. One has, of course, to pan it for the nuggets of pure gold to shine through the waste; and even then there will be much argument as to what is, and what is not, worthwhile. The percentage of nuggets is nevertheless, by general agreement, high.

But this music was light music, and as such has been considered insignificant, in comparison with the mainstream European musical movements, in whose shadow it has lain. These developments may have expanded the language of music, concentrated the intensity of its effect, and multiplied its purposes. But in the process, the composer and his audience might well part company. British light music, on the other hand, was largely content with its inherited language, has not wanted to disturb its audience, and has kept to its function of entertainment. It remained listener-friendly.

This light music was expertly tailored for its purposes; if it had not been, it would have been ruthlessly discarded.

The essential strength of so much of it is attested by its survival in the face of endless arrangements for all manner of forces, and countless performances of dubious quality. The sheer variety of both arrangements and performances points to the reasons for its growth in the first place. For it was rooted in need. The theatre, the parlour, both amateur and professional singer, the seaside pier, the bandstand and the music hall all need music. Later, the need encompassed the gramophone, radio and cinema.

When, in the second half of the twentieth century, the circumstances which had nurtured this music changed, it withered. Scorned by new audiences which had other needs, it was marginalized; banished from live performance, to survive precariously in the museum (for such it is) of recording.

It is a fine legacy – far too interesting and pleasurable to lose. Beyond its entertainment value and sheer quality, it can incomparably recall, and even define, its times; more intensely, perhaps, than the written word or the visual image.

GS

Acknowledgements

I should like to express my gratitude to Boosey & Hawkes Music Publishers Limited for their permission to reproduce short music extracts from the following works:

Shepherd Fennel's Dance	(Balfour Gardiner)
In The Shadows	(Herman Finck)
Bal Masqué	(Percy Fletcher)
Nights of Gladness	(Charles Ancliffe)
Sylvan Scenes	(Percy Fletcher)

My thanks are due also to Schott & Co. Ltd, London, for their permission to allow me to quote from *Salut d'Amour* (Elgar).

I am grateful, too, to Stainer & Bell Ltd for their consent to the reproduction of short extracts from:

From the Bavarian Highlands	(Elgar)
Sinfonietta	(Gordon Jacob)
Overture for a Masque	(E.J. Moeran)

The examples from *God Make Me Kind* (Haydn Wood. Words: Desmond Carter), *Calling All Workers* (Eric Coates) and *Country Tune* (Arnold Bax) are all reproduced by kind permission of IMP Ltd. (All rights reserved).

Finally, I should like to thank Pam and Adrian Self for producing the music examples, and Ellen Keeling for her unstinting help and advice.

Every effort has been made to trace all the copyright holders of the music examples, but if any have been inadvertently overlooked the publishers will be pleased to make the necessary arrangements at the first opportunity.

CHAPTER ONE

Roots and Reasons

When Alban Berg's opera *Wozzeck* was first given in London, one respected critic described its effect on him as like losing a pint of blood. *Wozzeck* is clearly not light music. It is disturbing, disquieting and carries a powerful electric charge. It is a major serious work.

Light music, in contrast, should divert rather than disturb; entertain rather than disquiet. If it does not, it fails in its purpose. It may have other functions which do not necessarily require concentrated listening. We might dance to it, eat to it or even buy to it. If we are stacked in a phone system, we may be regaled with it while we wait.

In all these functions, the music is catering to a real need, even if a created need. In contrast, the need for Beethoven, Wagner or Berg is not as readily apparent. Here, it was rather a question of a need on the part of the artist himself to create.

While it has shared the same language with serious music, light music has emphasized those aspects of that language which are immediately attractive. Of these, tune is clearly the most important. The catchiness and then the memorability of tunes is an elusive subject, worthy of a separate study in itself. Some composers – Schubert, Gershwin, Tschaikowsky or Kern, for example – have shown an apparently inexhaustible flair for such memorability. But this musical quality is not necessarily the preserve of the musically trained. A dip into any collection of folk-songs – and especially British folk-songs – will yield many instantly memorable tunes to which no authorship can be ascribed.

If we were to leave it as just a question of tune, we would have no distinguishing marks between light music and popular music. The former must obviously aspire to popularity with some, otherwise it will not meet the criterion of need. But it will have qualities of craftsmanship not necessarily to be found in mere popular music. To a degree, it will have the same mastery of harmony, counterpoint and orchestration to be found in more weighty work.

But not too much counterpoint. The American bandleader Artie Shaw observed on the subject of fugue:

> As the instruments come in one by one so the audience goes out one by one.

With a few exceptions, the great masters all wrote their share of light music, to which they brought the same technical resource to be found in their more serious work. Handel, writing for a stately progress up the Thames or for a great celebration with fireworks, used somewhat less counterpoint than he would have thought

1

fitting for a sacred subject; Bach, on the other hand, had few such scruples. The kind of aria he deemed suitable for his rare ventures into secular cantata (such as the *Peasant* Cantata) would as easily fit into the *Magnificat*, given a suitable text. Certainly in his Masses and confronted by dreary dogma, Haydn would happily intone the text on one note while giving free rein to his invention, letting his orchestra romp through what is indisputably light music.

Kapellmeisters such as Bach or Haydn would have enjoyed a little more economic security than a composer/impresario such as Handel. Certainly, composers emerging in the first flush of nineteenth-century Romanticism found such positions increasingly rare to come by – if indeed they ever wanted them in the first place. As composers became emancipated from employers, money became a problem, and was therefore a factor in the gradual separation of light music from what, for want of a better description, we must call serious music. But the former had to feed the latter. Beethoven cannot much have enjoyed arranging quantities of Scottish, Irish and Welsh airs for voice and piano trio at the behest of George Thomson, the Edinburgh publisher, but the work paid well and doubtless made possible the last piano sonatas and the *Missa Solemnis*. Elgar said that each time he wrote an oratorio, his family would starve for a year. An exaggeration, probably, but the fact remains that had he not sold his *Salut d'Amour* outright, neither he nor they might have felt the chronic insecurity that afflicted him.

There are many examples of composers who laced their major work with light offerings. Sibelius interspersed the pantheon of symphonies with such well-crafted trifles as *Suite Mignonne* and *Valse Triste*; Brahms, who revered the work of the waltz-king Johann Strauss, wrote his own set of waltzes (Opus 39) and, of course, indulged himself with the Hungarian Dances. Even the uncompromising Delius compromised at the start of his career, permitting the publication in Florida of the polka *Zum Carnival*, which he would, no doubt, have preferred to have stayed there.

The writing of light music, within our necessarily limited arena, was from the beginning of the nineteenth century widespread if not universal among those composers whose principal expression was through the symphony or symphonic poem. But, as Constant Lambert pointed out, composers as diverse as Mozart and Chabrier had shown that:

> seriousness is not the same as solemnity, that profundity is not dependent on length, and that wit is not always the same as buffoonery, and that frivolity and beauty are not necessarily enemies.[1]

If a more serious attitude to music was taken anywhere, it was doubtless in the Austro-German domain. There was a moral force and philosophic power to the music of Beethoven, Schumann, Brahms, Bruckner, Wagner and Mahler. Their work was (and is) seen as profound, and as such it dominated not only their own musical scene but also that of Britain. This country's own creative profundity in the nineteenth century seemed to favour poetry, painting and literature rather than music. This may have been just chance; but the lack of opportunities for a musical education and for a real musical career did not offer much encouragement.

Successive studies of early to mid-nineteenth-century British music have found little but mediocrity in it, before the arrival of Stanford and Parry, and then the 'Second English Renaissance' figures. And indeed, in the absence of any equal to such major continental figures as those mentioned above, we may well have to accept that one factor that cannot be overlooked is a sheer lack of creative genius among our early Victorian composers.

And yet the trickle of recordings now beginning to appear, of long-forgotten yet rewarding works by, for example, George Macfarren (1813–1887), Hugo Pierson (1815–1878) and others, suggests that such a condemnation may be far too wholesale.

The continental composers were purposive; even their lighter music had weight and was anything but inconsequential. Their work achieved in Britain something akin to the same acceptance as had been enjoyed by the great classic figures of Haydn, Mozart and Beethoven before them. If some of their music presented difficulties of understanding, there was as an alternative the less demanding manifestation of German Romanticism: Mendelssohn.

With court patronage to reinforce his command of the moral heights and his own awesome fluency both as performer and as composer, Mendelssohn wielded enormous influence. His *Elijah* and *Hymn of Praise* came near to rivalling *Messiah* in popularity. But his was just the highest profile of a succession of continental composers who visited these islands, perceiving the growing wealth of an emerging middle class faced with a virtual famine of good quality indigenous music. Handel, in the vanguard, had settled here. Haydn's two visits were financially profitable to him, and artistically so to us. Leopold Mozart had seen the possibilities for his prodigy-son. Weber saw them for himself a few decades later, writing *Oberon* for us. Beethoven never came, but his cordial relationship with the Philharmonic Society was instrumental in the completion of the Ninth Symphony. Liszt toured the country revealing undreamed-of possibilities of keyboard virtuosity. Chopin came too. (Where did they find adequate instruments on which to play?) Wagner, escaping from Riga and his creditors, found refuge here and returned years later, first to conduct the Philharmonic Society and then to raise money for Bayreuth. Bruckner came to play the organ of the newly built Royal Albert Hall, and Tschaikowsky to receive a Cambridge degree. Dvořák conducted at the Crystal Palace and at the Three Choirs Festival.

Naturally, it was expected that all these masters would present their own music. But purely performing musicians flocked here too: Michael Costa, Louis Jullien, Joseph Joachim, Charles Hallé, August Manns, and later Ignaz Paderewski and Hans Richter. At the lower end of the market, there were the ubiquitous German bands as well as bands of other nationalities – although some of the members of these were often British musicians in disguise.

For the aspiring young British composer, learning his craft was beset with problems. Some who later achieved distinction, such as William Sterndale Bennett and George Macfarren, studied at the Royal Academy of Music, founded in 1822 and for fifty years the only conservatory of music in London. But to many others, it seemed natural and right that they should learn their trade on the continent, neither in France nor Italy but in Germany. For, as the foregoing has hopefully shown, Germany was the perceived fountainhead of all musical wisdom.

Sullivan, Cyril Scott, Roger Quilter, Ethel Smyth and Fritz (later Frederick) Delius all studied in Germany. Stanford, in periods of leave-of-absence from Cambridge, went there too. Elgar would have if he could, but financial hardship precluded such a course for him. Among the performers, Walter Bache went over to study with Liszt and Mathilde Verne with Clara Schumann, while the young Adrian Boult went to Leipzig where Nikisch admitted him to his rehearsals. Where is was impracticable to study in Germany, some adopted German-sounding names, until the First World War made this imprudent. Henry Wood settled for trying to look like Nikisch, as his early photographs show.

The Germans appeared to hold the secret of greatness in music, and the British, with varying degrees of success, aspired to emulate them. The horizon was scanned for He-That-Should-Come. Sir George Grove thought he had perceived him in the young Arthur Sullivan. August Jaeger (himself from Dusseldorf) was nearer the mark in his advocacy of Elgar.

The specifically Austro-German hurdle of the symphony was leapt at by many; usually but once, if only because it was required as an academic exercise. But cantatas poured out in profusion – many from obscure cathedral organists and most destined for oblivion. 'Grand' opera lured some of the most distinguished figures – among them Stanford, Delius, Smyth, Sullivan and, later, Holbrooke – despite the fact that, if staged at all, their operas were likely to be roughly handled by touring companies, some of which were of appallingly low standard. But then, they had their eyes set on continental rather than home production. For there was in Britain still a vociferous minority who 'identified opera with idolatry and likened theatrical pleasures to deadly nightshade'.[2]

The figure of Sullivan conveniently demonstrates both the aspirations of a mid-nineteenth-century British composer and the uncomfortable realities of the true nature of his ability. Sullivan was really an entertainer, albeit one of genius. But from his Queen downwards, those who thought they knew best were continually urging him to lift his eyes to the hills of oratorio. They did him no service.

It is Sullivan, too, who equally conveniently suggests 1870 as a date for the start of a study of British light music. Specific dates for topics are notoriously misleading but 1870-with-blurred-edges is near enough to the start of the Gilbert and Sullivan partnership; to the beginnings of the coming renaissance of British music generally; to the emergence of the new teaching establishments; and to the vast expansion then beginning in the sheer quantity of music provision, as musicians and publishers struggled to meet the demands of domestic households, choirs, bands, festivals, spas and seaside piers.

The extent of that expansion is revealed in the statistics.[3] In 1871, a census showed 19,000 musicians and music masters; by 1911, it was 47,000. In 1856 there had been six brass band festivals; by 1896 there were over 240. In 1840, pianos were still a rare luxury. By 1910, there was one for every 10–20 of the population.

Once a demand is apparent, musicians are no slower than other trades or professions to satisfy it. The demand was satisfied but, in the process, the divergence already apparent between serious music and light music became ever more marked. Eventually, at one extreme would be such men as Eric Coates and Albert Ketèlbey aiming only to please their public; at the other would be Elisabeth Lutyens and Humphrey Searle, choosing uncompromisingly to ignore the tastes of the common herd. Many others would prefer to be in-between, writing their masterpieces, but catering to the public when they perceived a chance. One at least – Granville Bantock – somewhat shamefacedly hid under a pseudonym his efforts for the music-hall star Marie Lloyd. And while Lutyens' work continues to baffle all but the academics, it was found to be eminently suitable as background music for horror films.

* * *

Had there been no Industrial Revolution, the ensuing musical revolution would hardly have taken the course it did. The centralization of machines into factories led directly to migration from rural areas to towns, which then expanded with unprecedented rapidity. It was the conglomeration of people in towns and cities that turned music into a social activity, facilitating the growth of bands, orchestras and choirs.

The creation over a very short time in the early and middle years of the nineteenth century of a network of railways not only allowed the movement of groups such as choirs and bands from one town to another, but also led to the growth of seaside resorts. With regard to music itself, it might be argued that, without the growth of cheap railway travel, the Folk-Music movement, which was such a feature of the late nineteenth and early twentieth centuries, would never have taken place. Vaughan Williams and Holst might trudge from village to village in their song-collection forays; others would prefer the train as it snaked its way through deepest Dorset or Suffolk. The railways themselves often built a hotel at the terminus of their lines, around which in due course a resort would grow. Those who didn't come to stay could come as day-trippers, and were even celebrated in music; Frank Musgrave's *Excursion Train Galop* (mid-1840s) is an example. Both resort and spa needed entertainment. The bandstand in the park, the winter gardens, pavilions and piers – all needed music.

By the mid-1860s, many towns already had assembly rooms; now the new choral societies needed something better. Rooms especially designed for them began to appear, with raked seating for the singers and an organ for their accompaniment.

The new industrial towns often combined in one building a town hall and a room suitable for a concert hall.

In the last quarter of the century, there was a boom in theatre building, both in London and the provinces. These theatres in turn generated a demand for musical entr'actes and incidental music. The combination of music and drama meant grand opera, but it could also mean the more approachable operetta and thus down-market to musical comedy. The more popular bits of these could go lower still, as acceptable items on a music-hall bill-of-fare.

It had been a hazard of theatrical life that theatres burned down with monotonous regularity. D'Oyly Carte used electric lighting for the first time in his new Savoy Theatre, considerably reducing the fire risk. Other theatres soon followed.

The burgeoning middle classes had aspirations of both education and culture; they were enjoying, too, a little more leisure time than had their forebears. Their homes, cluttered to modern eyes, bear witness to their diligent devotion to crafts, to collecting, to curiosity – and to music. The piano became not only a prized object but a symbol of status. German ones were perceived as the best, but a thriving British piano industry could built on the knowledge that Beethoven had thought highly of Broadwood's instruments.

Orchestral concerts, supported by individual subscription, had a much longer history, pre-dating Haydn's two epoch-making London series in the last years of the eighteenth century. In the nineteenth, the dignified face of orchestral music was represented by the Philharmonic Society. In the north, the *nouveaux riches* textile manufacturers attempted to match London concert life with an orchestra of their own. Charles Hallé in Manchester created the orchestra which still bears his name today. When he died, Sir Frederick Cowen took over, but it was unthinkable to the management that anyone but a German should ultimately succeed Hallé – Hans Richter first, then Michael Balling. One Briton, though, saw no reason why his son should not conduct as well as, or better than, the Germans. Sir Joseph Beecham, the St Helens pharmaceutical manufacturer, promoted the early career of his son Tho-mas, to the delectation of generations of music-lovers thereafter.

Orchestral music could also display a popular face. Henry Wood's Promenade Concerts (founded in 1895) have proved to be enduring, yet they were but the latest in a history of such concerts, encompassing such figures as Louis Jullien and Michael Balfe. Jullien, indeed, maintained that it was his promenade concerts that educated the London public in musical taste. For his part, Wood proceeded cau-tiously and methodically. In his early Promenade seasons he programmed a preponderance of light music, and for some years afterwards he tended to devote the time after the interval to it.

From 1856, the Crystal Palace, in the centre of the growing middle-class suburb of Sydenham, offered popular Saturday concerts under the direction of August Manns. They ran from 1856 until the orchestra's dissolution in 1901. A bandmaster from Stolzenberg, one of a number who made the transition from band to orchestra, Manns promoted much British music. The vastness of the Crystal Palace allowed huge audiences and, indeed, gargantuan performances when the triennial Handel festivals took place there.

It is arguable whether or not these developments stimulated a desire to sing and play, encouraged advances in instrument design and primed the explosion in music-printing, or whether they themselves were stimulated by them. In this chicken-and-egg situation, the stimulation was probably mutual.

Singing was seen as both morally and physically healthy. By the mid-nineteenth century, penny singing classes were popular in the teeming new towns. They were often promoted by the Temperance movement as a way of keeping a labour force bereft of hope from straying into despairing dissolution. At first it seemed that tonic-solfa, promoted by the Curwens, would be more digestible than staff notation, and so it was for straightforward diatonic music. But as compositions became more complex, staff notation proved more pliable and gained the upper hand.

From the mid-1840s onwards, sheet music grew progressively cheaper. The London firm of Novello pioneered inexpensive music printing – of oratorios, anthems and cantatas. Huge collections of the familiar buff-coloured octavo books are still to be found even today, mouldering in many a church or chapel music cupboard. Something like a paper war was fought between Novello (through its house magazine *The Musical Times*) and Curwen (house magazine *The Musical Herald*). Curwen in particular was always very touchy whenever it saw criticisms of its system.

Improvements in instruments, and indeed newly invented instruments, were themselves the results of new processes developed in the Industrial Revolution. New engineering processes benefited wind instrument manufacture, and Theobald Boehm and Adolphe Sax applied logic to their design. The new instruments made possible the brass band. The band movement, with its frequent and countrywide competitions and festivals, could only have grown with the spreading railway network already mentioned.

Pianos were found to hold their tuning better with an iron frame rather than a wooden one. Upright pianos took up less room than grands and were thus more suited to the aspirations of the lower middle classes, whose houses were 'downsized'. But what were the hordes of domestic pianists to play? Many of them had but limited technique and much of the repertoire of classical and romantic piano music had been written by virtuosi for their own use. Some of Mozart, Chopin and Schumann was reasonably approachable from a technical point of view but much Beethoven, Schubert, Weber and almost all Liszt were inaccessible. To meet the demand, publishers pumped out albums of 'morceaux', 'reveries', 'fancies' and Beethoven's or Weber's 'Last Thoughts'. Mendelssohn filled a real need with his succession of *Lieder ohne Worte*, subsequently often derided but offering short, not-too-demanding pieces of great charm. Soon they were to be found on every parlour piano.

Learning to play adequately, however, still took a few years of study. For the more faint-hearted, the need for this disappeared when, in 1904, Edwin Welte invented a player-piano, at which one could sit and appear to play. A less than honest alternative to this was adopted by those who advertised piano 'methods' which, they said, took 'the drudgery of practice' out of learning.

In the earlier nineteenth century, many church services were still accompanied by bands of instrumentalists, varying in size and constitution from place to place. These, described so vividly by Thomas Hardy,[4] were to die out as the century progressed, to be replaced by barrel organ or harmonium in the poorer churches. Those more richly endowed installed an organ, at first 'tracker' action and then pneumatic.

Such was the musical world Arthur Sullivan both inherited and worked for. It was an expanding world, both in its demands and in its resources, but it was also fragmenting. Sullivan would attempt to keep his footing on each fragment.

Notes

1. Lambert, Constant (1934), *Music Ho*, Faber & Faber, p. 141.
2. Mackerness, E.D. (1964), *A Social History of English Music*, London, p. 187.
3. Russell, Dave (1987), *Popular Music in England: 1840–1914*, Manchester University Press, p. 1.
4. Hardy, Thomas (1935), *Under the Greenwood Tree*, MacMillan: Cottage Library.

CHAPTER TWO

Sullivan and the Dilemma

In some ways, Sullivan typifies not only the acceptable face of the Victorian age but also its hidden side. He was a man of great personal charm and as a composer, conductor and administrator he dominated the musical world of his time. Beyond his music, he became an intimate of the aristocracy and through it, of the royal family also. It was no mean achievement to be simultaneously liked by Queen Victoria and both her sons the Prince of Wales and the Duke of Edinburgh. He was admired even by the Prince's detested nephew, the Kaiser. Victoria saw him as the saviour of British music, a worthy recipient of the sacred torch passed on from Mendelssohn, whom she and Albert had so cultivated. It is doubtful whether Prince Bertie was much interested in Sullivan's music, but he would have found Sullivan the gambler, card-table addict and man-about-town much to his taste. Audiences would have known little of Sullivan's habits, any more than they would have known of his chronic ill-health, which caused him such constant pain. They would have seen a dapper, genial man who had written not only *The Lost Chord* and *Onward, Christian Soldiers* but also the Savoy Operas.

As a composer, Sullivan was superbly equipped technically. His father had been bandmaster at the Royal Military College, and the young Sullivan had learned to play many of the instruments to which he had access in the band. As a chorister in the Chapel Royal he learned to sing, and as a Mendelssohn Scholar (the first) he learned composition and conducting at the Leipzig Conservatory. On his continental travels, he had met Rossini, and played cards with Liszt.

While today he is remembered primarily as the musical half of the Gilbert and Sullivan partnership, he was an acknowledged and established master well before 1869 when Frederick Clay first introduced the sharp-witted playwright to him. Clay was a musical amateur of talent, who had already collaborated with Gilbert on an operetta, *Ages Ago: a Musical Legend*. This was produced on 22 November 1869 at an establishment in London's Regent St, run by Thomas and Priscilla German Reed and called the Royal Gallery of Illustration. Both Clay and the German Reeds have claims to have acted as midwives to the Savoy Operas. *Ages Ago* indeed anticipated *Ruddigore* with a plot in which phantom ancestors materialize from their portraits. Wits of the time would say that Gilbert and Sullivan were 'cradled among the Reeds'.

At the age of twenty-seven, Sullivan was already a leader of his profession, selling the songs, ballads and hymn-tunes with which a young composer might hope to make a living. *It Came Upon the Midnight Clear, Onward, Christian*

Soldiers and the song *Orpheus with his Lute* were all written before his thirtieth birthday. He had been first noticed in 1861 with his music for *The Tempest*, a student work, written at Leipzig. The following year, he was working on an opera, *The Sapphire Necklace*, which was completed but never performed. Its overture has survived, albeit via an orchestration based on a military band arrangement. The work is valuable because it is an early example of Sullivan's instrumental work; the grave beauty of its minuet-style introduction is particularly striking. The Concerto for violoncello and orchestra, the overtures *Marmion* and *In Memoriam*, together with a Symphony are all works of his early years, and all testify to an intention to make his mark as a serious composer.

Soon after his first meeting with Gilbert, he had a short work produced at the 1870 Birmingham Festival. This was the overture *Di Ballo*, arguably the finest of all British light overtures, and a work which, while not overtly influential, yet stands as the progenitor of a whole line of light music which followed it into the twentieth century.

Di Ballo is a waltz-overture in the form of an introduction, waltz and galop-style coda. As such, it nods gracefully in the direction of Weber's *Invitation to the Dance*. Weber's music is not, perhaps, an obvious influence on Sullivan, but it is nevertheless there – in, for example, the closing bars of the *Iolanthe* overture. (Weber had been teacher and friend, respectively, of Sir Julius Benedict and Sir George Smart, who had both been instrumental in securing the young Sullivan his Mendelssohn scholarship.) In the clarity of its orchestration and in the elegance of its string-writing, *Di Ballo* is a foretaste of two of the most striking features of the instrumental writing to be found in the Savoy Operas. Its rhythmic subtleties and gentle syncopations would similarly meet their match in Gilbert's polished phrases. Its happy combination of apparently disparate themes would be repeated with effortless ease whenever Gilbert gave Sullivan the opportunity. And Sullivan's contact with Liszt went beyond the card table when he absorbed the Hungarian composer's thematic transformation technique – in *Di Ballo* conjuring a galop from a waltz (Ex. 2.1).

Sullivan was to be diverted from light orchestral music, of which *Di Ballo* is such a delectable example, to operetta, to oratorio and to time-consuming bureaucracy. But the characteristics of his instrumental melody follow through into the Savoy Operas. From time to time – in, for example, the ballet suite *Victoria and Merrie England* – he returned to instrumental music. When he did, the deft touch was as apparent as it had ever been.

Few directly British influences are discernible in Sullivan, although he was not above borrowing ideas when they suited his purpose. There is, however, a strain of 'Old English' pastiche, seen for example in the madrigal in *The Mikado*, and reflecting a general view of what Elizabethan music was supposed to be like before Canon Fellowes revealed its true nature. This imaginary world had made an early appearance for Sullivan in the masque *Kenilworth*, written for the Birmingham Festival. He was not alone in his exploitation of never-never halcyon times. Through

Ex. 2.1 Sullivan: *Overture Di Ballo*

a) **Tempo di Valse**

b) **Tempo di Galop**

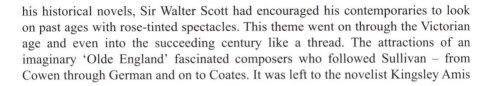

his historical novels, Sir Walter Scott had encouraged his contemporaries to look on past ages with rose-tinted spectacles. This theme went on through the Victorian age and even into the succeeding century like a thread. The attractions of an imaginary 'Olde England' fascinated composers who followed Sullivan – from Cowen through German and on to Coates. It was left to the novelist Kingsley Amis

2.1 A cigarette card showing the Pirate King from a set of Gilbert and Sullivan characters

many years later in *Lucky Jim* to ridicule the nonsense of the cult. But historical truth might not have led to such attractive music.

The attractiveness was rooted firstly in the melody and secondly in its harmonic setting. Melody is an elusive phenomenon even to begin to analyse, but its effectiveness probably runs in direct proportion to its memorability. Sullivan scores heavily on memorability: so many of his tunes we seem to have known all our lives.

While Liszt and Wagner tended towards chromaticism in their melodies (*O Star of Eve*, from *Tannhaüser*, for example, or the opening of Liszt's Piano Concerto in A major), Sullivan's tunes are often sturdily diatonic. It is in modulation – often via a modulating sequence – that Sullivan's work is so striking. Beyond that, he is rarely at a loss for that 'aftersong' which, as Hans Sachs advised Walther (*Die Meistersinger*) is so necessary. An example from *The Mikado* illustrates both attributes (Ex. 2.2).

The nearest parallel for such melodic felicity is to be found in the work of Schubert. Sullivan's knowledge of Schubert was fostered by his great friend George

Ex. 2.2   Sullivan: *The Mikado* (Act II)

Grove, who had a passionate love for the Austrian's music (so intense a love that he and Sullivan journeyed to Vienna to search – successfully – for the missing *Rosamunde* and other Schubert music). Sullivan's happy knack of finding an unexpected modulation builds on Schubert's own facility in this regard. The sharply defined accompaniment figures that are so psychologically or descriptively fundamental to Schubert would be inappropriate for operetta, but Sullivan will nevertheless sometimes use an onomatopoeic figure, as, for example, in Phoebe's first appearance in *The Yeomen of the Guard*, sitting at her spinning wheel. More often, he will restrict himself to the simplest of Verdi-style figures, in order not to obscure Gilbert's words. Gilbert himself sought their audibility ruthlessly:

> … there were two or three words which failed to reach me quite distinctly. Sullivan's music is, of course, very beautiful and I heard every note without difficulty, but I think my words are not altogether without merit and ought to be heard without undue effort.[1]

Sullivan was familiar with early Verdi, whose style he parodied from time to time. This is most obvious in *The Pirates of Penzance*, where Mabel's song *Poor Wandering One* adopts the coloratura manner of *Ah, Fors' è Lui* (*La Traviata* – The Wayward One). There is even parody of Handel – one of the most untouchable Victorian icons – in *Princess Ida*, at the point where the three young stalwarts dispense with their armour. The chorus, in true Handelian style, encourage them:

> Yes, Yes, Yes
> So off that helmet goes.

Iolanthe, too, has elements of parody. There are shadows of Wagner's Rhinemaidens in Sullivan's treatment of his watery heroine. The Fairy Queen, too, has something of Brünnhilde about her. Any parody is gentle, for Sullivan admired Wagner. *Die Meistersinger* was in his view the greatest of comic operas.

There was, however, no element of parody in Sullivan's responses to Rossini and Mendelssohn. From the former he learned the deft pointing of a phrase – very often a propulsive series of repeated notes with a tight rhythmic 'finishing' (Ex. 2.3).

He was indebted, too, to Mozart, for one of the glories of the Savoy Operas – the Act finales. These superbly constructed extended ensembles, deploying all the soloists and chorus, demonstrate a complete mastery of the general 'fuss' music which had been so much the preserve of his great predecessor.

While Sullivan's woodwind writing owed something to Rossini, the main influence on his orchestration was that of Mendelssohn, whose exemplary clarity he rarely fails to match. Such a passage as that in the *Iolanthe* overture (one of the few overtures Sullivan wrote entirely himself, such was the usual panic to have everything ready on the opening night) where the *O Foolish Fay* tune (Fairy Queen) appears in the cellos, with wind doubling while the flutes cavort joyously aloft, is a text-book model, which has an ancestor (in its principle) in the last movement of Mendelssohn's Violin Concerto in E minor. But after the early *Midsummer Night's Dream* overture, Mendelssohn rarely matches either Sullivan's humour or his wit.

Ex. 2.3   Rossini's *Semiramide*; Sullivan's *The Mikado* (Nanki-Poo)[2] and *Iolanthe*

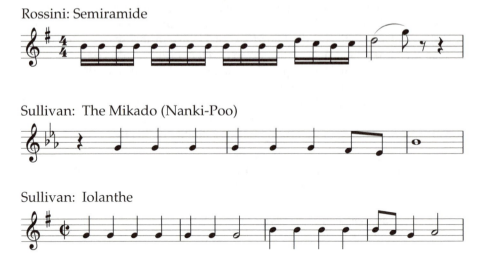

Rossini: Semiramide

Sullivan: The Mikado (Nanki-Poo)

Sullivan: Iolanthe

Perhaps the humour is a little heavy-handed in, for example, the treatment of heavy-footed Penzance policemen, but the wit is matchless in *The Mikado*'s school-girls, who have clearly never been near Japan, but are very familiar with South Kensington and Harrods. Their Trio (No. 7 in the Chappell vocal score) affords a choice example of Sullivan's happy use of modulation mentioned above, where at the words:

> From Three Little Maids Take One Away

the music veers from its basic C major into E flat major, and then as effortlessly back again. Nor will any true Savoyard miss the tiny touch where, breaking the symmetry of his two-bar phrase structure, the composer throws in an extra bar; silent would it be, but for a flurry of chuckling bassoonery (Ex. 2.4).

Such details were the bane of those who, in the absence of copyright laws, would plague Gilbert, Sullivan and Carte with piracy. A hack writer could probably achieve an approximation of the words; a hack musician could have some success in noting down the tunes. But the textures of the music and its orchestral clothing,

Ex. 2.4   *The Mikado* (Three Little Maids)

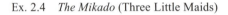

together with the detail of the ensembles – these were beyond copying. They justified Carte in presenting authentic performances of the operettas in any place where spurious and inaccurate imitations were given. The public could thus appreciate the superiority of the real thing. Gilbert, too, bitterly resented any departure from his stage business.

Sullivan's gifts were dazzling enough, but he had limitations which he appeared not to grasp or, at any rate, not to accept. He was incapable of writing in an emotional context without becoming either hymn-like, mawkish or sentimental. In this respect Mendelssohn, so admirable a model for most aspects of technique, was hardly a good example to follow. Mistakenly, Sullivan saw no lasting value in the Savoy Operas and grew ever more uncomfortable in the partnership with Gilbert. Increasingly, he weighted his own contribution towards a grand opera style. He never saw himself as anything but a serious composer obliged by necessity to dirty his hands in the muddy waters of popularity.

The expectations placed on his shoulders by everyone from the Queen down to his musical peers were daunting. At the beginning of his career, an early love, Rachel Scott-Russell, spurred him on towards her vision of greatness:

> I want you to write an opera. Such an opera – a grand, vigorous great work. O strain every nerve for my sake.[3]

He was continually urged to do better; there was always the lurking suspicion that what he had done was not quite the great work British music-lovers were yearning for. His oratorio *The Prodigal Son* prompted Sir John Goss to write:

> All you have done is most masterly. Some day you will, I hope, try another oratorio, putting out all your strength – not the strength of a few weeks or months. Show yourself the best man in Europe![4]

The pressure became even more intense when in 1883 he received his knighthood. As the *Musical Review* put it:

> Some things Mr Arthur Sullivan may do, Sir Arthur Sullivan ought not to do. In other words, it will look rather more than odd to see announced in the papers that a new comic opera is in preparation … A musical knight can hardly write shop ballads either; he must not dare soil his hands with anything less than an anthem or a madrigal; oratorio, in which he has so conspicuously shone, and symphony must now be his line.[5]

Tongue in cheek? It seems unlikely. Even his great friend Grove joined in publicly, with an exhortation in his *Dictionary of Music and Musicians*:

> Surely the time has come when so able and experienced a master of voice, orchestra and stage effect – master, too, of so much genuine sentiment – may apply his gifts to a serious opera on some subject of abiding human or natural interest.[6]

And then there were those who not only were not prepared to humour Sullivan for musical peccadilloes but actually decried him for breaching the moral ramparts. Lewis Carroll was one of the more vituperative, especially when *The Children's*

Pinafore was staged at the *Opéra Comique* in December 1879. Hearing the child-captain utter 'the big, big D', he marvelled that Sullivan 'could have prostituted his noble art to set such vile trash'.[7] He was not to know that this child-production by Gilbert and Sullivan themselves would be a forerunner of tens of thousands of twentieth-century school productions.

A year later, and *Punch*, in parody of the Judge's Song (*Trial By Jury*), could sardonically observe:

> So I packed off to Leipsic, without looking back
> And returned in such classical fury
> That I sat down with Handel and Haydn and Bach
> And turned out *Trial by Jury*.[8]

Sullivan became the victim of a climate of opinion – sadly, the climate of those whose approbation he craved. His situation was exacerbated by his own financial problems – in part stemming from his own insatiable gambling addiction, but in part also from his unfortunate choice of stockbroker.

He had abandoned writing purely orchestral music (with the exception in 1893 of the *Imperial March*) quite early, and he craved the opportunity to attempt a grand opera. He longed to write a work which would have strong human interest – probably the one thing he was least well equipped for. Failing that, there was the challenge of oratorio and of dramatic cantata. Undaunted by this peculiarly English musical graveyard, he chose subjects which did, indeed, have strong human interest: *The Martyr of Antioch*, *The Prodigal Son* and *The Golden Legend*. But for a period of nearly thirty years (1866–95) he had perforce to divide himself into a number of parts as he tried to reconcile the worlds of operetta, cantata and oratorio – and then to squeeze all three into the opposing worlds of festival conducting and educational administration. In later years all were carried out against a background of recurrent pain from kidney trouble.

His first operetta collaborator was not Gilbert, but F.C. Burnand, with whom he wrote first *Cox and Box* (1866) and then *The Contrabandista* (1867). *Cox and Box* still gives delight, often as a curtain-raiser to *HMS Pinafore*, but *The Contrabandista* had little success, even when Sullivan and Burnand revised it in 1894 under the title *The Chieftain*. Burnand's words simply did not have Gilbert's sharp edge; but when the diamond-hard facets of Gilbert's lyrics met Sullivan's melodic genius, the composer's tunes leapt to meet the poet's phrases.

Precision was a Gilbertian quality. For *HMS Pinafore*, for example, he visited Portsmouth to check that every detail of his stage set was ship-shape. He even went to the length of having his officers' uniforms made by a Portsmouth naval tailor. He would come to the first rehearsal of a new production with a vision of every movement already clear in his mind, having worked it out on his own model stage. Rarely would he permit the slightest deviation from his 'business' – let alone from his text. Throughout the run, he would look in unannounced at the theatre, to check that standards had not fallen nor text and production had been adulterated. Eric Coates, describing him as a 'peppery little writer', remembered him calling an extra rehearsal of *Iolanthe* in the middle of a run, getting the whole of the Savoy Theatre into a state of nervous tension.[9] Nevertheless, in terms of sheer professionalism, he has claims to be the father of modern theatrical technique.

His first collaboration with Sullivan came in 1871–72. *Thespis* achieved a run of 80 performances at the recently built, and huge, Gaiety Theatre. The music has mostly disappeared, although one particularly bright jewel was rescued, to reappear as *Climbing over Rocky Mountain* in *The Pirates of Penzance*, and another (*Little Maid of Arcadee*) was published as a ballad. Both show how Sullivan almost instantly found a style which was hardly to change over the whole period of the partnership.

With the closing-down of *Thespis* it is unlikely that the Gilbert and Sullivan partnership would have continued, were it not for the vision of a third figure, Richard D'Oyly Carte, at thirty-one in 1875 younger than either Sullivan (thirty-three) or Gilbert (thirty-nine). During the four years after *Thespis*, Sullivan had progressed steadily in the world of serious music, in which, despite his youth, he was a major force.

Gilbert, by his own admission, knew little of music when he showed his *Trial by Jury* script to Carte: 'I know two compositions; one is God Save the Queen and the other isn't';[10] he had thought of asking Carl Rosa to set it.[11] At the time, Carte was managing a run of performances of Offenbach's *La Périchole*. The work was a little too short for an evening's entertainment and, perhaps as a consequence, business was poor. Carte realized that *Trial by Jury* would fit his bill and that, if set by Sullivan, his name would have sufficient prestige to bring in the crowds. Consequently it was sold on Sullivan's name rather than on that of Gilbert. Audiences came to see the appetizer rather than the main course, which was soon dropped, to be replaced by Lecocq's *La Fille de Madame Angot*.

It was in *Trial by Jury* that Sullivan first exercised his gift for parody – of Handel and, in the sextet, of the Verdi of *Rigoletto*. Such parody would have been pointless if the audiences of the day had not been culturally aware. Advances in education were beginning to have their effect; Gilbert's targets for satire presumed an intelligent audience, and in this early collaboration, notwithstanding that Sullivan had the higher billing, and that the work is unique in the pantheon for being sung throughout, it is arguable that the book rather than the music makes the greater effect.

The same is true, perhaps, of *The Sorcerer* (Opéra Comique, 17 November 1877). It succeeded *Trial by Jury* which had been brought to an untimely close by the death of Sullivan's brother Fred, who had played the Judge. Based on Donizetti's *The Elixir of Love*, Gilbert's book for *The Sorcerer* contained many of the ingredients – love potions and magic spells among them – against which Sullivan would eventually rebel. His approach to music for magic was conditioned by the early German Romantics. Clearly he was familiar with the scene in the Wolf's Glen from Weber's *Der Freischütz*. The pattern for successive patter-songs, whose pedigree is music-hall out of Rossini, is firmly established in *My*

Name is John Wellington Wells, but the ballad style of Alexis' *It is not Love*, fashioned so that it could be taken out to be published and performed separately, would need to relax its stiffness considerably before it would attain the effortless ease of *Take a Pair of Sparkling Eyes* or *A wand'ring Minstrel I*. *The Sorcerer* was the first product of Carte's new Comedy Opera Company, of which his eminent composer and distinguished librettist were the chief assets. A company was brought together to perform the work, which included two artists destined to become almost indispensable over the years: George Grossmith and Rutland Barrington. Not only did the assembled talents dictate who would do what and the style in which they would do it, but the characters in that second operetta would themselves become prototypes for the stock Gilbertian figures who would follow.

The company had been established with borrowed capital, on which the investors expected a return. This shackled Sullivan to a treadmill, for as attendances over the months fell off, a replacement opera was required. This recurring demand he would find increasingly irksome. But the successor to *The Sorcerer*, first performed on 25 May 1878, became the first runaway success of the triumvirate.

Gilbert's target in *HMS Pinafore* was not just the Navy, nor even class distinction in the Navy, but more particularly the British habit of appointing amateurs to professional positions. Here the unspoken victim was the newsagent and bookseller W.H. Smith, appointed by Disraeli as First Lord of the Admiralty. Gilbert, of course, denied that Smith was his target. At first, the new opera seemed to falter; if it had failed, that would probably have signalled the end of the partnership then and there. But business picked up after Sullivan conducted a selection from it at the Covent Garden Promenade Concerts. After this, it is said, ten thousand piano scores of the work sold in a single day. *HMS Pinafore* settled into the first really long Gilbert and Sullivan run.

Its very success caused the chronic problem of piracy which, in the days before any effective law of copyright, plagued the triumvirate. Carte went to the USA, to try and terminate pirated versions there (at one point, eight unauthorized productions were running in New York alone). He never found much support in American law; in one test case a few years later (concerning *The Mikado*), one Judge Divver in the New York court handed down the following uncompromising ruling:

> Copyright or no copyright, commercial honesty or commercial buccaneering, no Englishman possesses any rights which a true-born American is bound to respect.[12]

The directors of the Comedy Opera Company themselves sprang a mutiny on 31 July 1879, when Carte was in the USA. Although they were doing very well from their investment, the success of *HMS Pinafore* led them to believe that they could do better if they put on their own production. That night, they invaded the official production bringing men and vans; there was a pitched battle as they attempted to remove the scenery. This rival production turned out to be a miserable caricature – as were many others, whether in Britain or in America.

The eventual answer proved to be for Carte to take an official production, directed by Gilbert, to the USA, and to arrange for the first performance of the succeeding opera – *The Pirates of Penzance* – to be simultaneously produced in the USA with a copyright performance in England (at Paignton). Even then, a violinist in the New York orchestra told Sullivan that he had been offered one hundred dollars if he would supply his part to one illicit publisher. Another unscrupulous printer had his tame hack attend to note down what he could, and subsequently brought out some of the tunes arranged as quadrilles.

As the date of the first performance approached, Sullivan still had much music left to write; a situation aggravated by the fact that he discovered too late that he had left all the last act sketches back home in England. And, of course, he had to send the completed score back to Paignton for the copyright performance. In the small hours of New Year's Eve, there was still no overture. Sullivan and Alfred Cellier sat down to compile one, with Gilbert and Frederick Clay copying out parts until they dropped out from sheer exhaustion.

The Pirates of Penzance proved, after such birth pangs, to be one of the great Gilbert and Sullivan triumphs, expectedly perhaps in Britain, but in the USA unexpectedly and particularly. In 1880, while Ragtime and Black jazz styles were on the American horizon, no truly national style had yet achieved dominance there. In its absence, such a tune as *Come, Friends, who Plough the Sea* passed for a time into the American folk-soul. Gilbert's words were discarded; it lent itself to others, from college fraternities:

Hail! Hail! the gang's all here

to pub crawls:

All go the same way home (don't break up the party)

Gilbert's targets in *The Pirates* (under the umbrella of a general gibe at the virtually untouchable Victorian ideal of duty) were the army and the police. His comically heavy-footed policemen seem to have strayed from the world of burlesque, while their progeny a few years later were probably Fred Karno's Keystone Cops. The stock Gilbertian characters from *HMS Pinafore* translated easily from sea to land. As Sullivan himself admitted, all was 'beautifully written for music, as is all Gilbert does'.[13] Just as in *Don Giovanni* Mozart was able to mock his own *Marriage of Figaro*, so here Gilbert was able to have a little fun from his Major-General, who, though antiquated in military skill, could 'whistle all the airs from that infernal nonsense *Pinafore*'.

On 23 April 1881, after a run of 363 performances at the Opéra Comique, *The Pirates of Penzance* was succeeded by *Patience*. The targets here were Walter Pater, Oscar Wilde and the aesthetic movement; a late thought, for until quite a long way into his libretto, Gilbert had intended to make fun of the established church. The aesthetic movement had already been caricatured in *Punch*; in the persons of Maudle (a painter) and Jellaby Postlethwaite (a poet). The aesthetes

Ex. 2.5   Sullivan: *Patience*

were distinguished by their romantic, flowing clothing, made from Messrs Liberty's fabrics. Gilbert himself sketched the designs and in his passion for authenticity, purchased the materials from the respected Regent St store.

In *Patience*, perhaps for the first time, we can sense Sullivan's realization of his power to affect radically the force of his partner's words. In *Pinafore* he had been content to go along with Gilbert's ridicule of Buttercup, the Bum-boat woman, by setting her to an absurd waltz. But Sullivan was never at ease in lampooning women and in *Patience* Lady Jane fares better than Buttercup; she may look ridiculous playing her cello, but Sullivan ensures that her song will be seemly and beautiful (Ex. 2.5).

By now, the triumvirate were wealthy. Gilbert spent his share on his yacht and on a splendid house, Sullivan gambled his, and Carte built a new theatre. The Savoy Theatre, the first to be lit electrically, opened on 10 October 1881, with the transfer of *Patience* from the Opéra Comique.

In the next opera, Carte lit not only the theatre electrically but also the ladies of the chorus, enhancing immeasurably their effect as young fairies. Opening at the Savoy on 29 November 1882, the cast believed right up until the final rehearsal that it was to be called *Perola*. At that point, Gilbert told the company, to its consternation, the real name – to be used thereafter and throughout. It was to be *Iolanthe*.

This ploy had been part of the defence against the continuing piracy menace. Again, there was a simultaneous opening in both New York and London but, as usual, Sullivan was late in completing the music. The company – and the score and parts – had left for the USA before Sullivan had written the overture. Alfred Cellier, who was to conduct in New York, cobbled one together; but the overture with which we are familiar today was written by Sullivan himself for the London performances.

Iolanthe is a satire on parliament in general, and the peerage in particular. The central idea of the possibility of disrupting parliamentary business seemed merely amusing at the time, but within thirty years, the threat of Asquith and Lloyd George to create a majority of Liberal peers brought the unlikely into the realm of the distinctly feasible.

Many authorities on Gilbert and Sullivan would agree that *Iolanthe* is the finest purely comic opera of the series. The Lord Chancellor's two patter songs show

Gilbert's verbal virtuosity at its most brilliant, and Sullivan's setting of them at his most inventive. This is particularly true of the accompaniment to the Nightmare Song. In its mastery of ensemble, Sullivan's first act finale is hardly excelled anywhere in the series, while both pastoral and 'fey' elements found sympathetic resonances within him. The Fairy Queen's reprimanding aria *O Foolish Fay* shows how far Sullivan had advanced in his treatment of the ballad form, while the Sentry's Song was in many ways a model male comic song; a style which both came from, and would return to, the music-hall.

At this point in 1882, Sullivan had worked with Gilbert for some five years. He would have liked to withdraw from the partnership but his broker was bankrupt, and he was in consequence financially embarrassed. He respected Gilbert, but he liked Carte. Accordingly, he signed on for another five years. But he would resist, as far as he could, Gilbert's topsy-turvydom, magic lozenges and plot-identity problems caused by baby-swapping.

Princess Ida (first performance 5 January 1884) was less successful than some of the others in terms of run, although many thought it musically at least the equal of its predecessors. It differed from them to the extent that the book was in blank verse, and in three acts. But like them, it was satirical. The Forster Education Act (1870) had testified to a society increasingly avid for advancement of understanding, learning and self-improvement. The position of women in this came under scrutiny as colleges specifically for them were contemplated. Could women be intellectuals? The cornerstones of knowledge were being undermined by Darwin. Could we all really have sprung from apes? The apparently unrelated subjects of blue-stockings and evolution were in Gilbert's sights for *Princess Ida*.

In it, Sullivan took a further small step in the direction of grand opera. The music exhibits a hitherto unnoticed suggestion of savagery – the savagery of elation apparent in the chorus. There is in *Princess Ida* a perceptible extension of Sullivan's range, in evidence again in the next opera *The Mikado*, where the chorus *With Joyous Shout and Ringing Cheer* (Ex. 2.6), heard in both act-finales, goes well beyond both Victorian decorum and the usual voice limits of chorus sopranos.

Sullivan had flatly and finally refused to set a Gilbertian 'magic lozenge' plot, but in *The Mikado* (opened 14 March 1885) he had perhaps fallen into a Gilbertian trap. The possibilities for exploiting oriental colour in a Japanese subject seemed to offer much musical opportunity; but Gilbert had no intention of going very far east of the Strand. The costumes and names of the characters would be pseudo-Japanese but the Seminary of the Three Little Maids would sit more happily in Kensington than in Kyoto, and the Chief Executioner would bear some resemblance, if only in malice, to Gilbert himself. The recent Japanese Exhibition in Knightsbridge was superficially exploited, but Gilbert's satire on bureaucracy and its accompanying cruelties was firmly rooted in England.

The Mikado is musically unsurpassed in the Savoy operas. Nowhere is this more marked than in the treatment of the solo arias, where there is a striking further extension of Sullivan's range and technique. The treatment of *A Wand'ring Min-*

Ex. 2.6   *The Mikado (With Joyous Shout and Ringing Cheer)*

strel I demonstrates a virtuoso response to Gilbert's various challenges of masque. At the other extreme is the virginal innocence of Yum-Yum – simple chords and a pentatonic tune, with no worldly chromaticisms to corrupt her (Ex. 2.7).

Ex. 2.7   *The Mikado* (Yum-Yum's Aria)

Confident in the expectation of a long run for *The Mikado*, Sullivan now turned to Longfellow and *The Golden Legend*: a cantata for Leeds (1886) 'putting out all his strength', as he thought, and as Goss had asked. It was well received but when he looked to Dame Ethel Smyth for agreement that it was his best work, she felt forced to point to *The Mikado* as his masterpiece.

For his next book, Gilbert turned once more to Cornwall for his setting, finding the improbable fishing village of Rederring. *Ruddigore* was poorly received (for Gilbert and Sullivan, that is) and it has been one of the Cinderellas of the series, revivals constantly showing it to be unjustly neglected. It has remained in the shadow of *The Yeomen of the Guard* (first performance 3 October 1888), which possesses little, if any, satire and little comedy either, beyond the fact that Jack Point and Elsie are strolling players whose boast is that they can turn their hand to any entertainment. Musically, the work is very strong, with a depth of technical resource and an orchestral richness paralleled in the series only by *The Mikado*. Sullivan's stylistic progress had been slow but there was now a fresh breeze of originality – to be heard, for example, in *Here's a Man of Jollity*, or in the Tower Warders' chorus from Act One. The rejection and collapse of Jack Point, who 'sighed for the love of a ladye' at the opera's conclusion as the rest of the cast heartlessly conclude their song of triumph, is moving beyond words.

The success of *The Yeomen of the Guard* encouraged Sullivan in the great ambition of his life: the composition of a grand opera. Between him and its fulfilment stood the sparkling *The Gondoliers* (opened 7 December 1889), the last great success, if not the last opera, of the Gilbert and Sullivan partnership. Its musical score was, if anything, even more sparkling than its predecessors.

Much to Gilbert's annoyance, Carte had set about building yet another opera house. It would provide Sullivan with his chance. For its opening, he finally wrote his grand opera: *Ivanhoe*. The work itself is outside the scope of this book. Suffice it to say that London seemed then as now unable to sustain a run of performances of one grand opera. But the fact of it, together with the so-called 'carpet' quarrel, brought about a final severing of the partnership of W.S. Gilbert and Arthur Sullivan which, although patched up for *Utopia Ltd* and *The Grand Duke*, never really recovered.

*   *   *

In the succeeding century, the Gilbert and Sullivan operas took on a new lease of life as amateur productions proliferated (the first appears to have been that of the Harmonists' Choral Society, who gave *HMS Pinafore* in April 1879 at Kingston-upon-Thames, Surrey). Until the new generation of musical comedies became available, the Savoy Operas provided the standard fare of amateur societies, many of which were formed specifically to perform them. They were translated into German, French and even (for Philadelphia) Dutch. In Germany, the Kaiser could quote from them. Even the philosopher Nietzsche loved *The Mikado*. Koko's complaint: 'A nice mess you've got us into' was to be echoed some forty years later by Oliver Hardy, in reproach to Stan Laurel.

Yet while in Britain his music was played from bandstands to barrel-organs, something prevented Sullivan's countrymen from acknowledging that greatness in music is not the total preserve of the profound. Sadly, Sullivan also seems to have thought this. It was not generally recognized in his time just what Sullivan *had* achieved; a style and an art form that was, as Grove had looked for, an expression of the English national character. He had also laid the foundations of an English light music style that would not be lost on his successors, as they analysed and responded to that style. Some would approach it from a background of a similar rigorous technical training and expertise as Sullivan himself had enjoyed. Others would content themselves with aspiration merely to the tunes; but hardly in such profusion, and rarely with such finish and craft in presentation.

Notes

1. To Durward Lely, rehearsing as the first Nanki-Poo.
2. This phrase appeared as early as the *In Memoriam* overture (1867).
3. Sullivan might have married Rachel Scott-Russell, had not the opposition of her father discouraged such a union. One of Sullivan's earliest songs – *O Fair Dove! O Fond Dove!* – is dedicated to Rachel.
4. Sir John Goss (1800–1880), organist of St Paul's Cathedral, and composer of much church music.
5. Quoted in Leslie Baily (1952), *The Gilbert and Sullivan Book*, Cassell & Co., p. 224.
6. Sir George Grove (1820–1900). His *Dictionary of Music and Musicians* appeared in four volumes over the period 1879–89, and in subsequent editions by other hands.
7. Quoted in Arthur Jacobs (1986), *Arthur Sullivan*, O.U.P., p. 123. Two years before in 1877, Carroll had received an unenthusiastic response from Sullivan when he had approached the composer with a proposal to make a musical dramatization of *Alice's Adventures in Wonderland*.
8. Quoted in Leslie Baily, p. 173.
9. Coates, Eric (1953) *Suite in Four Movements*, Heinemann, p. 95.
10. This well-known statement appears in at least two different remembered versions. The version quoted in the text is from Arthur Jacobs, *Arthur Sullivan*, p. 63. Leslie Baily (*The Gilbert and Sullivan Book*, p. 89) has it thus: 'I know only two tunes, and one of those is *God Save the Queen*'.
11. A fellow-student with Sullivan at Leipzig. He had that year (1875) founded the opera company that bore his name.
12. Quoted in Leslie Baily, *The Gilbert and Sullivan Book*, p. 256.
13. Sullivan to his mother: 2 January 1880.

CHAPTER THREE

Down into the Market-Place: Sullivan's Followers

The musical comedies which succeeded the Savoy Operas had little of the latter's elegance and ensemble construction, and still less of their orchestral and textural detail. Nor did they have that pungency which, as E.D. Mackerness has pointed out,[1] was missing from mid-nineteenth-century comic opera until the advent of Gilbert and Sullivan.

Yet the new confections were but a response to changes in taste – changes which were already apparent to Gilbert as the partnership was coming to its end. The comparative failure of *Utopia Ltd* and *The Grand Duke* had been a portent. Intrinsically, they are not much below the very high average of quality of the other Savoy Operas. As Carte wrote, lamenting the demise of *Utopia Ltd*, 'What the public wants now is simply "fun" and very little else'.[2]

A few composers followed in Sullivan's footsteps, tackling either comic opera or cantata. One of these was the Shropshire-born musician Edward German Jones, known as Edward German (1862–1936).[3] He enrolled at the Royal Academy of Music primarily as an organist and violinist, but it was his rigorous training in harmony and counterpoint under the pedagogue Ebenezer Prout that equipped him to be a composer. Like Sullivan and, a few years later, Samuel Coleridge-Taylor, German made an early reputation as a composer of songs and incidental theatre music. In 1887, August Manns had conducted his first symphony at the St James's Hall. A second, the *Norwich*, was given at the 1893 Festival in that city.

Although he had dipped a toe in the waters of light opera with *The Rival Poets* (St George's Hall, London, 1885), he was in his fortieth year when, on 27 April 1901, his opera *The Emerald Isle* (book by Basil Hood) was produced at the Savoy Theatre. Sullivan had started on the music for it but had completed only two numbers and sketched the tunes of fifteen more before his death on 22 November 1900. While critically well received, *The Emerald Isle* had only moderate success; the death of Richard D'Oyly Carte a few weeks before the opening night did not augur well for it. But the fact that German was asked to complete it demonstrates that, on the strength of his songs and orchestral work, he was seen to be in Sullivan's tradition and perhaps even his successor. Certainly it led to a further collaboration with Hood, which was to result in the most famous post-Sullivan light opera: *Merrie England*.

Composed in 1902, it was first produced that year at the Savoy Theatre. The conductor was Hamish MacCunn, and the cast included some old troupers from the

Gilbert and Sullivan days, among them Henry Lytton and Rosina Brandram. But it had only a short run (24 November 1902 to 17 January 1903), and its future success – which has been considerable – was to be among amateur societies. And those societies would generally prefer to offer concert performances, which is a pity because the concert version is virtually meaningless in plot and story.

In this work, and in some of his theatrical incidental music (to be discussed in Chapter 5), German cornered a small but significant market in period pastiche: the creation of a sound world with little basis in squalid reality, but a much more desirable one in what we would all have liked our history to be.

Merrie England aped a dominant aesthetic of its time. It reflected the neo-Elizabethan houses of Lutyens, the work of William Morris, the resurrection of Tudor period instruments by Arnold Dolmetsch, the researches into folk-dance and song by Cecil Sharp and into late Tudor and Jacobean vocal music by Edmund Fellowes. But whereas there is a sturdy solidity about Lutyens' country houses, a plain honesty about Morris's domestic drapings, a care for detail about Dolmetsch's instruments and an intellectual rigour about Fellowes' transcriptions, there is a certain complacency about *Merrie England*, with its implied suggestions that the age of which it sings was in some ways a golden time.

The whole back-to-the-golden-age movement catered to what people thought they wanted. For Elgar, it was still all around him when he lovingly sang its requiem a few years later in his Violin Concerto; in many other cities and towns it had already vanished, and for urban dwellers could only be recalled in the illusory worlds of theatre and romantic novel.

Edward German had prodigious talent; perhaps even a touch of genius. But its nature was not such as to equip him to be Sullivan's successor, as the Savoy Theatre quickly discovered. Nor was Basil Hood's work a match for Gilbert's theatrical instinct and flair. Hood and German had produced a pastiche of arrant olde Englishe nonsense involving the Earl of Essex, Walter Raleigh and Queen Elizabeth, with Robin Hood and the ghostly Herne the Hunter threatening to appear, given half a chance.

While the work does follow in that English pastoral vein already to be found from time to time in Sullivan, German does not have Sullivan's wit and humour. Nor does his operetta have much comedy about it. If Gilbert, in his heyday twenty years earlier had written the book, he would probably have mocked and satirized the yearning for the golden age. Mockery was certainly beyond Basil Hood; but then, in the political climate of early Edwardianism as Britain faced up to the realities of growing Teutonic menace, such an approach might well no longer have been acceptable. What German could offer was melodic skill and ingenuity of ensemble, expressed with the craftsmanship and orchestral virtuosity of a master. The score is full of good things, such as the splendid waltz-song, the sheer sweep and physical excitement of the finale to Act One, and the Dances. Viewed from a vantage point of nearly a century later, he seems nearer to Elgar than to Sullivan in that, with such contributions as *O Peaceful England* and *The Yeomen of England*, he touchs a particularly sensitive aspect of the English psyche not readily found elsewhere.

A further stage work – *A Princess of Kensington* – opened at the Savoy on 22 January 1903. The very title attempts to reflect, and attract, a growing clientele among the *nouveaux riches* middle classes moving into the fashionable villas in that then-desirable district.

With German's third theatrical venture, *Tom Jones* (opened in Manchester on 3 April 1907 and a fortnight later at the London Apollo Theatre), a new producer appeared on the scene. This was Robert Courtneidge who over the next few years would move to the centre of theatre life at a time when new theatres were proliferating in London. *Tom Jones*, in which Fielding's frolic was largely sanitized in A.M. Thomson's book, still enjoys the occasional revival, and is remembered especially for its fine waltz-song; a luckier fate than was to befall German's next venture for the stage.

Fallen Fairies opened at the Savoy on 15 December 1909. If at this distance in time we did not know the librettist, we would surely guess it from that title. W.S. Gilbert had failed to persuade Sullivan to enter the world of fairies one last time, and had, indeed, failed to persuade any other composer from Elgar downwards to try it until, a dozen years or so after his last libretto (*The Grand Duke*), he ensnared German. It proved to be a last musical stage work for both of them, surviving into the New Year for a few weeks only.

Sullivan had not found it necessary to debase his musical standards, and until his very last years, there had been little falling-off in audience support for him. Working a quarter of a century later, German probably should have gone down-market in order to succeed; but to his credit, he did not. He paid a price for it, for the theatregoing public no longer wanted the quality he represented. Sadly, the effect on him of such rejection by the public was to inhibit all his output. He wrote very little more music of any kind.

But if there were things Sir Arthur could not do, there were certainly things Sir Edward Elgar – with Lady Caroline Alice firmly at his elbow – would not be allowed to do. Coleridge-Taylor, too, was conscious of his dignity. While musical comedy and the prospect of a comfortable living from it beckoned, these composers, and others like them, resisted the temptation. For, as Gilbert had foreseen, the new musical comedy audiences were prepared to settle for standards of craftsmanship far lower than those maintained by Sullivan and German.

The first true musical comedy to be seen in Britain is thought to be the American importation *In Town* (1892) but the most influential was probably *The Belle of New York* (Gustav Kerker 1857–1923) which arrived in 1898. The man who did most to establish musical comedy in Britain was George Edwardes, of the Gaiety Theatre. Edwardes had learned theatre management from Richard D'Oyly Carte, whose assistant from 1875 he was. This position also afforded him the opportunity of observing at first hand the methods of W.S. Gilbert who, sensing a possible rival, became jealous of him. Edwardes subsequently went into business with John

Hollingshead at the Gaiety, which was specializing in burlesque: a less respectable relation of the Savoy Operas, using French musical scores and featuring beautiful girls in costumes more risqué than Gilbert would ever have allowed. In the hope that they would acquire some American zest and energy, Edwardes would send his Gaiety Girls, half-a-dozen at a time to see their counterparts in *The Belle of New York*.

Raising the money to buy out his partner, Edwardes tried his luck with a cross between light opera and musical comedy. It was called *Dorothy*, but its fortunes were so modest that he sold it outright for one thousand pounds to the Prince of Wales Theatre. Here the cast was changed, whereupon it became a great success. Edwardes learned the lesson; that fickle audiences were now to be attracted not by the book, the music, or the ensembles, but by the stars engaged to perform. A comedian rather than a comic character was now needed; in addition, there should be a female actress and singer of strong personality. The era of the 'post-card queens' had arrived. Stars such as Gertie Millar (*The Quaker Girl*), Edna May (*The School Girl*) and Ada Reeve (*Florodora*) adorned many thousands of postcards.

The sheet music of the period confirms the dominance of the stars. You have to look hard to find the name of the composer, but the 'queen' who first sang the song will fill the cover with her image, while any remaining space will be taken up with lists of other prominent artists who performed it; often with a dedication to one of them. Of these 'queens', and other Gaiety Girls, over twenty married into the aristocracy.

The original Savoy company had had its stars, too, but had been based essentially on the ensemble as a whole. In contrast, the house-styles of George Edwardes's Gaiety and Daly's theatres are reflected in the 'girl' titles of the shows: *A Gaiety Girl*, *The Quaker Girl*, and *The Shop Girl* (which was set in a thinly disguised Knightsbridge Royal Stores called *Garrods*). These musical comedies featured a love story with a slender plot, which avoided anything remotely historical. Gilbert's plots may have been improbable but were at least strongly defined. The polished wit which had distinguished a Gilbert libretto now gave way to rather obvious puns. In the music, there would be no counterpoint to distract, and little or no ensemble to confuse. The accompaniments ranged from generalized arpeggii to simple vamping. The orchestration was basic.

But there had to be a good waltz-song, for waltzes were all the rage. In them, at a time of loosening bonds of propriety, you could dance quite close to your partner, and the girl might even reveal her ankles. Musical comedies were up-to-date, especially in their clothing fashions. Scenery was important. Exotic settings were sought, but English or European backgrounds would do, if they could be a little unusual. Thus, *A Gaiety Girl* has scenes at a Royal Garden Party and on the French Riviera. Their appeal, and Edwardes's success, may be judged from the meteoric rise in Gaiety Theatre shares in the last decade of the old century.

Sullivan at least had the satisfaction that, even when Cellier had to help him by cobbling together an overture, the main body of his operetta, including the orches-

3.1 Gertie Millar

tration, was largely his own. With the new musical comedies, it was more a question of a corporate effort, in the sense that, quite often, a work would come from the pens of two or more composers. The staff composers employed by George Edwardes included Ivan Caryll, Lionel Monckton, Howard Talbot, Sidney Jones, Leslie Stuart and Paul Rubens.

Ivan Caryll (1861–1921) – real name Felix Tilkins – was of Belgian nationality, and had received thorough musical training in his own country. In 1894, Edwardes appointed him music director at the Gaiety Theatre. In this position, he became one of the principal driving forces of musical comedy. His professionalism was of a standard to impress Elgar, who in 1899 dedicated his *Serenade Lyrique* 'to Ivan Caryll's Orchestra'. Today, Caryll is remembered for his Valse, *The Pink Lady* (Ex. 3.1). While many will recall the tune, rather fewer will be able to put a name to the composer.

Ex. 3.1   Caryll: *The Pink Lady* Valse

Extravagant in his tastes, clothes and life-style, and generous as a host, Caryll made much money and lost it as easily. He went to the USA, where he was as successful as he had been in England. P.G. Wodehouse, with whom he collaborated, dubbed him 'Fabulous Felix'. Unusually for a Victorian musical comedy composer, his appeal lasted well into the twentieth century. He even achieved some post-First World War success with his operetta *Kissing Time* (1919), which linked two of the old pre-war stars George Grossmith and Phyllis Dare with coming new ones such as Leslie Henson and Yvonne Arnaud.

George Bernard Shaw's judgement of Caryll is harsh, but penetrating:

> He has energy and determination, which he puts into his composition in an intelligent, mechanical way; but even the most impetuous pages have not a smile on them. His orchestration is clever, active, full of traits and points, but certainly not smooth and beautiful, and often uneasy, self-conscious and obtrusive. There is no pretence of novelty in the melodies and rhythms.[4]

Working with Caryll, and in due course perhaps even surpassing him in popular esteem was Lionel Monckton (1861–1924). Educated at Charterhouse and Oxford, Monckton had a rather different background to that of Caryll. With aristocratic forebears, he became a barrister and in the society in which he moved was regarded as something of both a wit and a gourmet. His musical training was sketchy, but he played the organ and wrote musical criticism for the *Daily Telegraph*. He managed to be both a Wagnerian and an admirer of Sullivan, whose friendship he enjoyed. Herman Finck, indeed, thought his music to be 'in the true Sullivan tradition'.[5] His interest in the theatre had been kindled at Oxford, where he had joined the OUDS. At first, Edwardes employed him to write additional material for the shows, and also to be on hand to produce alternatives when a particular part of a show was seen to be sagging. He lacked the technical skill to do his own orchestrations but did have an undeniable knack of thinking up attractive tunes, trite though some of them seem today. Monckton came into his own with *The Quaker Girl* (Adelphi: 1910). Its waltz-song *Come to the Ball* enjoyed phenomenal popularity in the spas and on the piers.

As well as collaborating with Caryll, Monckton worked also with Howard Talbot, to whom on occasion he entrusted his orchestration. After some false starts, first as a medical student and then as an apprentice in the silk trade, Talbot had enrolled at the Royal College of Music. He was, wrote Eric Coates who had played in his orchestra, 'full of fun, liked a good story and knew how to tell one, wrote delightful music and was popular with his orchestra'.[6] Highly regarded in the profession, he was engaged by Edwardes in 1904 to direct the Prince of Wales Theatre orchestra. He wrote a succession of musical comedies for Edwardes:

Wapping Old Stairs	(1894: Vaudeville)
Monte Carlo	(1896: Avenue)
A Chinese Honeymoon	(1901: Strand)
The Blue Moon	(1905: Lyric)
The Belle of Brittany	(1908: Queen's)

Of these, only *A Chinese Honeymoon*, exploiting the oriental vogue left over in the wake of *The Mikado*, achieved a long run (1076 performances).

In 1909, Talbot and Monckton wrote a new work for Robert Courtneidge, the impresario who two years before had produced Edward German's *Tom Jones*. Opening at the Shaftesbury Theatre on 28 April 1909, *The Arcadians* was an immediate success, which held the stage for over eight hundred performances. It has been described as 'the first musical comedy in which plot, music and characters were fully integrated'.[7] While the book, by Arthur Wimperis, clearly derived from Gilbert's world of fairies and mortals, it was fresh as new paint, making much effect with an aeroplane landing in Arcadia, a horse race at 'Askwood' and the grand opening of an Arcadian restaurant.

The Arcadians (Ex. 3.2) was unusually rich in catchy tunes, some of which approached Sullivan's rhythmic pointing.

Monckton also worked with Sidney Jones (1861–1946). Like Sullivan, Jones was the son of an army bandmaster.[8] He was a clarinettist who himself became a bandmaster, before Edwardes contracted him to take over the forty-member or-

Ex. 3.2   Lionel Monckton: *The Arcadians*

Fol-low, fol - low,   fol-low   the   mer-ry, mer-ry pipes of   Pan.

chestra of Daly's Theatre. He had been responsible in 1894 for the score of *A Gaiety Girl*. Two years later, he was joined by Monckton in writing the music for *The Geisha*. In this the English heroine, somewhat foolishly dressed in Geisha costume, has to be rescued by a resourceful British naval officer. It was another manifestation of that oriental trend which showed itself everywhere, from furniture to crime novels, and would eventually have its apotheosis a few years later in *Chu Chin Chow*. The young Eric Coates played his viola under Jones in the orchestra for *The Geisha*. Coates much admired him, especially for his first-class orchestrations. He noted, too, the 'fabulously large cheques' Jones recieved as royalties for his work, no doubt remembering them when in due course he had to decide whether or not to attempt to earn his living from his compositions alone.

Leslie Stuart (?–1928, real name: Thomas Barrett) made his reputation writing music-hall songs, of which the 'coon' song *The Lily of Laguna* (written for Eugene Stratton) was probably the best and certainly the most celebrated. Another was *The Soldiers of the Queen*, which was played everywhere and in the Boer War was to become almost a second National Anthem. But he was versatile; he had been a church organist and had promoted and conducted 'people's' concerts of popular classics in Manchester. He scored a musical comedy success with *Florodora* (Lyric Theatre: November 1899), an unlikely tale of a stolen perfume formula – the Florodora of the title. It made him a rich man. One song from it, which became very popular, was *Tell Me, Pretty Maiden* (Ex. 3.3). It tapped a vein of Sullivanesque delicacy. Even Sullivan, though, did not often divide one tune between two groups of singers so neatly.

Ex. 3.3   Leslie Stuart: *Florodora*

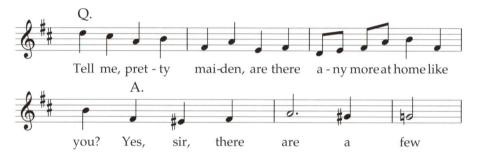

Q.

Tell me, pret - ty   mai-den, are there   a - ny more at home like

A.

you?   Yes,   sir,   there   are   a   few

Stuart wrote other musical comedies, *The Schoolgirl* (1903), *The Belle of May-fair* (1906), *Havana* (1908) and *Peggy* (1911), but none matched the success of *Florodora* – which was inconvenient for him as his tastes, like those of Caryll, were extravagant and the fortune made for him by *Florodora* soon melted away. His songs – he wrote over sixty of them – found a ready market among the great music-hall stars and indeed towards the end of his life when his first fame had faded, he enjoyed an Indian summer appearing on the variety stage, sitting at the piano. Here, to general pleasure, he would accompany his daughter May as she sang 'Leslie Stuart's Dream Songs'.

Contributing a few songs to *Florodora* was Paul Rubens (1875–1917), whose career in some ways paralleled that of Lionel Monckton. He studied law at Oxford, and acted there as well as writing music for the dramatic efforts of his fellow students. He collaborated with Talbot in Robert Courtneidge's first London production *The Blue Moon* (Lyric: 28 August 1905). He wrote songs, and also some incidental music for Beerbohm Tree's production of *Twelfth Night*. He added some songs to Monckton's *The Country Girl*, but he was also capable of penning *Algy's Simply Awfully Good at Algebra*. Professionalism indeed.

He first achieved prominence as a composer of his own show with *Three Little Maids* (Apollo: 10 May 1902). Subsequent work included *Miss Hook of Holland* (Prince of Wales Theatre: 31 January 1907), and *The Balkan Princess* (Prince of Wales Theatre: 20 February 1910), in both of which he also had a hand in writing the lyrics. *The Sunshine Girl* was written for his mistress, the post-card queen Phyllis Dare.

Herman Finck, who orchestrated much of Rubens's work, thought and hoped that, had he lived, Rubens might have stemmed the growing tide of imported American musicals. But he was sickly, and his short life was clouded in its last years by tuberculosis.

Caryll, Monckton, Talbot, Jones, Stuart and Rubens – these were the most prominent musical comedy composers of the pre-1914 era. Despite their successes, it is difficult to escape the conclusion that none of them exhibited the skill of Sullivan, or even of German. Nor did they maintain the consistency of standard shown by those masters. Rarely did they attempt work in the more demanding instrumental forms. They needed the stimulus of words, but the words they were offered had not the rhythms of a Gilbert; rhythms which could prompt potent musical phrases. Their work was essentially ephemeral – due not so much to the lowly ambitions of the music, as to the nature of the books. The more topical the book, the faster would it become dated. Some of them survived a number of years going the rounds of the amateur societies. But even amateur supporters had become sparse by the post-1945 years.

Their work took advantage of the gradual thawing of strict morality towards the end of Victoria's reign and at the onset of that of Edward. D'Oyly Carte ran the Savoy as a successful business which nevertheless did not compromise artistic standards. In musical comedy, the balance of interest tilted towards purely commercial considerations, which took precedence over artistic ones. The commercial market identified was in the first place London, and in particular the middle classes of its burgeoning suburbs.

But those same audiences could be fickle. A portent of how easily they might change their loyalty could be seen in the success of Franz Lehár's *The Merry Widow* (Daly's Theatre, 8 June 1907), which proved to be the harbinger of an Austrian musical invasion, an invasion so penetrating that it was only finally countered when three decades later, Ivor Novello and others themselves went to Ruritania. Lehar's tunes were quite easy to sing and play, and had a Europe-wide appeal. It is said that at one time, *The Merry Widow* was playing at some four hundred theatres worldwide. Where the Victorian and Edwardian British musical comedy simply dated, *The Merry Widow* acquired a nostalgia which has ensured repeated revivals.

The home-grown product had another chance when the onset of the First World War terminated the importation of European musicals and operettas. But what remained of the story-line in them vanished when in 1916 *The Bing Boys Are Here* (Alhambra, 19 April 1916) established a vogue for revue. The new revues had as great a need for hit tunes as musical comedy had done. The success of *If You Were The Only Girl In The World* demonstrated that.

Notes

1. Mackerness, E.D. (1964), *A Social History of English Music*, London, p. 190.
2. D'Oyly Carte to W.S. Gilbert, early in 1894. Quoted in Alan Hyman (1978), *Sullivan and his Satellites*, Chappell, p. 116.
3. He altered it to Edward German because, when he enrolled at the Royal Academy of Music, there was another Edward Jones among the students.
4. Bernard Shaw, George (1932), *Music in London*, Volume 3, Constable, pp. 64–65.
5. Finck, Herman (1937), *My Musical Memories*, Hutchinson.
6. Coates, Eric (1953), *Suite in Four Movements*, Heinemann, p. 91.
7. Russell, Dave (1987), *Popular Music in England 1840–1914*, Manchester University Press, p. 72.
8. J. Sidney Jones, Conductor of the Grand Theatre, Leeds, and bandmaster of the Leeds Rifles.

CHAPTER FOUR

Music-Hall Songs: a Social Mirror

The image of music-hall that we may well have today is of a large smoke-filled room filled with diners, drinkers and serving women, with a crude entertainment at one end presided over by a chairman. This Master of Ceremonies would be doing his best to ensure some semblance of order, that the artists might stand a chance of being heard. The image will do as a starting point, but is a blanket for many refinements, variations and subtleties.

The music halls had their origins in the London Song and Supper Rooms, such as the Cyder Cellars (Maiden Lane), The Coal Hole (The Strand) and Paddy Green's (Covent Garden). The Variety Saloons were slightly different in that they were licensed by the magistrates to stage not just music but any entertainment, except, oddly, Shakespearean drama. The Eagle (the City Rd), the Effingham (Whitechapel Rd) and the Apollo (Marylebone) were examples.

The Theatres Registry Act (1843) brought them to an end, forcing proprietors either to run theatres without auditorium refreshments, or to become music halls where drink and food could be served but no stage plays were permitted. The subsequent history of the latter was clouded with unending trouble, both with the forces of moral outrage and their most potent weapon: the law. Since the Act made no provision for the prohibition of drinking and smoking in music halls, tavern owners, where they were able, found it profitable to buy up an adjoining property and turn it into a music hall in which to sell their beer. Some of them, however, aspired a little higher. Charles Morton, one of the earliest music-hall proprietors, hoped to attract a respectable, even high-class, clientele when in 1849 he started concerts at his newly purchased Old Canterbury Arms in Lambeth, to which he added the Canterbury Hall in 1852. Here, ladies were admitted every night – the sexes being separated (up until then, there had been specific 'Ladies' Nights'). Sixpence bought a refreshment ticket. But the premises, ill-lit by gas, decrepit and none too clean, can hardly have been inviting.

The kind of music Morton offered was far from the stereotype our opening image above might suggest, including as it did madrigals, glees and 'classical selections'. For many people, indeed, their first and only experience of opera and cantata would have been at the Old Canterbury, or in a similar institution. In 1859, for example, Sterndale Bennett's cantata *The May Queen* was heard there, as were excerpts from Meyerbeer's *Dinorah* and Gounod's *Faust*.[1] The remarkable thing about this is that *Dinorah* and *Faust* had only appeared that year. In the case of *Faust*, shortly to become one of the pillars of the operatic repertoire, it seems possible that it was the first occasion on which any music from Gounod's opera was heard in England. Some of the music halls were thus quite enterprising in their attempts to lift the tone of what they offered. Some of the new theatres, too, were daringly adventurous.

In 1909, *The Musical Times* could report that Madame Albani at the London Hippodrome was 'heard with attention and appreciation, especially in the simpler items … '. In 1911, the recently opened London Palladium introduced excerpts from *Carmen* and from 'some of Wagner's music-dramas'. Later still, the virtuoso Mark Hambourg was to be heard at the Coliseum, 'playing the finest piano music to enthusiastic audiences' (1916), and was an 'enormous success' at the Birmingham Palace of Varieties (1917).[2]

The interaction of the two worlds of popular entertainment and serious music went on intermittently throughout the remainder of the nineteenth century and into the twentieth. For as the new century progressed, many serious composers experienced a growing and perhaps insuperable problem of communicating with their public and looked with envious eyes on the ease – in fact much more apparent than real – with which music-hall artists overcame this; for these artists, it all seemed so direct. Some serious composers embraced the music halls: Joseph Holbrooke – composer of operas, tone-poems and chamber-music – appears to have revelled in their outrageousness. Holbrooke (1878–1958) played at both the Old Bedford and Collins' Music Halls, and wrote songs for such stars as Dan Leno and Lottie Collins: 'I wrote hundreds of comic songs and scored them for eight to ten instruments for an inclusive fee of five shillings each'.[3]

The halls spread rapidly. By 1866, there were thirty-three in London alone, and by 1870 most of the larger provincial towns had at least one. Many of the institutions which called themselves music halls actually provided a source of culture to be experienced elsewhere only at great expense. Nor were their standards unacceptable. No less a figure than Sir Richard Terry (Director of Music, Westminster Cathedral) expressed his view that the music halls had an 'efficiency which in many cases falls little short of the marvellous'.[4] But side by side with this, and certainly as early as the 1860s, a number of specifically music-hall artists had begun to emerge. Their material, which they either wrote themselves or commissioned, was aimed directly at the hall audiences and their tastes, with no element of uplift or education in mind. Known as the *Lions Comiques*, these early music-hall stars were led by George Leybourne and 'The Great Vance'. The rivalry between them was immense. Many years later, it would be the basis of the Cavalcanti/ Tommy Trinder film *Champagne Charlie* (1944, see Ex. 4.1 on page 38) (a film, incidentally, for which Lord Berners wrote a splendid pastiche music-hall song).

The songs commissioned by Leybourne and Vance became the prototypes for hundreds of others that followed. The lyrics of their songs and those of their successors, moreover, together form a body of data that no sociologist examining the late Victorian and the Edwardian eras would wish to ignore. George Leybourne's most famous warhorse was the song from which Calvalcanti's film would take its name: *Champagne Charlie*. The cover of its printed music score tells us a lot of the trend. Most of it is taken up by a picture of Leybourne himself. He brandishes a bottle of the effervescent brew, pointing to it almost reverently with his cane. Most of what little space remains is allocated to his name as performer. Beneath that, in print several points smaller, we learn that the music was written by Alfred Lee. He also wrote the words, but we are not told that on the cover.

The point is thus established that, in the music-hall era, the performer – the star – was dominant. Some, like Albert Chevalier, Charles Coborn or Harry Lauder, wrote their own material, but most 'bought in' their songs. The writers – of the words and of the music – were, however, reduced in status to that of mere word-monger and tune-smith respectively. Coborn himself, when writing for others, was content to describe his role as merely that of a 'tradesman supplying a public want'. The material would be acceptable or not to the star according to its topicality, its catchiness and the extent to which the star could impose his or her personal style on it. One music-hall songwriter, Felix McGlennon, expressed unequivocally the importance of catchiness:

I will sacrifice everything – rhythm, reason, sense, sentiment – to catchiness.[5]

There were in England hundreds of hack writers, and between them they ended the use in the halls of existing or traditional tunes. Some of these writers were prolific. Among the most prominent were Joseph Tabrar and G.W. Hunt. The latter – the creator of The Great McDermott's War Song ('We don't want to fight, but, By Jingo, if we do …) – reckoned that, over a twenty-year period, he had produced over seven thousand songs. Over a similar span, Tabrar – best known for *Daddy Wouldn't Buy Me A Bow-Wow*, written for Vesta Victoria – claimed to have eclipsed this with seventeen thousand, writing up to three a day, and selling them for a shilling each. Holbrooke (see above) was, on the face of it, more richly rewarded with his five shillings, until it is remembered that he was also providing the orchestral material for that sum.

Much of the work was wasted. Marie Lloyd – the acknowledged queen of the music halls – considered that ninety per cent of the songs she saw proved to be of no use to her. She could tell at a glance what would register with her public, and whether it would strike home. One of the problems for any professional song writer is that the impulse for the song must be a genuine one, for the public has an unerring capacity to detect insincerity:

No composer can write a popular tune with his tongue in his cheek and get away with it.[6]

Artists of Marie Lloyd's popularity and quality did need a mass of material – which had to be topical and therefore constantly renewed. The greatest of these artists would appear at two or more halls each night. Their schedule of appearances was thus complex, involving precise timings as they rushed from one hall to the next.

The authentic music-hall song favoured either the march or the waltz, and its form is almost always verse:chorus (Marie Lloyd in fact seemed to sing a consider-

able number of songs based on the polka rhythm). If the chorus was catchy – and
this was a fundamental requirement of a good hall song – the star would hope that,
by the second or third repetition, the audience would be joining in with him. For
this reason, the chorus would ideally be restricted in its tessitura, and would be
rhythmically forthright. Charles II is said to have enjoyed the foot-tapping dotted
rhythms of the French styles of his day. It is notable how many music-hall choruses
employ dotted rhythms; that of *Champagne Charlie* shows the manner.

Ex. 4.1   Alfred Lee, *Champagne Charlie*

It is centred around the notes of the tonic triad, and is instantly memorable. Too
good for the Devil, thought General Booth, forgetting for a moment the eighth
commandment as he appropriated it for the Salvation Army.

In the favoured form of verse:chorus, vestigial traces of the operatic recitative
and aria can still be heard. The recitative is formalized into an introductory passage
in which is developed what will be the subject matter of the song. The aria has
become the chorus, which comments on the subject matter, rather as the operatic
aria had expressed its character's emotions at that point in the story.

Since people went to the music halls for entertainment, the tunes had to be
attractive and the subject matter non-contentious. Subjects such as trade unionism
or pacifism were best avoided, while Womens' Suffrage could be joked about but
not treated seriously. Moreover, the star would have to fine-tune his material and
his treatment of it to the particular hall in which he was performing. A London East
End hall would have a predominantly working-class clientele; a West End one
might be patronized by a lower middle-class one. The stars themselves came from a
variety of backgrounds. George Leybourne and later Sir Harry Lauder, for example, were from the working class while Charles Coborn and Albert Chevalier were
from the middle class.

By the early years of the twentieth century, music-hall had spread through the country to become a national institution. As it did so, the element of class – certainly in the audiences – became less marked. Music-hall songs spread beyond their original homes, as did their performers. The songs were featured in the end-of-pier pierrot shows and, with Marie Lloyd and Dan Leno leading the way, the artists themselves appeared in pantomime.

*   *   *

It is possible to identify three principal categories of music-hall song:[7] (1) social comment; (2) topical; and (3) patriotic.

While social comment songs often invited the audience to feel pity for those who suffered in an unjust society, it is difficult to find any that advocated revolution, or indeed any change to the status quo. Rather do they reveal an acceptance that there were very rich people and very poor.

Work was the curse of the drinking classes, it was said. And indeed George Leybourne, in his *Champagne Charlie* character, seems to have been thoroughly approved of by the more lowly in his audiences. While they themselves were unable to afford Charlie's favoured tipple, they would happily sing along with him in its praise. Unearned wealth, while envied, was not yet generally resented – rather as that other fraudster Horatio Bottomley was envied but not at first resented, and might himself have sung along with Charlie:

> A bottle in the morning
> Sets me right then very quick.

Champagne Charlie took its place in a long line of drinking songs – not very surprising in the halls, where most of the profits came from selling drink. There were other champagne songs such as 'The Great Vance's'[8] *Cliquot, Cliquot.* (Charlie had preferred the rival Moet vintage.) But there was a progression down-market to beer, where, no doubt, the brewers hugged themselves with delight on the occasions when their own brand was specified in the lyrics by name, as in *Barclay's Beer*, sung by Harry Clifton.

The halls could find time for more than one approach to the delights and consequences of alcohol. At first, there were pure drinking songs, to express the bonhomie of the ale-bar. They held the platform in most halls, but had a long pedigree; from the opera house, through operetta and thence to musical comedy. These songs led naturally to a division between those who perceived humour in drunkenness and those who saw moral, physical and social danger in it. Gilbert's pirates had poured the Pirate sherry in Penzance; Gus Elen – rather more downmarket – preferred *'Arf a Pint of Ale* (written and composed by Charles Tempest):

> I never zeen a man get drunk in me life on cocoa, corfee or tea.
> You think I'd pay one and eight a pound for tea –
> Why the thought makes me feel queer!
> When I think what you gets for another two and six –
> Such a pretty little barrel of beer.

With such a song as this, it is the words that matter, and the tunes are correspondingly often of the most banal nature. This is even more striking when drunkenness
is treated comically, as in Tommy Armstrong's Geordie song *Wor Nanny's a Mazer*
which relates what happened when Wor Nanny sampled Holland's gin. With such
scintillating lines as:

> She sat an' she drank till she got tight; she sez, 'Bob man, Aa feel varry
> queer,
> Aa sez 'Thoo's had nine glasses o' gin to me two gills o' beer

no one was going to worry that the tune was nothing more than a variant of *The
Blaydon Races*.

While the Salvation Army appropriated the best of the tunes, the Temperance
movement generally was well served by the strong meat of melodrama, and by the
fact that the music-hall audiences were not too sophisticated to wallow in the pathos
of domestic scenes which reflected, in heart-string-tugging fashion, the evils inflicted
by over-indulgence in drink. Such examples as *Please sell no more drink to my father*
(1886) or *Don't go out tonight, dear father* (1864?) suggest a lost innocence:

> Don't go out tonight, dear father,
> Don't refuse this once, I pray;
> Tell your comrades mother's dying,
> Soon her soul will pass away;
> Tell them, too, of darling Willie,
> Him we all so much do love,
> How his little form is drooping
> Soon to bloom again above

In the late nineteenth century, expectation of life was still comparatively short
and in consequence death – especially in poorer families – was an ever-present
reality. The great killers were diseases such as tuberculosis (consumption) and, in
an age which relied heavily on steam-power and its associated heavy machinery,
accident. Within a few years, the early twentieth century would replace these with
war.

While darling Willie in the above song had clearly 'gone into a decline' – a
Victorian euphemism for tuberculosis – death by disease is not often found as a
subject for a song. It was not a dramatic event. Accidents were another matter;
especially those in the mines. These inspired both industrial folk and music-hall
songs. Generalized mining songs included *Don't Go Down The Mine, Dad*, *The
Collier's Life* and *Heroes of the Mine*. Half a million copies of the last-named had
sold by 1914. But the immediacy of a specific major disaster at Senghenhydd
(1918) in South Wales, in which 436 miners died, prompted *Only a Few More
Broken Hearts*, the bitterness of which is apparent from its subtitle: *The Same Old
Story*. A few years later, a similar catastrophe called forth the song *The Gresford
Disaster*.

Except in the coalfields themselves, the prayers of society do not seem to have
included pleas for those toiling underground, where hymns 'for those in peril on

the sea' were widespread. The image of ships foundering on the coast was familiar from postcards which brought an immediacy of impact. But it took the overwhelming disaster of the loss of the *Titanic* in 1912 to generate music. This ranged from George D'Albert's song *Be British* – 'dedicated to the gallant crew of the *Titanic*' – to Lawrence Wright's descriptive piano solo *The Wreck of the Titanic*. (This, and works similar to it, could make use of lantern slides readily available from the publisher.) Such a story caught the public imagination as much for its horror as for its heroism. The bravery of Captain Scott and his companions succumbing to the forces of Nature in Antarctica were similarly commemorated in *'Tis a Story That Shall Live For Ever*.

The 1914–18 war would force a revision of male attitudes to women. Dame Ethel Smyth might stand at the window of her prison cell conducting, with her toothbrush, the other female inmates in her Suffragettes March; but she had to contend with responses which trivialized both the Suffrage Movement and its philosophy – in, for example, such offerings as *The Suffragette's Two-Step*. While the movement focused on the all-important vote, it reflected the liberalizing of women's activities in all spheres from employment to physical exercise. It is clear from Dan Leno's song *The Swimming Master* (see Ex. 4.2; words and music by Herbert Darnley – the music in fact an illegitimate offspring of a union between an unwritten Mozart horn concerto and a well-known march) that neither he nor his male listeners perceived the latent threat to their entrenched positions.

Ex. 4.2   Herbert Darnley, *The Swimming Master*

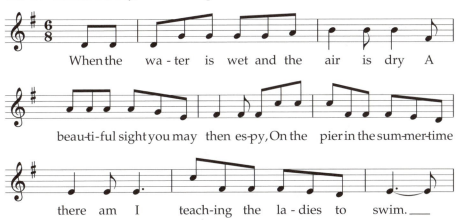

When the   wa - ter   is   wet and the   air   is   dry   A

beau-ti-ful sight you may   then es-py, On the   pier in the sum-mer-time

there   am   I   teach-ing   the   la - dies   to   swim. ___

At the time of writing, the end of the twentieth century, the rate of technological change and the immediacy with which television informs us of current events have produced a kind of mental numbing in which no innovation or happening seems worth putting into song. Such blasé sophistication had no place in either the music halls or on the musical comedy stage. In consequence, their material provides both a social and an historical mirror of their times. The first aviators are an example of this. Aeroplanes – novelties in the first decade of the century – were toys for grown-ups to race:

> *The Great Air Race*
> Sensational Descriptive Fantasia for the piano by Lawrence Wright[9]
> Title in Colours
>> Synopsis:
>> 3 AM. The dawn of a great day, motors dashing towards the aerodrome – great excitement – the airmen take their seats whilst mechanics start the propeller – now they're ready. Hip!Hip! Hooray! Airmen bid adieu to their wives and friends – See! They're off, o'er hill and dale, faster than an express train, at the mercy of the winds, now running smoothly, a neck and neck race. The Frenchman takes the lead, at the finishing point a machine appears above the hills – Who's the winner? – The Frenchman – enthusiastic reception. See the conquering hero (aero) comes – The Victor carried shoulder high – Hurrah! Grand Finale.

Within another decade, the potential of the flying toy as a weapon of war would be all too graphically revealed.

On a purely domestic level, music-hall songs provide an endless series of cameos of London life. Although the halls had spread so widely by the turn of the century, London remained incomparably their chief home. The very streets of the metropolis were celebrated, as we all went down the Strand or Knocked 'em in the Old Kent Road. As the tenements and back-to-backs crowded in on one another, it was still possible to wring some wry and bitter humour from their awfulness, as Gus Elen did when he contemplated the view from his backyard (Ex. 4.3).

Ex. 4.3   George Le Brunn and Edgar Bateman, *If It Wasn't for the 'Ouses in Between*

Even for such hovels, the rent had to be found. Harry Champion, in *Have You Paid the Rent* (words and music by L. Silberman, Herbert Rule and Fred Holt) advised:

> Here's a wrinkle when the landlord is about
> Send the kiddies down to say that mother says she's out.

If all else failed, there was nothing else to do but a 'moonlight flit' which, given the propensity for a poverty-stricken woman to drown her sorrows in drink, could be even more disastrous than the destitution which caused the problem – as Marie Lloyd lamented so memorably:

> Off went the cart with the home packed in it
> I walked behind with my old cock-linnet
> But I dillied and dallied
> Dallied and dillied
> Lost the van and don't know where to roam
> (*Don't dilly-dally on the Way*, 1919, Charles Collins and Fred W. Leigh)

If it is a characteristic of music-hall song to drag humour from human tragedy, these songs also reveal and reflect widely held attitudes to such topics as morality, marriage and relationships. Albert Chevalier was something of a specialist, and his *My Old Dutch* exudes a kind of sentimental truth which can move us even today. *The Future Mrs Hawkins* has weathered less well. Set for the most part to a minimal melody (by Chevalier himself), it reveals the perceived barrenness of spinsterhood – soon to become commonplace after the decimation of a generation of young men in the 1914–18 war:

> Oh! Lizer! Sweet Lizer! If yer die an old maid
> you'll 'ave only yerself to blame!

Chevalier hymned the joys of working-class marriage. Marie Lloyd's bitter experience of the all-too-frequent reality of it is always clear. The kindest and most generous of artists, she suffered at the hands of her violent husband, but, great trouper that she was, turned all to comic account:

> Outside the Oliver Cromwell last Saturday night
> I was one of the ruins that Cromwell knocked about a bit
> (Harry Bedford/Terry Sullivan)

She was making the best of it. And indeed, music-hall songs reflect – even advocate – an acceptance of one's lot. You worked, enjoyed the present as best you could, and generally took little account of the future. Cheat in marriage and you would be punished – more especially if you were a woman. Women were expected to be loyal, even if – like Marie Lloyd – ill-treated. Sex was treated with nothing like the frankness of many folk-songs. But the innuendo of music-hall suggestiveness was infinitely more powerful than the explicity of folk-song – that is, if you could find an unexpurgated one after Cecil Sharp had finished cleaning them up. With a past-mistress such as Marie Lloyd, it was all conveyed in the minute inflections of the voice, and in what we would now call body language (see Ex. 4.4).

There are in this the vestigial remains of a Sullivan patter song, which serve to show what a gulf had opened up between run-of-the-mill music-hall song and one of its progenitors: comic opera. Many of the music-hall songs were little more than musical doggerel, of which the best that could be said was that they didn't obscure the often far more diverting words. But, just occasionally, there would be tunes of pure gold, that have stayed with us long after most have been forgotten. Leslie

Ex. 4.4   K. Hoschna and O.A. Haverbach, *Every Little Movement*

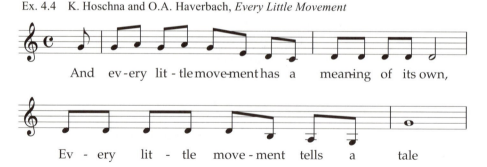

Stuart's *The Lily of Laguna*, written for Eugene Stratton, comes in this category. But even here, the verse melody is ordinary; it is the chorus that leaps into life. Vesta Victoria's *Daddy wouldn't Buy Me a Bow-Wow*, written for her by the prolific Joseph Tabrar, and Marie Lloyd's *Oh Mr Porter* may not, as the Leslie Stuart song can, offer a moving experience, but both have proved to be memorable and durable.

It is significant that we remember these as Vesta Victoria's *Daddy* and Marie Lloyd's *Porter*, and it is clear from the comments of those who heard the great music-hall artists that it was the performance that made the song. Max Beerbohm noted Marie Lloyd's rhythmic sense and her 'exquisitely sensitive ear, impeccable phrasing and timing',[10] which George Bernard Shaw confirmed, adding that 'her intonation and the lilt of her songs are alike perfect'.[11] But this supremacy of the performing artist marked the beginning of a new period of lowly status for the composer.

Notes

1. Russell, Dave (1987), *Popular Music in England: 1840–1914*, Manchester University Press, p. 88.
2. *The Musical Times*, noted in Scholes, Percy (1947), *The Mirror of Music*, Novello and Oxford University Press, p. 508.
3. Freeman, Michael (1993), 'Holbrooke', *British Music*, 15, 1993, pp. 72–3, quoting an interview with Holbrooke in *The Star*, 19 August 1924.
4. *The Musical Times*: ibid.
5. McGlennon, Felix (1894), 'A chat with Felix McGlennon', *The Era*, 10 March, p. 16.
6. Hughes, Spike (1946), *Opening Bars*, Pilot, p. 221.
7. Dave Russell, ibid., pp. 96–111.
8. Real name: Alfred Stephens.
9. A publisher, better known under his composing pseudonym: Horatio Nicholls.
10. Beerbohm, Max (1922), *Around Theatres*, London.
11. George Bernard Shaw review in *The World*, 19 October 1892.

CHAPTER FIVE

Theatre Music

That same 1843 Act that so influenced the path of music-hall had as great an impact on theatres and their music. Prior to 1843, only three London theatres were permitted – at any rate, in theory – to produce what was termed 'legitimate' drama. These were the Theatre Royal, Drury Lane, the Haymarket and Covent Garden. They were considered to be the major theatres. By 'legitimate' drama was meant a five-act play without music. In practice, it seems that only the Haymarket abided by the rules; the others found music too popular to leave out, and added it if it suited their purpose. The remaining theatres – the 'minor' ones – added songs and accompanying music even in Shakespeare's tragedies (over and above, that is to say, the already quite extensive written-in requirements). The resulting productions were sometimes described as *burlettas*. These and other productions, and very often the plays themselves, have now largely been forgotten. But the incidental music, arranged into suites, has occasionally acquired a life of its own, quite independent of the play for which it was written. As such, it now forms a substantial part of our light music repertoire, and is the justification for a brief consideration of the theatrical circumstances which gave it birth.

In London, and also to an extent in the other burgeoning cities, a boom in theatre-building took place in the later years of the nineteenth century. This followed in the wake of the general migration from rural districts to towns and cities which was such a dominant feature of nineteenth-century demography. The spread of the railway network encouraged this. In London especially, the suburban services meant that villages five or ten miles away from the centre of the metropolis were effectively within half-an-hour's journey from it.

The need for entertainment was not lost on the more perceptive and enterprising entrepreneurs. Such a huge potential, and captive, audience created its own market. Among the theatres that were built in London (many within a very few years of each other) were:

The Gaiety (1868)
The Criterion (1874)
The Savoy (1881)
The Royal Court (1888)
The Garrick (1889)
The Palace (1891)
The Duke of York's (1892)

Her Majesty's (1897)
Wyndham's (1899)
The Albery (1903)
The Globe (1906)

Many of these are still thriving today. Their auditoria are of much beauty and are greatly prized. Especially is this true of the theatres designed by the Newton Abbot-born architect Frank Matcham (1854–1920). He was responsible for the Richmond (1899), the Hackney Empire (1900), the Hippodrome (1900), the Coliseum (1904), the Palladium (1910) and the Victoria Palace (1911).

These theatres could be powered and lit electrically (the first, as noted in Chapter 2, being the Savoy). There was a beneficial by-product in that they didn't burn down as frequently as they had done before. They had orchestra pits and their orchestras fuelled an ever-growing appetite for instrumentalists. Fortunately, the Royal College of Music (1883), the Guildhall School of Music and Drama (1880), and Trinity College of Music (1875) had joined the Royal Academy of Music (1822), and all were on hand to assuage it. Each annual intake of young musicians probably dreamed of becoming the new Mendelssohns or Paganinis; realism would soon dictate otherwise.

Eric Coates (1886–1957), a product of the Royal Academy of Music, did go on to become the most distinguished light music composer of his time. But he was originally a viola-player, and as such second in virtuosity only to his teacher Lionel Tertis. Possessing, too, a literary talent denied to most of his fellow instrumental-ists, he has left a vivid account of what it was like to play in a theatre pit. He had gained entry in the time-honoured way, by deputizing – in his case at the Vaudeville Theatre. The front-of-house may have been plush and glittering; back-stage was very different:

> I groped my way down the dirty, evil-smelling staircase, past the evil-smelling lavatory on the left, and found myself at last in the evil-smelling bandroom ... The orchestra-pit which had to be negotiated by crawling through an under-sized door which threatened to knock your brains out if you were incautious in your approach, proved to be just as dirty as the bandroom, though being more or less open to the inside of the theatre, it was fortunately not quite so unpleasant from the point of view of odour ... [1]

Coates was, and remained, fastidious.

As in other aspects of Victorian and Edwardian life, it was a question of what could, and could not, be seen. Coates soon noticed that most of the Vaudeville audience was in full evening dress. The orchestra was just visible from the auditorium. Those members of it who turned out with white tie earned six shillings and sixpence a night; sixpence more than those who did not. Since the object was to cram as many ticket-chargeable seats into the stalls as possible, orchestra pits were generally cramped, and this in turn determined the size of the theatre orchestras themselves.

In a lecture to the Musical Association,[2] Norman O'Neill, one of the most distinguished theatre-music directors of his time, suggested that, in the bigger

theatres, an orchestra of around twenty-four to twenty-six players might be allocated as follows:

Strings: 4.3.2.2
Woodwind: 2.1.2.1
Brass: 2.2.1
Percussion: 1

There might also be a harp and celesta – with one player offering both instruments.

Pointing out that this number is a 'comparative luxury' he goes on to discuss
plays in which there is no intrinsic music, but which have entr'actes (or intervals)
only. Here, an orchestra of around eighteen players might be sufficient:

Strings: 4.2.1.2.1
Woodwind: 1.1.1.1
Brass: 2 horns, 1 trumpet

In many theatres, the orchestra would be even smaller than this, and the players
would need to be versatile, doubling-up on certain instruments. Indeed, when the
conditions of work are taken into account, the standards of musicianship must have
been remarkably high:

> I found myself one night serenading the lovely Lily Elsie with the viola part of Franz
> Lehár's delightful music to *The Merry Widow* … It takes a good deal of ingenuity to
> look at a lovely woman, at the same time watching the conductor, reading at sight a
> badly-copied manuscript, transposing one number a tone up and another half-a-tone
> down, looking out for cuts and turning over for the leader … [3]

There were, too, some excellent conductors. Coates instanced Howard Talbot,
Barter Johns and the Vaudeville conductor Teddy Jones – the same Edward Jones
for whom Edward German relinquished the 'Jones' of his own name. Among the
orchestrators, Coates singled out the now-forgotten I.A. de Orellana for special
praise.

It is clear that some of these theatre orchestras were very good indeed. Just as
had been the case with the early music-halls, it was possible during the interval at
some theatres to hear a miniature concert. At the Lyceum, for example, during the
interval of a matinée of Henry Irving's presentation of *Much Ado About Nothing*
(on 24 March 1883), the Music Director Meredith Ball offered a selection from
Bizet's *Carmen* and Gounod's march: *La Reine de Saba*. But if you had been
present at Squire Bancroft's Theatre Royal, Haymarket, two months before (20
January 1883), you would have had even better value. With Ernest Bucalossi
(1859–1933) presiding in the pit, the interval music extended to Bizet's *Scene du
Ballet*, Mendelssohn's Wedding March (from *A Midsummer Night's Dream*) and
two overtures: Auber's *Masaniello* and Rossini's *La Gazza Ladra*.

* * *

In the course of his lecture, O'Neill identified three separate classifications of theatre music. These were:

1. Incidental music (which may or may not have been specifically written for the production).
2. Entr'actes and interlude music.
3. Music specially written for and therefore an essential part of the production.

It is the third category which concerns us here. Some of the greatest musicians have turned their attention and talents to writing music which would be integral to, and would enhance the effect of, the drama. Beethoven and *Egmont*, Mendelssohn and *A Midsummer Night's Dream*, Bizet and *L'Arlésienne* and Grieg and *Peer Gynt* are just a few of the most distinguished examples. In Britain, an honourable history of the genre goes back to Purcell and beyond. Actor-managers such as Squire Bancroft, Henry Irving and Herbert Beerbohm-Tree perceived the importance in their productions of music, and commissioned from composers who they believed at the time to be the best available.

Sullivan, however, wrote his first set of incidental music virtually as a speculation, no doubt having observed the effectiveness of Mendelssohn's *A Midsummer Night's Dream* music. Sullivan's work for *The Tempest* dates from 1861, when he was still a student at the Leipzig Conservatory – an institution of which Mendelssohn had been the first director, and where his influence was still all-pervading. *The Tempest* music also served as an examination exercise for Sullivan, who conducted six of its twelve movements in the Conservatory end-of-year concert in April 1861, and thereby gained his diploma a few days later.

On his return to England, Sullivan showed the score to George Grove. As secretary of the Crystal Palace Company and with considerable influence over its concert programmes, Grove promoted the work, with the result that August Manns conducted it at the Crystal Palace on 5 August 1862. Such was its reception that Manns repeated it a few days later. As the twenty-year-old composer said: 'It is no exaggeration to say that I woke up next morning and found myself famous'.[4]

The music was used for a stage production at the Princes Theatre, Manchester, in October 1864, and its success then was probably remembered in 1871 when the same theatre asked him to write some music for *The Merchant of Venice*. But it was his music for *The Tempest* which was instrumental both in establishing him before the public and in revealing a composer with a marked affinity for the needs of Shakespearean drama as they were perceived in the last quarter of the nineteenth century.

Manchester sought him again in 1877 – this time the Manchester Theatre Royal – for *Henry VIII*. A few years later in 1888 he was well established as the musical half of Gilbert and Sullivan, but his hankering for high seriousness led him to find time for Irving's *Macbeth* (Lyceum Theatre: December 1888), even though he had *The Yeomen of the Guard* to compose. Irving had immense prestige, and spared little in his production costs. With thirty-five musicians, his orchestra was larger

5.1 *Caste* programme – outer front cover showing music selection

than most. But he had incurred some criticism with his production of *Faust*, which had used music by Berlioz, Spohr and Marschner, together with some work by the theatre's not-too-distinguished Director of Music, Meredith Ball. *The Musical Times* had suggested that, for subsequent productions, music should be commissioned from 'one of our foremost composers'. Irving took the advice. His choice naturally fell on Sullivan, who provided for *Macbeth* an overture, four act-preludes, all necessary choral settings, 'melodrama' music (background for speech) and various incidental passages, as well as the many drum and brass fanfares required. It was an elaborate score.

Sullivan was to write two further sets of incidental music: one for Irving and one for the American producer Augustin Daly (1838–99). The Irving production was *King Arthur*, first performed at the Lyceum Theatre in January 1895. That for Daly was *The Foresters*, presented at Daly's Theatre, New York, in March 1892. Sullivan had met Daly in California during his 1885 trip to the USA. By 1890, the Savoy Operas were well established in America, and Sullivan would have been an obvious choice as a composer to approach for Tennyson's verse play about Robin Hood and Maid Marian.

Until very recently, Sullivan's incidental music has tended to be overshadowed by the Savoy Operas. This has been a loss, because those sets of his theatre music which are available for study reveal a composer of greater range than would be apparent from the operettas and works for chorus and orchestra alone. *The Merchant of Venice* music, for example, provides for one scene of revelry during which Jessica escapes from her father's house to elope with Lorenzo. What Sullivan has written for this scene reveals a ballet-music composer of striking genius, in work which appears to have no British ancestry but does owe something to early Verdi and even, perhaps, to the mid-century French masters. Certainly among nineteenth-century British composers, none excels him in such delicacy as we can hear in, for example, the Graceful Dance from his *Henry VIII* music. There are resonances, too, which are echoed in the operettas themselves. The dotted rhythms of the *Henry VIII* March may have been in the back of Sullivan's mind when, two years later in 1879, he was evolving the *tarantara* fanfares for his comic *Pirates of Penzance* policemen.

*   *   *

Sir Hubert Parry is most usually thought of as the creator of noble oratorios, rather than of theatre music. Yet, over a period of some thirty years, he too wrote for the theatre: six scores of incidental music, which favour classical Greek rather than modern English drama. His scores comprise *The Birds* (1883; revised 1893), *The Frogs* (1891; revised 1909), *Hypatia* (1893), *Agamemnon* (1900), *The Clouds* (1905) and *The Archarnians* (1904). Vaughan Williams followed his teacher in 1909 with another Aristophanic play, *The Wasps*, from which the onomatopoeic overture achieved popularity.

Working within the time-span of Parry's theatre work was Edward German. A chance meeting with the conductor and singing teacher Alberto Randegger (1832–1911) led to German's appointment in the autumn of 1888 as conductor at Richard Mansfield's Globe Theatre. By the theatre standards of the time, Mansfield's orchestra ranked high, consisting as it did of some twenty-nine players. It was hard work for German; compounded when Mansfield decided to produce *Richard III* in 1889.

German thought that neither Mansfield nor his stage manager had much idea of the complexity of producing an orchestral score:

they speak of music as though it could be turned on and off like waterworks.[5]

Nevertheless, the production settled in for a run of some seven months, which meant that German's overture (written in one week), entr'actes and other incidental music were heard by a large number of people, thereby establishing his reputation as surely as *The Tempest* had established that of Sullivan.

Irving had heard the *Richard III* music and was impressed with it. When he announced in the press that he intended to present *Henry VIII*, the somewhat diffident German assumed that Irving would buy the music Sullivan had written for the Manchester production. It was German's sister Rachel who pressed her brother to approach the actor-manager with an offer to write the music. In accepting, Irving proposed a fee of two hundred guineas; an enormous sum for a young composer in 1892. German, unable to believe his luck, accepted with alacrity. But a few days later, Irving's manager Bram Stoker[6] astonished the young composer by raising the fee to three hundred guineas, because that was the sum they had paid Sir Alexander Mackenzie a few years before for his *Coriolanus* music.

The Lyceum connection continued for German when Johnston Forbes-Robertson (who had taken over as actor-manager) commissioned music for *Romeo and Juliet* (1895). For this, German wrote a Pavane, Pastorale, Nocturne and Dramatic Interlude. There followed music for *As You Like It* (1890), and *Much Ado About Nothing* (1898) for Sir George Alexander at the St James Theatre. The music for *As You Like It* included, of course, the duet setting of *It Was a Lover and His Lass*, together with a masque for the final act (Woodland Dance, Children's Dance and Rustic Dance). *Much Ado About Nothing* had an overture, bourrée and gigue as its principal contributions.

German wrote two further sets of theatre music: *Nell Gwyn* (The Prince of Wales Theatre: 1900) and *The Conqueror* (Scala Theatre: 1905). With Forbes-Robertson in the lead, the Duchess of Sutherland's dramatic fantasy *The Conqueror* included a Romance, Entrance and Dance of the Children, a Satyr Dance and a Berceuse. The music for *The Conqueror* is rarely heard today; indeed, it was not heard much in 1905, as the play folded within a fortnight. But the *Nell Gwyn* Dances are still heard, and once enjoyed huge popularity. Anthony Hope's play *English Nell* was written for Marie Tempest, who stipulated that the music should be by Edward German.

The overture German wrote for the play was the forerunner of a number of 'London' overtures, tone poems and other works, whether or not some of these were specifically named for the capital. Its influence is readily apparent, for example, in Albert Ketèlbey's *Bank Holiday ('Appy 'Ampstead)* movement from the *Cockney* Suite (1924). Ketèlbey's subsidiary idea may well reflect German's primary one (see Ex. 5.2).

German had the happy idea of weaving the traditional tune *Early One Morning* into his overture. The combination of an original tune with a traditional one was

Ex. 5.1   Edward German's *Nell Gwyn* overture; Albert Ketèlbey's *Bank Holiday ('Appy 'Ampstead)*

a) German:

b) Ketèlbey:

"Nell Gwyn" Cartoon by Downey
in "Sporting and Dramatic News" 1900

(*Reproduced by kind permission of the "Illustrated Sporting and Dramatic News."*)

5.2   Edward German cartoon

not lost on Eric Coates, who did the same thing with *Cherry Ripe* when he came to write his *Covent Garden* movement in the *London* Suite (1932). And Elgar, who much admired German's work, was surely aware of the *Nell Gwyn* overture when, one year later in 1901 he came to write the lovers' music in his *Cockaigne* overture (*In London Town*).

Edward German possessed a masterly composition technique. The mastery is in the lyrical flow of ideas and in the transparency of their expression. Particularly is this true of his orchestration – marred only by the occasional over-use of the cymbals. And even this may perhaps be forgiven by theatrical custom and usage, for it is a feature, too, of the Sullivan incidental music discussed above. Essentially, his music depends on memorable melody, supported by strong bass movement – such as would have been insisted upon by his Royal Academy of Music training. Whatever movement may occur in tune or bass, the whole is usually held together by a fairly static inner part; often a sub-melody in its own right. There is also the stock-in trade of sequences and pedal points common to most light music compos-ers of the time; but these are used by German with particular skill, so that the textures are always spare and of exemplary clarity.

His incidental music lent itself to issue in the form of suites, and these suites were published for all manner of instrumental combinations. But they adapted especially well for piano, and the *Nell Gwyn* and *Henry VIII* dances in particular made albums which sold in many thousands.

Edward German did not enjoy robust health, was diffident in manner and suf-fered much from depression. He wrote little after the 1914–18 war, and nothing in the last dozen years of his life. His bitterness at the lack of recognition of his powers as a symphonist must have been a factor in this. He is on record as advising his fellow composer W.H. Bell that it was futile to offer the public anything but rubbish. Whatever vision he had of jolly swains and milkmaids disporting them-selves on the too-hygienic village green no doubt seemed inappropriate to him after the recent carnage of the war.

Elgar's admiration for the work of Edward German was as unbounded as it would be a few years later for that of Eric Coates. This remained undimmed when his own publisher (Novello) suggested he himself attempt something on the same lines and style. He particularly liked the *Henry VIII* Dances; as he wrote to German:

> … you would have found me here alone … smoking a pipe and listening to your 6/8
> Henry VIII with all the exquisite pleasure I have always derived from it.[7]

The '6/8 Henry VIII' was the Shepherd's Dance. We may hazard a guess that two aspects of it appealed to Elgar, the first being technical. It is the manner in which, at one point, the phrases pile up imitatively much as they do in the Minuet from Mozart's Symphony No. 40 in G minor, a work which Elgar admired so much as to use, phrase by phrase, as a model for an early composition exercise. Beyond this, and intangible, is the mood, which the Worcester master was to match a few years later in his *Falstaff*. Neither Elgar nor German were really concerned with either

Plantagenet or Tudor England. They were concerned with their own responses to the rural England of their own time – '*O Peaceful England*', so soon to be lost.

Elgar's destiny lay elsewhere, and there is something wistful in his admiration for the great masters of light music. His own early career had been devoted almost entirely to light music, and he himself also wrote some theatre work. His first venture into this field came in 1901, when George Moore asked him for a 'horn tune' to use in a production at the Gaiety Theatre, Dublin, of a play he and the poet W.B. Yeats had written, *Grania and Diarmid*. Elgar did better than a mere horn tune. He produced some incidental music, a song for Act One and the magnificently sombre funeral march. 'Wonderful in its heroic melancholy', wrote Yeats to Elgar.[8] This was music of profound import. His next incursion into the theatre can reasonably be considered as light music.

In 1912, Oswald Stoll asked him to write some music for a masque, *Crown of India*, to be performed at the London Coliseum to mark the impending visit to India by the King-Emperor George V. The commission came at a bad time for Elgar; he was about to start work on *The Music Makers*, commissioned by the Birmingham Festival, which was just nine months away. But at huge expense, he had on New Year's Day 1912 moved his family into Severn House, Hampstead. Stoll's commission was too financially attractive for him to turn down; Elgar was under pressure. The task involved trawling through old material to find anything usable – any superfluous sketches discarded from other work. Many of these sketches date from 1902 and, although jumbled, they are sufficiently explicitly labelled as to leave little doubt where they were originally intended. *The Dance of the Nautch Girls*, for example seems to have started life as a possible episode for *Falstaff*. Elgar had gone to the trouble of consulting the Ranee of Sarawak about oriental dances (she was, it is true, a fine musician, but his apparent belief that anywhere within a couple of thousand miles of India would be local enough is disturbing). *The Entrance to Delhi* appears to have been intended originally for a possible second *Cockaigne* overture. It is likely that one tune (in E flat) in the *Crown of India* march was conceived for the Second Symphony, and another for an unwritten *Pomp and Circumstance* march.

The ability to find grist for the mill in unlikely places is one of the marks of a true professional. Despite its origins and its speed of composition, the *Crown of India* music made an attractive orchestral suite, testifying to a dramatic flair that makes the fact that Elgar never proceeded with a projected unnamed opera in 1909 or with the Ben Jonson *The Spanish Lady* in the last years of his life all the more lamentable. The point takes even more force when we come to the music for *The Starlight Express*.

In November 1915, the 1914–18 war was at its most black, with no end in sight. It was at this point that the actress Lena Ashwell[9] (Ex. 5.3) suggested to Elgar that he write music for a production of *The Starlight Express*, an adaptation for stage of Algernon Blackwood's novel *A Prisoner in Fairyland*. It was a piece of Barry-like whimsy in which a group of visionary children are the victims of blinkered,

5.3 Lena Ashwell

misunderstanding parents. The children believe that, when they are asleep, their spirits roam at will, collecting the stardust freely available in star-caves. Without it, nothing worthwhile in life can be achieved.

The play opened at the Kingsway Theatre on 29 December 1915, where the run was to be conducted either by Julius Harrison or his deputy Anthony Bernard, with the opening performance under Elgar himself. The reason given for Elgar not, in the event, conducting was that Lady Elgar had suffered some concussion as a result of a taxi accident. But both Elgar and Blackwood had been horrified when, two days before the opening night, they had seen the stage sets (by Harry Wilson) which in their view entirely misinterpreted the essence of the play. There can be no doubt that the spirit of Blackwood's fantasy hit Elgar at his most vulnerable and susceptible; within only a month, a flood of music poured from him – three hundred pages of score containing more than an hour's music.[10]

The escape into an imaginary Elizabethan idyll that had been offered by Edward German had found resonances in the Edwardian nostalgic mood; how much more powerful must Elgar's yearning nostalgia for lost childhood have seemed to those sensitive enough still to feel it in the numbing circumstances of mud, squalor and death in the Flanders trenches. Some of the music was recorded in 1916, and one officer, having played the record for the twelfth time, wrote to Elgar to tell him that it brought back 'the days that are gone' and that it helped him 'through the "Ivory Gate" that leads to Fairyland, or Heaven, whatever one likes to call it'.[11]

Is it light music? An arguable point, when the work can make such an impact. But directness of appeal is one of the attributes of good light music, and such an appeal need not be limited to superficial titillation.

Elgar went on to provide music for the Old Vic production of Binyon's *King Arthur* in 1923, and the Birmingham Theatre Royal's production of *Beau Brummel* (B.P. Matthews) in 1928. Both found Elgar again quarrying his old notebooks for ideas, and perhaps for this reason were for many years undervalued. But while the ideas are those of a callow youth, the experience and technique of a great master were on hand to present them.

Frederick Delius's work for the theatre was in the main operatic but he wrote two sets of incidental music – one at the outset of his creative life and the other in his later years. Delius felt an intense affinity with 'The Great Solitude'[12] of Scandinavia, and many of his friends – including the Norwegians Grieg, Sinding and Strindberg, and the Swede Munch – were from the region. In 1897, great political tension existed between Norway and Sweden; a tension into which Delius walked when the Norwegian playwright Gunnar Heiberg asked him to write some incidental music for his play *Folkeraadet* (The People's Parliament). This play satirized Norwegian parliamentary government. It was presented in Christiania (now Oslo) in October 1897 and caused a riot among students each night, for they thought Delius's music parodied the Norwegian National Anthem. Delius had, indeed, founded his music throughout on the anthem, but mostly used that part of it which bears a distinct resemblance to the Welsh *Deck The Hall* (or, depending on your background, *Father's Pants Will Now Fit Willie*). A few days into the presentation, Delius wrote to Jelka Rosen:

> Every night in the theatre there is a pitched battle when the music begins. Hissing and Hurrahs. There was some talk of lynching me but no-one has yet dared to attack me in the street.[13]

Someone did fire a blank at the conductor, however, and Delius was ordered out of the hotel where he was staying.

Apart from some minor items, Delius provided for this play an overture and preludes to acts two, three and five. The music is not characteristic of him; that is to say, it is too early for the miraculous transformation of his style which was, even so, in the process of crystallizing at that time. But it is interesting in its own right. The overture – a lively fugato – testifies to Delius's contrapuntal studies with Thomas Ward in Florida, and to his professional training during his eighteen months at the Leipzig Royal Conservatory. The second movement is an attractive *scherzando*, while the third is a fine *Allegro Energico*. The last movement – a mock funeral march for the parliamentarians – is probably the one that caused most offence. Divorced from the play, the music inevitably loses its satirical force, but is invigorating and enjoyable even without its allusions.

The poet James Elroy Flecker (1884–1915) is remembered today for his poetic drama *Hassan*. Its story – a complex one – concerns a poor Baghdad confectioner (Hassan) who helps his Caliph escape the clutches of Rafi, the king of the beggars, who in his turn is captured by the Caliph's police. Rafi is offered his freedom if his beloved and beautiful Pervaneh will join the Caliph's harem. Alternatively, after one day together, both Pervaneh and Rafi will be put to death. They choose death. Hassan reviles the Caliph, and takes the Golden Road to Samarkand.

The play was offered to Sir Herbert Beerbohm Tree (1853–1917) who, perhaps seeing no sufficiently meaty part in it for himself, declined it. He passed it on to Basil Dean, who not only saw its possibilities, but also realized it would need a distinctive music score. Ravel was asked but declined. Then Dean happened to hear Delius's *A Village Romeo And Juliet*. It was immediately apparent to him that the plight of Sali and Vrenchen bore similarities to that of Rafi and Pervaneh, and that Delius should be his composer. After production in Darmstadt and New York (where it failed), the play reached London in September 1923, where it ran for 283 performances at His Majesty's Theatre.

Just as Elgar found the nostalgia for childhood innocence in *The Starlight Express* irresistible, so Delius was unlikely to decline a play in which there would be not only a kind of Persian *Liebestod*, but also a procession into the oblivion of Samarkand. The play – and indeed some of Delius's music – descends in places to a *Desert Song* level. The Persian market beggars are sometimes nearer to those imagined by Albert Ketèlbey than we would expect from the aristocratic Delius. But much of Delius's music is pure gold. The score is elaborate, ranging from the purely orchestral Introduction, Serenade and Interlude, to baritone solos, unaccompanied chorus, and male and female choruses with orchestra. The exquisite Serenade is well-known; the wordless unaccompanied chorus finds Delius still in *Song of the High Hills* mode, reaching now as then for similarly elusive sounds and harmonies. The Prelude to Act Three seems to hark back to the Nocturne *Paris*, or even to *Appalachia*. *The Procession of Protracted Death* is intriguing. In 1913, Delius had attended the first performance of Stravinsky's *Le Sacre du Printemps*, describing it later as 'an anti-musical pretentious row'. But are there not echoes of Stravinsky's *Rite* in Delius's *Procession*?

The *Hassan* music was some of the last on which Delius was able to work before paralysis overcame him, and until the arrival of Eric Fenby. The extent of his achievement in *Hassan* – and the yawning gap between genius and mere competence – may be thrown into relief when it is compared with the work of another

5.4   Scene from *The Garden of Allah*

worthy musician working on a similar 'Desert Song' project about the same time. Landon Ronald was a superb, and sometimes under-rated, conductor. He was asked to write the music for a 1920 production of Robert Hichens's play *The Garden of Allah*. The plot – preposterous in its unlikely escapism – concerned the love of a wealthy society woman for a lapsed monk, in the Algerian desert. Ronald's music yielded a suite of five movements, including a *Dance of the Ouled Nail* and *Music to Sand Storm*. The audience may well have been distracted from the sheer awfulness of Ronald's music by the menagerie of live animals employed: donkeys, sheep and even camels. They certainly would have been in the sand storm scene. To create the effect, fine meal was blown on the stage by powerful electric fans. Unfortunately on the opening night no one remembered to lower the transparent curtain which was intended to protect the audience.

In suite form, Ronald's music was extremely popular for a while, but today it seems very dull. Even Holst's repetitive flautist in his *Street of the Ouled Nails* (*Beni Mora* Suite: 1912)[14] holds more interest than Ronald's *Ouled Nail* (Ex. 5.2).

Ex. 5.2   Landon Ronald: *The Garden of Allah* (*Dance of the Ouled Nail*)

Scherzando ma non troppo presto

Beerbohm-Tree held sway at Her Majesty's Theatre, where his productions were renowned for their lavishness and spectacle. While he did not know a great deal of the technical processes of musical composition, he did recognize the composers of his time who were held in highest regard. In 1900, he perceived the twenty-five-year-old Samuel Coleridge-Taylor.

Two years before in 1898, Coleridge-Taylor had achieved enormous prestige with his cantata *Hiawatha's Wedding Feast*. As the offspring of a brief union between an impoverished white woman and a newly qualified black doctor who abandoned them both to return to his Sierra Leone homeland, Coleridge-Taylor's background throughout his short life was one of financial insecurity. During his training at the Royal College of Music (paid for by his patron Colonel Herbert Walters – a true Victorian philanthropist, the more admirable because he was not especially wealthy), he produced a series of distinguished chamber and orchestral

5.5   Beerbohm Tree

works which seemed to suggest a future for him as a kind of English Dvořák, a composer he much admired and who much influenced him.

The possibility of work from one of the leading actor-managers of the time was a golden opportunity. Although Coleridge-Taylor had at that time no theatrical experience, Tree commissioned him to write music for Stephen Phillips's *Herod*. From the music he provided for it, a Processional, Breeze Scene, Dance and Finale were published (Augener: 1901) but the reviews were not enthusiastic. Tree must have been pleased enough, however, since over the next three years, he commissioned three further scores for Phillips's plays: *Ulysses* (1902), *Nero* (1906) and *Faust* (1908).[15] From these, the published work was as follows:

Ulysses: Two songs: O set the Sails, for Troy is Fallen
             (Drinking Song) Great is he who Fused the Might of Earth and Sun
             (Novello)
             (Remaining in manuscript: an overture, part-song, Nymph's Song, interludes, entr'actes and Storm Music)
Nero: Suite: Prelude, Intermezzo, Eastern Dance, Processional March (Novello)
Faust: (For the production of *Faust*, music by other composers, as well as that of Coleridge-Taylor, was used)
             Suite of Three movements (Boosey)

Coleridge-Taylor's music for Stephen Phillips's plays had much currency in the early years of the century but never approached the popularity of Edward German's sets of theatre dances. Nor did his music for *The Eve of St Agnes* – a series of tableaux commissioned in 1912 by the Keats-Shelley Memorial Association – make much impact. Beerbohm-Tree also asked for music for Alfred Noyes's *The Forest of Wild Thyme* but he did not proceed with its production. Rather than waste the effort he had put into it, Coleridge-Taylor organized the music into a number of separate entities:

1.   Scenes From An Imaginary Ballet
2.   Three Dream Dances
3.   Intermezzo

The Forest of Wild Thyme music is variable in interest, but these three works represent the very best of it: light music of high quality. After Coleridge-Taylor's death, the remaining manuscript pieces appeared in print, doing the composer no service.

In 1911, Tree commissioned from him music for *Othello*. For this production, Coleridge-Taylor wrote a Prelude, Entr'acte, Dance for the Second Act, Prelude to Act Three, Willow Song, Introduction to the Fourth Act and a Part-song. All this material, wrote the *Musical Times* reviewer, would provide a suite which 'should last long after Sir Herbert's production has become historical'.[16] The publisher (Metzler) indeed thought so highly of it that he took the unusual course, for theatre music, of engraving a full score. The music poses interesting questions, which perhaps apply to much other incidental music of its period. Does it at any point suggest the darkly passionate world of Iago and Othello? For one listener, at least, it does not. But hearing it now, divorced from the play that generated it, this hardly seems to matter. For the music is hugely enjoyable purely as light entertainment. In particular, the Children's Intermezzo has now the charm of an antique, flower-garlanded postcard, while the Military March has the panache and swagger of Elgar in *Pomp and Circumstance* mode. In passing, it may be noted that, even for the none-too-demanding needs of incidental music, Coleridge-Taylor had regard for overall musical unity as he effected a thematic relationship between these two movements (see Ex. 5.3).

Ex. 5.3   Samuel Coleridge-Taylor: *Othello*, (a) Children's Intermezzo, (b) Military March

a) Children's Intermezzo

b) Military March

Sullivan, Parry, Elgar, German, Delius and Coleridge-Taylor. These were the giants who applied their art to the services of the theatre when asked to do so. Below them were the hordes of humble career theatre-musicians: men with technique, resource and sometimes more, who could compose, conduct, orchestrate and generally solve any musical problem put before them, usually at a day's notice or even less. Occasionally, they struck gold. Frederick Rosse (1867–1940) was one. After study at Leipzig, he became a complete man of the theatre, writing music for many plays, including *Monsieur Beaucaire* (1902) and *The Merchant of Venice*

(1905), both of which yielded suites. For years afterwards, many a young pianist thought, as did his fond parents, he had arrived when he could pound out The Doge's March from *The Merchant of Venice*. Norman O'Neill (1875–1934) was another – but he was out of the ordinary. Like so many musicians who drifted into humdrum positions, his musical training had been thorough; in his case under Ivan Knorr at the Frankfurt Conservatorium, where his fellow students included Balfour Gardiner, Percy Grainger, Cyril Scott and Roger Quilter. O'Neill's most distinguished theatre scores were for whimsical plays by J.M. Barrie (*Mary Rose*, 1920) and Maeterlinck (*The Blue Bird*, 1909). There was a fashion for whimsy in the first two decades of the twentieth century – especially that involving children; we have already noted Blackwood's *The Starlight Express*, and Elgar's part in it. A slightly earlier example was *Where the Rainbow Ends* (Savoy Theatre: 1911) for which Roger Quilter provided the music. Quilter was himself a somewhat child-like figure, whose sexual identity problems would in later life contribute to his personal disintegration. At the stage of *Where the Rainbow Ends* in 1911, his music exhibits a curiously sexless innocence. Probably, it made him an ideal composer for this story of Rosamunde and her brother setting out on a magic carpet in search of their lost parents – 'where the rainbow ends'. The children performing the play were from the Italia Conti Stage School. Among them was the twelve-year-old Noël Coward, whose name will recur in later pages.

Quilter extracted a suite from his work, as he did also from the *As You Like It* music he wrote for Lilian Baylis at The Old Vic in 1921. Both suites show him to be an immaculate exponent of 'Old English' pastiche; the melodies in the tradition of Edward German but the harmonies owing more to Delian chromaticism than German would have allowed.

While Quilter wrote theatre works, he was, unlike O'Neill, not a man of the theatre. There were many other worthy theatre musicians, but only rarely were they fired by the vital spark; and then, curiously, not always by their theatre music. Alfred Reynolds (1884–1969), Percy Fletcher (1879–1932), Herman Finck (1872–1939) and Arthur Wood (1875–1953) are typical of this company.

From the 1920s onwards, the 'straight' theatre orchestras were in gradual but distinct decline. To an extent, theatre economics dictated this but trends in production styles also had their effect. Moreover, the fantasy and whimsy plays, represented by *Mary Rose* or *Starlight Express* – for which music was an intrinsic part – had lost their vogue. Many musicians drifted for a while into the silent cinemas, or 'picture palaces' as they were called. Here, they would either use existing music or they would improvise. The better musicians found places in the rapidly proliferating dance bands – which were associated more often than not with hotels or clubs. For the variety theatres – as the old-style music halls had now tended to become – an orchestra was still essential. Some of these, such as that of the London Palladium, were of high quality.

In this brave new theatrical world, the old styles of incidental music had lost their place. After the Second World War, the situation declined still further. The bigger theatres which housed and hosted 'musicals' still maintained them, but the straight play had to make do with recorded music, when it was needed. A sad loss, which seriously diminished the special ambience of the theatrical experience.

Those musicians working for the Shakespeare theatres, such as Leslie Bridgewater (1893–1975) at the Stratford on Avon Shakespeare Memorial Theatre, still found an outlet for their art. Others would have to master the techniques of writing for radio drama and, once the talkies arrived, for film.

Notes

1. Eric Coates, *Suite in Four Movements*, pp. 87–88.
2. Since 1944, the Royal Musical Association. The lecture was given on 21 March 1911.
3. Coates, p. 91.
4. Quoted in Leslie Baily (1952), *The Gilbert and Sullivan Book*, London: Cassell, p. 32.
5. Scott, W.H. (1932), *Edward German: an Intimate Biography*, Cecil Palmer.
6. Author of *Dracula*.
7. Elgar to German, May 1916 (no day date).
8. Yeats to Elgar, 23 March 1903.
9. Lena Ashwell OBE (1872–1957). An actress who organized 'Concerts at the Front' for the YMCA. She raised money for the purpose, and in the first two years of the war sent out two thousand concert parties.
10. Northrop Moore, Jerrold (1984), *Edward Elgar: A Creative Life*, Oxford University Press, p. 691.
11. J. Lawrence Fry to Elgar, 5 October 1917 (Hereford and Worcester Record Office).
12. A section named thus in *The Song of the High Hills*.
13. Delius to Jelka Rosen, 22 October 1897.
14. Eric Coates had a low boredom threshold. To while away the time as a viola-player in the Queen's Hall Orchestra, he and his colleagues would make up words to fit the tunes they were playing. For Holst's *Ouled Nails* tune: 'Oh What a Dull Time We're Having'.
15. Phillips, in conjunction with J. Comyns Carr, after Goethe.
16. *Musical Times*, May 1912.

CHAPTER SIX

Balladry

Ballads have had a bad press; none worse than from some of their own interpreters. Nellie Melba's (1861–1931) alleged contemptuous advice to Clara Butt (1873–1936) on the occasion of the latter's first visit to Australia mirrors that of Edward German to W.H. Bell: 'Sing 'em muck – it's all they can understand'.[1] Here, her comment is all-embracing of her fellow country-folk, but there is little doubt what material she, and indeed many other singers, thought 'muck'. Sir Charles Santley (1834–1922) was scarcely less dismissive, when, in his autobiography, he described ballads as 'imbecile trash'. Eric Blom[2] dismissed all ballads indiscriminately:

> the words are by a hack writer set to music by a composer of no merit but that of easy melodic invention.

Blom thought music-hall vulgarity was preferable, and that *Champagne Charlie* or *A Bicycle Made For Two*, while not to be taken seriously as music, nevertheless 'surpass any amatory or horticultural ballad ever written'.[3] But, as Felix McGlennon, who wrote both music-hall and ballad fodder pointed out, 'There is a great art … in making rubbish acceptable'.[4]

The Victorian and Edwardian Drawing Room Ballad had a broad and mixed ancestry, with many august names to be found in its pedigree. Among them may be cited Charles Dibdin (1745–1814), James Hook (1746–1827), Charles Edward Horn (1786–1849) and even Haydn, who wrote a number of songs to English words. But the greatest influence was probably that of Mendelssohn (1809–1847), whose popularity in the middle years of the nineteenth century was unparalleled here. Sadly, the best of the ballad-writers rarely approaches in quality the least of the names above.

The demand for ballads was stimulated by the spread of pianos in middle-class parlours, and was amateur-led. The piano had become one of the symbols of status. It needed minimum maintenance, especially when the better ones began to be built on an iron frame. The piano was, so to speak, *in situ* and this meant there would always be an accompanying instrument to hand. Even the least talented and least vocally endowed were asked if they had brought their music; and some didn't wait for an invitation, despite their performing limitations. Jane Austen's dry Mr Bennett was placed by her in a time some years before balladry came into its own, but his exasperation with his daughter Mary, who inflicted vocal punishment on his assembled guests, could be matched in most ages: 'That will do extremely well, child. You have delighted us long enough … '.[5]

Balladry probably reached its peak of popularity in the first decade of the twentieth century, but had by then been in vogue for many years. Among the earlier successful ballad-writers were Sir Arthur Sullivan (1842–1900), Sir Paolo Tosti (1846–1916) and Sir Frederick Cowen (1842–1935). Both Cowen and Sullivan – Leipzig-trained – were comprehensive musicians to their fingertips. Tosti had not their technique, but he was a trained singer employed by both Queen Victoria and the Royal Academy of Music as a professor of singing. Some of their younger competitors would not be of this quality. Tosti's *Goodbye*, Cowen's *The Better Land* and Sullivan's *The Lost Chord* sold in huge quantities as sheet music. The last-named is reputed to have sold over half-a-million copies.

There are echoes of Elgar pursued by *Land of Hope and Glory* and of Rachmaninoff by the Prelude in C Sharp Minor in Cowen's attempts to escape the popularity of *The Better Land*:

> It has, like a Frankenstein monster, haunted me … It has followed me everywhere, cropping up at all sorts of unexpected places. When I have wanted to be quiet, a cornet has played it in the street. When I have thought to read a nice eulogium on myself in the papers, it has been the chief topic of the article. When I have made a new acquaintance, feeling perhaps rather proud of some recent composition, I have been introduced as the composer of it …[6]

Cowen thought he had done well to sell the copyright for three hundred pounds: 'not a bad sum for about an hour's work'. But had he not done so, he would have profited to the extent of several thousand pounds.

The endorsement of a ballad by the great singers of the day was necessary if sales on this scale were to be achieved. *The Lost Chord* was particularly associated with the New York-born Antoinette Sterling (1850–1904). So, too, was J.L. Molloy's *Love's Old Sweet Song*. She was contracted to the publisher Boosey, and would have received a royalty each time she included a song published by him in one of her programmes. These songs, therefore, were sometimes called 'Royalty Ballads', and the royalty would be a welcome addition to the singer's usual appearance fee. Miss Sterling had a little more concern for the quality of what she offered than some of her fellow singers. She shared the fervour of some eminent Victorians for moral uplight through education, and did her bit by including Lieder in her programmes. Such serious art-songs, however, were not popular and her audiences no doubt considered they were being improved enough by the ballads. It would take carefully structured improvement by Henry Wood in his Promenade Concerts for such a course to succeed.

Ballads generally used but a fraction of the technique available to the greatest of the late nineteenth- and early twentieth-century singers. Some of these artists were among the most distinguished in the history of singing. But such were the rewards of ballad-singing that few could afford to disdain them, however much they may have lamented sullying their vocal chords. Edward Lloyd, for example, would be paid the huge fee for the time (1899) of two hundred and fifty guineas – provided he agreed to sing *The Holy City*.

Apart from those already mentioned, these singers included such now-forgotten artists as Hubert Eisdell, Phyllis Lett, Topliss Green (a pupil of the ballad composer Wilfrid Sanderson) and Robert Radford. John McCormack's fame was based on his association with *I Hear You Calling Me* as surely as was that of Edward Lloyd on *The Holy City* and *I'll Sing Thee Songs of Araby* (Frederick Clay). Harry Dearth was so closely identified with Eric Coates's hugely successful *Stonecracker John* that he was often called 'The Stonecracker'. Bernard Shaw complained that Sims Reeves was always inviting Maud to 'Come into the Garden'; but in truth, Reeves was more famous for letting down concert promoters and for the frequency of his 'farewell' tours.

Before the establishment of the Performing Right Society in 1914, composers had a poor return for their work, especially if they sold it outright. Purchase of a copy conferred the right of performance – although publishers tried to 'ring-fence' their publications with all manner of restrictions. If, for example, you purchased Ivan Caryll's *Lazily, Drowsily* (from the burlesque *Little Christopher Columbus*), you were restricted:

> All Performing Rights in this opera are reserved. Single detached numbers may be sung at concerts, not more than two in one concert, but they must be given without Costume or Action. In no case must such performance be announced as a 'selection' from the Opera …

The publishers also tried to prevent parody. They could hardly stop George Grossmith amusing Frederick Cowen at a private birthday party, parodying the great man's *The Better Land*:

> I hear thee speak of a Better Land,
> Written by young Freddie Cowen's hand
> Mother, where did he get that tune?
> Where did he steal it, oh, tell me soon?
> Did it come from Handel's grand Messiah?
> Or Charlie Gounod's 'Ave Maria'?
> Not There, not there, my child.

Prices per copy varied. In the 1890s, Boosey was selling his ballads at two shillings a copy, but Hopwood and Crewe were charging double that for the Ivan Caryll song mentioned above. Robert Cocks and Co. ('Music Publishers to Her Majesty Queen Victoria and His Royal Highness The Prince of Wales') charged four shillings for Miss M. Lindsay's *The Bridge*; but for that, a superb cover was offered (see Fig. 6.1). In comparison with the wages and prices of the times, even two shillings was a considerable sum. Such a charge gives some indication as to who was best able to purchase; these songs were aimed at the increasingly prosperous middle classes.

Of the many publishers of ballads, two became pre-eminent: Boosey and Chappell. In order to promote their wares more effectively, these two publishers organized their own ballad concerts, John Boosey's commencing in 1867 and those of Chappell in 1894. The history of these concerts is complex and intertwined. Those of Boosey

6.1   A cover illustration for Longfellow's 'The Bridge', set to music in the late nineteenth century

were called the London Ballad Concerts, and were held at the St James Hall, Regent St, until January 1894 when they moved to the Queen's Hall, Langham Place, which had opened the year before. Here they stayed until Chappells took over the lease of the Queen's Hall; the London Ballad Concerts then returned to the St James Hall. In October 1904, with the decommissioning of that hall imminent, they returned once more to the Queen's Hall. In October 1907, they were transferred to the Royal Albert Hall, where they stayed until 1927. In the October of that year they returned to the Queen's Hall, where in February 1933 their final concert was held.

Chappells inaugurated their ballad catalogue in the 1890s, and started their own ballad concerts at the St James Hall in November 1894. Confusingly, they were managed by William Boosey, who had left the family firm for Chappells. (William Boosey was known to all musical London as 'The Emperor of Bond Street', such was his authority.) On securing the Queen's Hall lease in 1903, Chappells naturally transferred their ballad concerts there, where they remained until their closure in 1927.

These concerts were not entirely devoted to songs. To an extent, the Chappell concerts recognized this when, in 1923, they were renamed the Chappell Popular Concerts. On their platforms, such pianists as Solomon, Moiseiwitsch and Pachmann regularly appeared, together with string virtuosi of the order of Szigeti, Suggia and Kreisler. From 1916, the New Queen's Hall Orchestra under Alick Maclean would be in attendance too. Many ballads were therefore orchestrated, and then issued in boiled-down versions.

In Boosey's advertising, there was always a clear distinction made between ballads and 'artistic' songs. Usually, composers such as Warlock, Moeran or Britten came in the 'artistic' category. The 'selected' ballad had to be easy to sing, because the aim was to secure as much as possible of the huge sales generated by the market for home performance songs. In practice, this meant that many ballads were slow and soulful. It is easier for an amateur singer to be slow and soulful than light and agile. These songs were usually rhythmically enervated. Rarely did they set great poetry, for their composers could not in their music match the rhythmic energy which is a characteristic of the best English verse. Moreover, the accompaniments had little life of their own. A simple chord structure, often clumsily laid out, was the usual order of the day. This structure was often expressed in arpeggio patterns, and in this respect, Mendelssohn's example was not entirely understood. For him, the arpeggio was merely one element of an unparalleled armoury of composition technique. For the lesser imitators, it was all too often the only element. These ballad accompaniments merely support the singer; little attempt at illustrating aspects of the words – in, for example, the manner of Schubert – is made. Still less is there any penetration of the underlying psychology, as in, for example, the songs of Schumann. The word-setting itself was often cavalier; no ballad composer would sacrifice what he perceived to be a good tune for the sake of the words.

The subjects of the lyrics were surprisingly constricted. In late Victorian times, too, they could be mawkish to an extent that would not have been tolerated in the early twentieth century, let alone today. Cowen, who had few scruples about setting such material, was quite cynical about it:[7]

> One song I wrote, *The Children's Home*, was, I think responsible for more musical passings-away and transportations to heaven of little children than any severe epidemic of measles in real life ever could be. For a long while afterwards nearly all the songs were cast in this infanticidal mould and I was always afraid of opening any sets of verses sent to me in case I should be doomed to read about the inevitable little child, with a faded flower in its hand, occupying a prominent seat among the angels.

The subject of Love, in its many aspects, became in due course supreme. But songs hymning the virtues of the more beautiful regions of the country were also popular. *Glorious Devon* (Edward German), *Green Hills O' Somerset* (Coates) and *Mountains O'Mourne* (Percy French) are three of many. Gardens and flowers sent both poet and composer into ecstasy, especially if there were roses in it. Haydn Wood triumphantly managed to embrace all three approved subjects in one song: *Love's Garden of Roses*. He found further inspiration in *Dear Hands That Gave Me Violets, O Flower Divine* and *Daffodil Gold*. Eric Coates was drawn repeatedly to lunar contemplation. A selection by no means complete includes *Maid and the Moon, Brown Eyes Beneath the Moon, Moon Daisies, Moon Boat, Moonland Dreams* and *Little Lady of the Moon*.

The last five of the above titles all have lyrics by Fred Weatherly (1848–1933), by common consent the most sought-after ballad-poet of his times.[8] He was successful because he understood so well the needs and tastes of his listeners. These he said, were 'restrained contentment, warm affection, freedom from *angst*, the loveliness of common objects and familiar scenes, and the sanctity of Home'. Weatherly wrote hundreds of lyrics, including such famed ones as *Roses of Picardy* and *The Boys of the Old Brigade*. But lyric-writing was for him but a spare-time hobby. Born in Somerset, which he would celebrate from time to time in such poems as *Up From Somerset* (set by Wilfred Sanderson), *Green Hills O' Somerset* and *A Dinder Courtship* (both set by the essentially city-centred Eric Coates), Weatherly had taught at Oxford and was a barrister taking silk in 1925. His academic books included such titles as *The Rudiments of Logic: Inductive and Deductive* and *Questions in Logic: Progressive and General*. Eric Coates has left a vivid picture of the man. As a young unknown, he visited Weatherly in his Bloomsbury house:

> I walked bashfully into the pleasant study, and there, with his back to the light, in a window overlooking Woburn Place, sitting in a swivel-chair, was the famous author. He was one of the smallest men I had ever met and, for such a remarkably gifted man, strangely enough, was the possessor of a small head. He rose from his seat with the agility of a boy, shook me by the hand, offered me a cigarette and made me feel at home in a few seconds. I noticed on his desk two piles of papers; the one on his right hand looked like lyrics and the one on his left had the appearance of legal documents. I was right in both cases, for during the conversation which followed he told me he wrote poems while working out difficult problems of law.[9]

Coates was rewarded with *Stonecracker John*. He thought of a tune for it on the top deck of a horse-bus, on his way home. Two days later, he sold the completed song to Arthur Boosey for five pounds. This was in 1909. Some months later, Harry Dearth sang it at a Boosey concert in the Royal Albert Hall, to great acclamation. Thereafter, it sold in many thousands of copies. Boosey had at first been reluctant to publish it, for the song was in three/four time, when most popular ballads had usually been in common time. This tiny point of originality, however, proved to be a factor in its success. Both Arthur Boosey and Harry Dearth made much money from *Stonecracker John*; Coates made his five pounds. No wonder that, five years later, he was to be a founder-member of the Performing Right Society.

Weatherly was sufficiently a musician to set his own lyrics when he had a mind to. A number of distinguished singers could also write their own music. Peter Dawson (1882–1961) was one, writing under the pseudonym of J.C. McCall. He published a few songs, of which the most popular was his setting of *Boots* (Kipling). Nothing so clearly illustrates the division between popular taste and the trained musician's rejection of it as Sir Henry Wood's reaction when Dawson sang the song at the 1926 Promenade Concerts:

> I was about to take a bow because of the tumultuous applause when (Wood) stood in my way in a towering rage and shouted 'Don't ever sing rubbish like that here again. Boots, Boots … sing them songs that uplift them. Brahms or Schubert'.[10]

Yet until well into the 1930s, Wood did allow ballads in the Proms – after the interval.

Despite his success with the public as a composer – even if one of modest ability – Dawson remained primarily a bass singer. Other singer-composers were to be remembered principally as composers. These included Teresa Del Riego (1876–1968), Frederick Keel (1871–1954), Liza Lehmann (1862–1918) and, later, Michael Head (1900–1976).

Del Riego, of Spanish parentage, was a Londoner who often wrote her own lyrics. 'I think that the qualities most essential to success in composing songs are truth of expression, and harmony, combined with originality', she said. We may look askance at how far she met her own criteria; we can hardly question the phenomenal success of *Homing*, *O Dry Those Tears* or *Thank God For A Garden*.

As a boy, Frederick Keel had been head chorister at Wells Cathedral, and in due course he studied composition with Frederick Corder at the Royal Academy of Music. Subsequently he became a professor of composition there. His work was not restricted to ballads, but he did write a number of them – of which *Trade Winds* is probably the best known.

Liza Lehmann, herself the wife of the composer Herbert Bedford, gave up her singing career in 1894 in order to devote her time to composition. She wrote a musical farce *Sergeant Brue* and an opera *The Vicar of Wakefield*. Laurence Housman had adapted the Goldsmith story for her, but disgraced himself when he attended a performance by laughing immoderately at her effort. She was more successful with her songs, of which there are over one hundred and fifty. Many of them catch the popular infatuation in late Victorian times with all things oriental. Her song-cycle *In a Persian Garden*, setting quatrains from Fitzgerald's translation of the *Rubaiyat* of Omar Khayyam, was first performed in 1896. Originally written for mixed chorus and piano, it was soon rearranged for the more palatable and profitable form of solo song.

Michael Head came on the scene too late for the era of ballad concerts. He became a professor of piano at the Royal Academy of Music in 1927, and as a composer wrote light operas, children's operas, pieces for oboe and piano, and a cantata. But he found a niche for himself giving recitals of his own songs in which he accompanied himself; almost a cabaret performance, emulated in more recent times by Richard Rodney Bennett. These songs, dating mainly from the 1930s, reflect the psychological needs of an inter-war people, clinging to rural and domestic certainties. Today they may seem vapid. But an unassuming song such as *When Sweet Ann Sings* reveals a singer-composer who set English words with a care missing in the work of many more well-known balladiers.

While in the early nineteenth century women were prominent in the field of the novel, they were not as significant in other arts. But they certainly came into their own in the age of the ballad; although, even here, as in the case of some female novelists, a few thought it prudent to adopt a male name. Jules Brissac had been born Emma Mary Bennett, while Helen Mary Rhodes published her work under the pseudonym Guy D'Hardelot. Bernard Shaw exercised his wit on the latter:

> ... There was a composer who announced herself as Guy D'Hardelot, a name in which I confess I do not altogether believe. She accompanied Madame Inverni and Mr Isidor de Lara in a cycle of her love-songs – fluent and pretty outpourings of a harmless Muse with an unsuspiciously retentive memory. The two singers were quite equal to them, Mr de Lara, in fact, being considerably underweighted.[11]

At a century's distance, D'Hardelot's work seems featureless and bland, but in its time, such a song as her *Three Green Bonnets* was popular enough to be reprinted in the albums of the day.

It is in fact remarkable how many ballad composers regardless of sex chose to publish their work under pseudonym, almost as if they sought thereby to deflect the inevitable rapier thrusts of Shaw, Runciman, Newman and other mordaunt critics. Among them were Henry Trotter (publishing as Henry Trotère), Dotie Davies (Hope Temple), Mary Dickson (May Brahe, composer of *Bless This House*) and Michael Maybrick (Stephen Adams, composer of *The Holy City*). To balance this, it must be said that, at a time when women's rights were beginning to be asserted, most female composers were content to stand under their own names. Dame Ethel Smyth (1858–1944) blazed a trail for them, establishing a standard of sheer professionalism few of her sex would match until the early years of the twentieth century. But Dame Ethel, Leipzig-trained, wrote lieder not ballads. Much more down-to-earth were Amy Woodford-Finden (1860–1919) and Maude Valerie White (1855–1937), born in Valparaiso and Dieppe respectively.

White was thoroughly trained academically. She was a holder of the Mendelssohn Scholarship and studied in Heidelberg, Paris and at the RAM in London. She spoke fluent German, French and Italian, and of her three hundred songs, a number were set in these languages. Despite all this effort, she is remembered today only for her ballad *Until*. Some of her instrumental and choral music might, with profit, be given a renewed hearing today.

Woodford-Finden was just as prolific. Like Lehmann, her interest was the Orient, which for her ranged from Egypt all points east to Japan. Song albums poured from her, greatly enriching both her and Boosey, her fortunate publisher: *A Dream of Egypt*, *A Lover in Damascus*, *Indian Love Lyrics* (from which came the still popular *Pale Hands I Loved*), *Four Little Japanese Songs*. These titles show how she cornered a lucrative market. Many of the songs were issued in various keys, in versions for piano only, and as duets, and in arrangements for mixed chorus. Both piano and orchestral accompaniments were provided for.

The financial success of the balladiers was not lost on the great and good who laboured for little reward in the serious music market. Elgar memorably expressed their dilemma when he complained that, if he wrote a new oratorio, he and his family had to go without for a year. Elgar was incapable of writing below a very high standard of professional expertise. He was also a master of light orchestral music. But, among the patrons of the ballad concerts, his songs never achieved the popularity of some of the composers mentioned above. Nor did Sir Hubert Parry or Sir Charles Stanford fare much better when they tried their hand. Sir Frederick Cowen bore out Elgar's point when, as an old man, he wrote somewhat defensively:

> At that period [i.e. the late 1800s] serious music yielded very little money, and we musicians had to live![12]

It is, perhaps, more difficult to write down to a level than to write up to one. Hermann Löhr (1872–1943) could never have aspired to write six symphonies, as Cowen had done. Nor did he have the sheer musicianship to conduct an entire repertoire from memory, as Cowen had. He had nevertheless written *Little Grey Home in the West* and *Where my Caravan has Rested*. These were two of the more enduring ballads, and Löhr, unlike Cowen, would neither denigrate them nor apologize for them: 'A number of my humble efforts have, I am proud to say, attained a considerable degree of success'.[13]

Sir Landon Ronald (1873–1938) was a thrusting musician of the kind not afraid of getting his hands dirty in the mud of popularity. Any kind of music was grist to his mill. It is no surprise, then, that Ronald – an admired principal of the Guildhall School of Music (1910–1938) and a splendid conductor who, perhaps better than the composer himself found the rhythms of such Elgar works as the Second Symphony – wrote some three hundred songs. Even today, many older folk remember *Down in the Forest*; not so many will remember that it was written by Landon Ronald.

Edward German dipped a toe in the waters of balladry. The best known of his ballad-type songs is probably *Glorious Devon*. A four-square, sturdy song with clean-cut lines, it is typical of a strongly defined style already exploited in *Merrie England*, a style which was to have a marked influence on the ballads of Eric Coates.

Coates saw no reason why light music should imply a lowering of artistic or technical standards, and his training at the Royal Academy of Music under Frederick Corder had been rigorous. He wrote ballads throughout his career – around one hundred and sixty of them – although the rate of production did fall off drastically in the last two decades of his life. Despite the success of *Stonecracker John*, even Coates found it hard to progress in the world of ballads, dominated as it was by Guy D'Hardelot, Hermann Löhr and others. As he revealed, too, in his autobiography,[14] treachery at Chappells (his publishers) at first resulted in the work of the firm's other ballad composers being promoted over his own. Subsequently, he was given a con- tract by Chappells which required him to offer them three ballads each year, together with two orchestral works. This contract stimulated such ballads as *I Pitch My Lonely Caravan by Night* (Horley), *I Heard You Singing* (Royden Barrie) and *Birdsongs at Eventide* (Royden Barrie). Coates's work was in the repertoire of John McCormack, Alfred Piccaver, Hubert Eisdell, Richard Tauber and, indeed, most other singers of his day. It is, nevertheless, to be doubted whether the setting of words was his strongest suit; rather, instrumental work was his forte. The three songs mentioned above are arguably heard to best advantage in the Two Symphonic Rhapsodies for orchestra he wrote around them in 1933.

As Philip Scowcroft has pointed out,[15] Samuel Coleridge-Taylor faces us again – as did Sullivan, German and a number of others – with the problem of whether to regard him as a 'serious' or a 'light' composer. Like so many of his colleagues, Coleridge-Taylor had to write what the market demanded, rather than the quintets and trios of his student days (that luxury was enjoyed only by composers of inde- pendent means). What the market demanded were dramatic cantatas, salon morsels and ballads. The distinction between Coleridge-Taylor's ballads and his art-songs is a fine one. The splendid *Sorrow Songs* (1904), for example, are art-songs of great beauty, subtlety and craftsmanship. The once-popular *Eleanore* (Eric Mackay) – a vehicle for the tenor John Coates in his time – is perhaps on the border-line, but is nevertheless a ballad of considerable passion. Coleridge-Taylor himself had no doubt about his settings of Kathleen Easmon, the coloured artist and poet from his father's country, Sierra Leone. He called them *Fairy Ballads* – and these delightful child- innocent songs of 1909 are indeed such. But his finest ballad – and surely one of the finest of all ballads – is not named as one at all, but is set as the centre-piece of his early cantata: *Hiawatha's Wedding Feast*. The suberb tenor song *Onaway, Awake, Beloved* (Ex. 6.1) remains the benchmark of ballad quality, rarely equalled by others.

Frederick Cowen also set *Onaway* and achieved considerable success with it. Coleridge-Taylor thought his own setting to be superior. Posterity has agreed with him.

Ex. 6.1 Samuel Coleridge-Taylor: *Hiawatha's Wedding Feast* (*Onaway, Awake, Beloved*)

With the work of Roger Quilter (1877–1953), we begin to move out of the Edwardian period. Quilter's work is difficult to categorize, since, while it has some characteristics of the ballad style, he tends to set distinguished poetry rather than mundane ballad-fodder. His work, too, approaches the quality of such younger figures as Frank Bridge, Peter Warlock and E.J. Moeran. Characteristic of him are his Shakespeare settings, and his *Seven Elizabethan Lyrics*. Ballad-like or not, his approach to song-writing is light, but with no compromise in standards of craftsmanship. For his publisher Boosey he made many arrangements of folk-songs, but first attracted attention with his Herrick cycle *To Julia* (Op. 8), which dates from 1905. This proved to be a popular vehicle for one of the more sensitive musicians among singers: Gervase Elwes. Quilter was a fine pianist, and it was this understanding of the nature of the piano that helped raise the quality of his accompaniments above the level of many mentioned so far in this chapter. *Fair House of Joy* is an example: while it is by no means easy to play, its notes all seem to lie securely under the fingers. So, too, do those of *Go, Lovely Rose* (Edmund Waller), written for Hubert Eisdell, and *Now Sleeps the Crimson Petal* (Tennyson) – a song which has been sung with equal ease by either tenors or sopranos, but which found an especial place in the repertoire of Ada Crossley.

Frank Bridge (1879–1941) may appear to be an unlikely source for the ballad-hunter. Distinguished as a violinist, violist, conductor, and composer of fine chamber and orchestral music, he also wrote songs. Such an example as *E'en As A Lovely Flower* (Kate Crocker; after Heine) has some of the characteristics of a ballad about it: a simple, sustained melody supported by chords, lifted above the bland only by mild syncopation. Its rhythmic accompaniment pattern is maintained in all but six bars. But when we come to *Go not, Happy Day*, we find more sophistication. The delicate melody is poised over a murmuring accompaniment of subtle accentuation. For this, the description of ballad is hardly adequate – infectiously light though the song is. And when we take a further few steps to *Love Went A-riding* (Mary Coleridge), we have moved out of the realm of the amateur singer, and certainly well beyond her drawing-room accompanist. This exhilarating song, clearly intended to conclude a recital, needs a singer who can luxuriate in the long phrase, and a pianist of virtuoso technique.

Like Bridge and Coleridge-Taylor, Haydn Wood (1882–1959), seemed likely to make his mark as a composer of chamber music, and he was indeed a Cobbett prize-winner with his Phantasie in F for string quartet. He had won an open violin scholarship to the Royal College of Music, and studied composition there with Stanford. Subsequently, his career resembled that of Eric Coates, in that he divided his time between orchestral music and ballad-writing. Apart from the obvious financial spur in writing ballads, he had married the soprano Dorothy Court, who sang many of his two hundred or more songs. He had started writing them from the year of that marriage (1909) and continued producing them throughout his life, long past the great age of ballads.

His best-known song remains *Roses of Picardy*, a memorable melody made the more poignant by its indelible associations with the 1914–18 killing fields. Closely following it in popularity were *A Brown Bird Singing* and the already mentioned *Love's Garden of Roses*. The strength of his songs lay in their melodies, always written into the most telling registers of the voice. As if aware of their rhythmic deficiencies, his accompaniments try to promote movement through gentle, off-beat syncopation.

Into the 1930s he went, with few if any concessions to changing styles and fashions. A song such as *God Make Me Kind* (1932: Desmond Carter) still manages the triumphant conclusion, and even boasts countersubjects in its accompaniment (see Ex. 6.2). Sixteen years later find him, in *Song of a Thankful Heart* (1948: Richard Corrin) almost indistinguishable from his style of forty years earlier. He may not have changed, but unfortunately, audiences had.

In the 1920s, as balladry drew its dying breaths, the most distinguished British song composer of his time would, when financially embarrassed, write a 'beer-money' song. His devotees might recoil at the idea, but is such a song as Peter Warlock's *Passing By* (1929, Anon) anything other than a ballad, albeit a very distinguished one?

Over the 1920s and 1930s, sales of sheet music ballads began to decline, and the ballad-concerts themselves ceased. One of the most eminent of ballad-singers had no doubt as to the reason for this. Peter Dawson wrote:

> ... since the advent of wireless the making of one's own music in the home has steadily decreased.
> This is a deplorable state of affairs, and most damaging to the progress and development of the vocal art.[16]

The infant broadcasting industry was undoubtedly a major factor. But there were others. One of them was the spread in popularity of the gramophone. This may appear so paradoxical as to require further explanation. Until the introduction of electrical recording, sound quality was poor – although the human voice fared better in reproduction than most instruments. The Copyright Act of 1911 and the establishment of the Performing Right Society in 1914 began a process whereby the income from a composer's sheet music sales would decrease while that from mechanical processes (records, broadcasting, etc.) would increase. Where still being

Ex. 6.2   Haydn Wood: *God Make Me Kind*

written, ballads were directed more towards the professionals who would record them, and less towards the amateurs who might have bought sheet music copies. But with the advent of radio it was soon found that the microphone influenced styles of singing. Since the microphone itself provided the volume, a great voice trained to fill the Queen's and other halls seemed redundant. In the studio, an intimate quality proved to be more suitable. At its extreme in the 1930s, the crooner – even the 'whisperer' – who worked in conjunction with the microphone came into his own. In this country, crooners were accompanied by small combination dance bands, recorded at their hotels by the embryo BBC. Boosey and Chappell, finding their audiences dwindling, brought their ballad concerts to an end.

The great era of the ballad had passed. Haydn Wood and others still wrote them, but by the post-1945 years, the ballad had retreated to the provinces; to the chapel concert and to the competitive music festival, where the ballad class still attracts a large entry, and usually too, a large audience.

Notes

1. The memoirs of W.H. Bell (manuscript), quoted in Lewis Foreman (1987), 'From Parry to Britten' in *British Music in Letters 1900–1945*, London, 1987.
2. *Everyman's Dictionary of Music* (1946), Dent, p. 36.
3. Blom, Eric (1942), *Music in England*, Pelican, pp. 217–218.
4. McGlennon, Felix (1894), 'A Chat with Felix McGlennon', *The Era*, 10 March, p. 16.
5. Jane Austen, *Pride and Prejudice*, Chapter 18.
6. Cowen, Sir Frederick (1913), *My Art and My Friends*, Edward Arnold, p. 53.
7. Ibid. p. 105.
8. It was Fred Weatherly who was thought to have dubbed William Boosey with the title of 'The Emperor of Bond St'.
9. Coates, *Suite in Four Movements*, p. 118.
10. Dawson, Peter (1951), *Fifty Years of Song*, Hutchinson, p. 68.
11. George Bernard Shaw: *Music in London 1890–1894*. 12.7.1893 (collected edition, vol. III, 1932).
12. Cowen, Sir Frederick, 'Then and Now', *Musical Masterpieces* (1920s Instalment Encyclopaedia), quoted in Ronald Pearsall, *Edwardian Popular Music* (1975), London, p. 82.
13. Pearsall, *Edwardian Popular Music* (see n. 12 above), p. 86.
14. Coates, op. cit., pp. 185–187.
15. Scowcroft, Philip (1997), *British Light Music*, Thames Publishing, p. 38.
16. Peter Dawson in his preface to *Famous Baritone Songs*, London: Chappell.

CHAPTER SEVEN

Instrumental Music (1):
the Founding Generation

The orchestral repertoire written over the period 1870–1950 is the great glory of British light music. Within that period, few if any countries could offer a light music repertoire to stand comparison with it. This repertoire had expanded with a growing demand. It dwindled when that market contracted. In this, it followed well-documented precedents: Thomas Morley's exploitation of the music printing monopoly granted him by Queen Elizabeth I, for example, or Handel's exploitation of operatic fashions.

The growth of light music within the period just as surely bore a direct relationship to the changing nature of orchestral provision. And that provision itself derived from sociological and demographic trends.

In London, the Philharmonic Society ('Royal' from 1912) continued to hold its series of concerts each year, as it had done since 1813. The Society had an enviable reputation for introducing first performances and recent work, but it was rarely a shop window for light music. A much more promising platform for this was to be found at the Crystal Palace, in the South London suburb of Sydenham where from 1855 to 1901 August Manns held sway as Director of Music. Manns was adventurous. Despite his predilection for German music, George Grove, the Crystal Palace Secretary, is thought to have engaged him because, among his other qualities, Manns was known to be anxious to explore and promote new or unusual music.

Promenade concerts had been held in London from at least 1838, when a series of *Promenade Concerts à la Musard* (modelled on those held in Paris by Philippe Musard) took place. In 1840, Musard himself came over to direct. That year, Drury Lane Theatre instituted the *Concerts d'été* (subsequently *Concerts d'hiver*) under Louis Jullien (1812–1860). A master showman, Jullien's proms juxtaposed fine Beethoven performances with those of his own vulgar monster quadrilles. The opening of the St James Hall in 1858 led to the institution of the Monday Popular Concerts ('Monday Pops'), while 1895 saw the Queen's Hall (Langham Place: destroyed by bombing in 1941) institute the annual series of Promenade Concerts under the conductorship of the young and then unknown Henry Wood (1869–1944). Wood took note of the practices of his predecessors; after the first few years, the first half of his programmes was generally devoted to the major classics. But after the interval, there would be novelties, and here Wood offered a chance to composers of light music.

These series, together with the theatre orchestras and their interval music discussed in Chapter 5, constituted the professional orchestral resources available to a London composer.

In the provinces, concerts tended to group into festivals, and these festivals were rooted in choral music, albeit orchestrally accompanied. But purely orchestral works were also included, and as cities grew, some of them established their own orchestras, for the more progressive city fathers saw these as marks of status.

Liverpool's Philharmonic Society was established in 1840. Its policy was exclusive and intimidating. Until the first years of the twentieth century, commoners were allowed in the gallery of its Philharmonic Hall (built in 1849). But to occupy a stall or box, you had to be adult and also an army or navy officer, a priest, a business man or a 'proprietor' or a person featured on a displayed list of 'Gentlemen'. Not surprisingly, Elgar's friend Alfred Rodewald found a fertile soil when he initiated the more forward-looking and liberal Liverpool Orchestral Society in 1884.

The Lancashire cotton trade had attracted a number of German entrepreneurs, of whom Rodewald was an example. It was the German colony in Manchester which invited their fellow-countryman Charles Hallé to their city in 1849 to conduct the Gentlemen's Concerts. The orchestra waiting for Hallé was mediocre. He dismissed most of the members and started afresh, attracting better players from London. In 1858, Hallé took over the responsibility for the orchestra on his own risk. Both Liverpool and Manchester were orientated musically towards a German culture.

The present-day City of Birmingham Symphony Orchestra was established in 1920, but as early as 1873 William Cole Stockley had arranged a series of orchestral concerts. Sullivan, Parry and Stanford all appeared in his programmes, as did Elgar, who as a young man played in Stockley's orchestra.

At Glasgow, the Scottish Orchestra (now the Royal Scottish National Orchestra) was instituted in 1891. Its early conductors included George Henschel (1891–1895), Willem Kes (1895–1898), Max Bruch (1898–1900), Frederick Cowen (1900–10) and Emil Mlynarski (1910–16). Bournemouth on the south coast followed Glasgow two years later, when the authorities appointed a young bandmaster to found a military band of some thirty players. Within a year, he had transformed it into an orchestra. The Bournemouth Municipal Orchestra had been established and its bandmaster-turned-conductor was Dan Godfrey; destined to become the leading advocate of British composers in his time.

These organizations were not permanent year-round orchestras as they are today, nor did they all, with the shining exception of Godfrey, make much response to British music, let alone British light music. Hallé, for example, tended to programme the mainstream German repertoire for which his fellow-countrymen had summoned him to Manchester. But Manns at the Crystal Palace was ever open to the home-made product, and between them, Manns, Godfrey and Wood transformed the opportunities for British composers in the last decade of the nineteenth century.

There remains to be considered the Spa and other seaside orchestras, and the amateur organizations. The masochism of 'taking the waters' – so unpalatable were they – was no doubt eased by sweet sounds of music at Harrogate, Scarborough and Bath. There had been concerts of a kind at Harrogate since at least 1835, but it was with the opening of the Royal Spa Concert Rooms in 1898 that an erstwhile wind band became an orchestra of forty-two members. J. Sidney Jones[1] presided, with such composers as Mackenzie, Cowen, German and Coleridge-Taylor all putting in an appearance from time to time to conduct their own works at the Wednesday morning concerts. Bath can claim an even longer tradition of instrumental ensemble entertainment – back to 1704. But in both towns, it effectively came to an end in 1939.

Scarborough employed musicians at least from 1840. A military-style band played there from 1867 to 1912 – for the first thirty of those years under William Mayer Lutz (1829–1903), a musician who had graduated from music-hall at the Surrey Theatre in London. But in 1912, with the appointment of Alick Maclean (1872–1936), the pattern of Bournemouth and Harrogate was repeated as band changed into orchestra. Dubbed 'The God Of Scarborough' by his patrons and 'The Lightning Conductor' by his players (because, it was said, he knew only three speeds: quick, quicker and damned quick), Maclean remained in charge until 1935. In 1916, he was also given command of the Queen's Hall Light Orchestra. With both orchestras, he was a formidable exponent of light music, second perhaps only to Godfrey. Scarborough's music was never the same after him, and it petered out in the 1950s.

Since the eighteenth century, taking the waters at a spa had been perceived by the wealthy as a species of cure. But the practice also came to fulfil a social function, fitting easily into their seasons. With the spread of the railway network over the second half of the nineteenth century, holidays – as opposed to Holy Days when everyone had a day off work – became more feasible for all but the very poorest. At the seaside termini, resorts grew rapidly, catering for both the long winter stay and the week by the sea. Bournemouth was the leader, and its example was not lost on Eastbourne, Hastings, Worthing, Brighton, Torquay, Llandudno, New Brighton and others. Local councils became the preserve of shopkeepers, tradesmen and hoteliers who, in causing the creation of their esplanades and pleasure gardens, soon realized the drawing power of music. At the lowest level, a bandstand at least would be provided. Higher up the scale, there would be winter gardens, a pavilion or, best of all, as at Blackpool, a tower. There in the ballroom in the 1930s and 1940s, Reginald Dixon presided at the Wurlitzer organ, identifying Blackpool with *I Do Like To Be Beside The Seaside*. Sussex was also beside the sea, and had its song to tell us so. Other holiday areas weighed in. Devon was fortunate when Edward German's 1905 song *Devon, Glorious Devon* became popular. Hastings joined in later when its music director Julius Harrison presented it with the *Hastings Carnival Song* (1934). But the prize for banality must surely go to Teignmouth for its *Summer Song* (Ex. 7.1).

Ex. 7.1 *The Teignmouth Summer Song* (David Graves/George Hay)

Wind instruments are more effective in the open air than strings, and this was one reason why many resorts at first employed military bands or similar wind ensembles. Italian, German, Blue Hungarian, Red Hungarian – all proliferated, all in livery and with ever more exotic names. The German bands appear to have been dominant:

> The German bands have now taken possession of the whole coast of Kent and Sussex, and wherever there are watering places.[2]

Foreign musicians dominated some of the symphony orchestras, too. As many as twenty-four, for example, were employed in the later years of the Crystal Palace orchestra. This situation was something the public not only tolerated but seemed actively to want:

> Such is the prejudice against English musicians that I find that when I offer an orchestra of first-class players at the same price as men who are not fit to play at a dog fight and are dressed up like monkeys, the society lady prefers to engage the monkeys at a high price and thinks the competent musicians only worth a few shillings.[3]

Gustav Holst's experience as a trombonist in Brighton reinforces the point:

> At one time he joined the White Viennese Band, under Stanislas Worm. Most of the players were English, but they got more pay if they called themselves foreigners, and dressed up in a white uniform with brass buttons.[4]

The composers discussed in this chapter rarely dabbled in band music, and in consequence, much of the band repertoire consisted of arrangements. With the building of pavilions and winter gardens, and with the partial enclosing of band-stands, other resorts followed Bournemouth and Harrogate in changing their wind bands into orchestras from the last decade of the nineteenth century onwards. Nevertheless, as Kenneth Young has obseved,[5] musicians like Dan Godfrey at Bournemouth and Sidney Jones at Harrogate remained, in outlook at least, essentially bandsmen.

At Bournemouth, Godfrey seemed to hear of every new work, and if he did not give a first performance, he would surely give a second or third within a few weeks of it. Technically superbly equipped, irascible but fair-minded, 'Sir God Damn-frey', as Beecham is alleged to have dubbed him, remains one of British music's imperishable heroes.

Bournemouth set the pace, but other resorts soon followed. Torquay employed the young Basil Cameron (1884–1975) who, with Eric Coates, had learnt the repertoire from the inside, playing under Henry Wood at the Queen's Hall. Margate, Folkestone, Worthing and Weston-super-Mare all established orchestras. East-bourne had two: that of the Duke of Devonshire and, from 1932, that of the Corporation, of which Harry Amers was the most distinguished director. The Hastings Municipal Orchestra ran in tandem for some years with that of Harro-gate. Thus Julian Clifford directed both orchestras 1919–1923, as did Basil Cameron 1923/24–1930.

Some spa and resort conductors undoubtedly bridled at programming music they thought unworthy. Howard Carr, for example, resigned from Harrogate rather than play jazz. Godfrey, ever pragmatic, disapproved of his attitude:

> … only the superior person condemned such pieces wholesale; the conductor who did not wish his concerts to be a financial failure had to cater for all classes.[6]

Cameron was at Torquay for only two years (1913–14), but in that time managed to put on a Wagner festival; hardly a popular choice for balmy days beside the sea. At New Brighton, Granville Bantock used much rehearsal time to explore Richard Strauss and Sibelius when his men could play their waltzes, selections and fanta-sies well enough without more practice. Some musicians were offering what they wanted to play rather than what their audiences wanted to hear. A clash of interest was always inherent and pending as resort councils, dominated by 'rate-savers', tried to clamp down on expense and expected to see a direct relationship between their expenditure and the profits of their shops and hotels. By the late 1930s, a general trend was evident, presaging the end of what had been a golden era for resort orchestras. Fairly typical were the remarks of one Eastbourne alderman

(Edgar Hill) at a council meeting in January 1939. Regarding the municipal orchestra's home at the Winter Gardens, he said:

> If I were running Eastbourne, I would pull the rotten place down and build a really fine place, capable of holding really big conferences …

Economic pressure dictated that resort orchestras were rarely big enough to do full justice to some of the music they played. Eric Coates, in particular, lamented that there were never enough strings to balance the wind and thereby to produce the effects he envisaged. It was thus a luxury for him when, towards the end of his career, the BBC Symphony Orchestra occasionally played his music. Nevertheless, for half a century (1890–1939) the resort orchestras played a major part in laying before the public the riches of the light music school.

Last but by no means least in the market for orchestral music were the amateurs. From time immemorial, groups of musician friends had banded together to play concerted music. Elgar himself, together with his brother Frank and their friends, took part in such a group in Worcester every Sunday afternoon. This was in the early 1870s. Within the next twenty years, amateur orchestras sprang up in many towns and cities, taking the more formalized constitution necessary for playing the standard classical repertoire. These orchestras would aim to have, therefore, double woodwind, brass (horns, trumpets and the occasional trombone), percussion and strings. This established format, to be found in both professional and amateur orchestras, naturally influenced, even dictated, the forces for which both serious and light composers would write.

The Royal Amateur Orchestral Society was formed in 1872, with Queen Victoria's son the Duke of Edinburgh in the first violins, and sometimes even leading the ensemble. The Stock Exchange Orchestra was formed eleven years later in 1883. These were among the best of their day. On a more humble level, even a department store such as Marshall and Snellgrove could muster an amateur wind band. Elgar's Powick Lunatic Asylum Orchestra would have been typical of the earlier groups, in that it would have consisted of whatever instruments happened to be available among the staff, and perhaps the inmates. Its repertoire would therefore have been basic – waltzes, lancers and quadrilles, many written by Elgar himself; works which would have been playable and would make an acceptable effect whoever turned up to play. In 1897, the Worcester Philharmonic Society was formed by a group of Elgar admirers, as an instrument for him to conduct. One year later saw the twenty-three-year-old Coleridge-Taylor taking on the Croydon Orchestral Society.

Both Worcester and Croydon orchestras were amateur. Temperamentally, Elgar had difficulty in coping with amateurs. His frustration at being unable to obtain the results he wanted led to walk-outs and general mutual antagonism. Coleridge-Taylor, timid though he appeared, was made of much sterner stuff. After a few years, he simply dismissed the incompetents, and reformed his orchestra with largely professional wind players.

Amateur standards were, to say the least, variable. Sidney Jones Senior, who had much experience of the amateur movement in his early days, wrote in his memoirs:

> All the violins wanted to be first fiddles, and all other instruments must be first of their respective kind. Each of the violins had an individuality which was very diffi-cult to shake off; it was 'I play it this way, you can play it as you like' sort of thing with them.

Despite problems of standards, of missing instruments and of coping with a repertoire which had never envisaged amateurs in the first place, the amateur movement grew throughout the early years of the twentieth century, stimulated by the introduction of classes for amateur orchestras in the syllabi of competitive music festivals. The movement faltered in the 1930s, when economic conditions restricted the less well-provided members. By then, however, gramophone records of much of the standard repertoire were readily available and it could also be heard by courtesy of the BBC radio. Many amateur orchestras found that their audiences were falling off; they could not match the standards of their professional colleagues.

In Britain, choirs and brass bands have been largely amateur, and for many years attained superior standards to those of amateur orchestras. From the 1960s onwards until the 1980s, the amateur orchestra movement recovered to some extent, aided by the astonishing growth and expertise of Youth Orchestras. This growth reflected the pioneer work in instrumental teaching of Mary Ibberson and her Rural Music School Movement, in due course to be taken over by the more enlightened Local Education Authorities with their peripatetic instrumental teachers. And, in the last years of the millennium, just as surely abandoned when those same LEAs experienced starvation of funds.

It is against the foregoing background that we consider the light orchestral music composers, beginning in this chapter with those whose work was largely completed before the First World War. Each of them – from Sullivan, the founding father of the light music school onwards – strove for acceptance as a composer of serious music; of opera, oratorio, symphony or symphonic poem. In their own minds at least, these men were not primarily composers of light music at all. There was, nevertheless, a growing demand for light music and they endeavoured to take advantage of it.

Sullivan's immediate near-contemporaries were Sir Alexander Mackenzie (1847–1935), Sir Hubert Parry (1848–1918), Sir Charles Stanford (1852–1924) and Sir Frederick Cowen (1852–1935). Slightly later came Sir Edward Elgar (1857–1934), Frederick Delius (1862–1934), Sir Edward German (1862–1936) and Samuel Coleridge-Taylor (1875–1912). The first three suffered, with Sullivan, from the curse inflicted on so many creative musicians: bureaucracy. To an extent, this was true also of Cowen, but he at least escaped the fate of being an administrative pedagogue. In musical bureaucracy, a mutant of the 'Peter Principle' operates.[7] It works as follows: a musician with a creative talent is invited to become a conductor. Success at both composing and conducting leads to teaching appointments.

Success at these leads in turn to a professorial chair, or even a conservatoire directorship. At this point, the original creative talent is probably long extinguished. Worse, it may not even have been replaced by the administrative talent now required.

Both Elgar and Delius managed to avoid most bureaucratic chores in their mature years – if we discount Elgar's unhappy spell as Professor of Music at Birmingham (which he sensibly yielded to Bantock), and his brief connection as conductor with the London Symphony Orchestra. Elgar, who until his late thirties seemed likely to be remembered only for his light music, did achieve acceptance as a major master of symphony, concerto and oratorio. Delius, too, became a master of the tone, or symphonic, poem and of what might be termed philosophic choral and orchestral work. As for the others, only now, many years after their death, is their work being remembered and seriously re-appraised.

Of our eight composers, Mackenzie and Cowen have, perhaps, suffered most from neglect by immediate posterity. Mackenzie, like Elgar, Delius, German and Coleridge-Taylor, was a violinist. He also enjoyed considerable success as a conductor who, in 1896 gave the first performance in Britain of Tschaikowsky's *Pathétique* Symphony. As principal of the Royal Academy of Music for more than thirty-four years (1888–1924), he conducted the First Orchestra, encouraging the young Eric Coates, but unable to come to terms with some of the dangerous modernists – Bax was one – among his students. That his own music had a decidedly irreverent aspect is attested by *Hazell's Annual*, reviewing an 1894 Philharmonic concert. The Annual's comment also reveals something of a nineteenth-century audience's expectations:

> The nautical overture Britannia by Dr Mackenzie, a merry piece … extremely well received by the ordinarily severe listeners.

A delightful work it is, with a Mendelssohnian busy-ness about its snatches of every conceivable sea-song.

MacKenzie's music was long championed by Dan Godfrey, who had in part owed his position at Bournemouth to the Scottish composer's recommendation. Long forgotten works such as the *London Day by Day* suite[8] and the *Cricket on the Hearth* overture were programmed by Godfrey, together with such manifestations of the composer's rabid nationalism as the *Burns* and *Tam O'Shanter* rhapsodies, *The Little Minister* overture, the *Scottish* piano concerto and the *Pibroch* suite for violin and orchestra. Despite the Scottish ambience of the titles, the style of these works is primarily influenced by continental models. Particularly strong is the influence of Max Bruch, whose First Violin Concerto had made steady progress here since its first appearance in 1868, and who was himself to become the conductor of the Scottish Orchestra in 1898. His *Scottish Fantasy* for violin and orchestra, too, had gained much popularity, and must have been in Mackenzie's mind when he wrote his *Pibroch* suite for the virtuoso violinist Sarasate to play at the 1889 Leeds Festival. In Mackenzie's suite, the *Pibroch* itself forms the centre movement of three – modelled loosely on the traditional Highland bagpipe dance, and formed by Mackenzie into an air and variations.

Sir Dan Godfrey loyally supported the irascible old Scot despite changing fashions, at least until 1922, when he played the oddly named *Youth, Sport and Loyalty* overture at Bournemouth. But others had dropped him. As early as 1907, one influential critic had made a damning verdict on his work:

> … a considerable quantity of his music does not show any distinctive qualities of any kind … he seems to recognise the unworthiness of anything short of the highest ideal, without, save sporadically, being able to make any notable personal contribution towards its attainment.[9]

It would nevertheless be satisfying to make our own judgement by hearing his work from time to time, and fortunately, a trickle of recordings is now beginning to appear. Unfashionable British work appears to be banished to the recording studio, which is perhaps better than nothing. The more adventurous provincial societies programme it, but we may scan the prospectuses of the major London concert halls in vain, if we look for anything other than the *Enigma* Variations or, sometimes, *The Planets* Suite.

Parry and Cowen are two composers who have benefited from the attentions of the smaller recording companies in recent years. Perhaps only one example of Parry's orchestral work – which went principally into his five symphonies – can be considered light music, but it is a particularly fine one. *Lady Radnor's Suite* for string orchestra was written in 1894 for an amateur orchestra conducted by the Countess of Radnor, which met in Salisbury, Wiltshire. Formally, it is based on the baroque suite, with six movements: Prelude, Allemande, Sarabande, Bourrée, Minuet and Gigue. For Parry, as for many other late nineteenth-century composers, the unfolding revelation of Bach's stature was a major formative influence. Not that Parry's suite – except, perhaps, in the bourrée – ever sounds like Bach; it is more a question of Parry's assimilation of Bach's aesthetic. The work of Parry was itself an equally important influence on Elgar in, for example, its finely crafted sequences. But Elgar would never quite assume so naturally the aristocratic graciousness and understatement which here came to Parry, to the manner born.

Where Mackenzie and Parry were distracted from their creative work by the demands of their respective administrative positions, Cowen was lured from composition by conducting. Mackenzie and Parry conducted, but with Cowen it took a much bigger role in his life. For a period, he held a dominant position in British orchestral life: with the Philharmonic Society (1882–92 and 1900–1907), the Hallé Orchestra (1896–99), the Liverpool Philharmonic Orchestra (1895–1913) and the Scottish Orchestra (1900–10). As a conductor, the wonder is that Cowen survived the merciless wit of Bernard Shaw:

> Mr Cowen's worst enemies have never accused him of impetuosity or vivacity in conducting; and as to *entrain*, he has cultivated to perfection a habit entirely fatal to

it; that is to say, he checks the band in every bar between the first and second beat. I do not say the interval is long enough to eat a sandwich in; but sometimes, when I am in my best critical condition, with my rhythmical sensitiveness highly exalted, it seems to me, even during a *presto*, that Mr Cowen always allows time somewhere in the bar for all ordinary exigencies of turning over, using one's handkerchief, nodding to an acquaintance, or the like.[10]

We have already noted Cowen's work as a composer of ballads. Both here and in his operas and symphonies, his light touch was remarked on early:

> the style is in many respects a sort of combination of Sterndale Bennett and Sullivan, with the addition of elements of Cowen's own

wrote Ernest Walker in 1907.[11] Cowen's first set of *Four English Dances in the Olden Style* appeared in 1896. There are Stately, Rustic, Graceful and Country Dances. His work sometimes lacks the point and concentration that would be features of such successors as German and Coates.

Ex. 7.2   Frederick Cowen: *Four English Dances in the Olden Style* (*Stately Dance and Country Dance*)

a) Stately Dance

b) Country Dance

It is difficult, too, to see what is specifically English about the dances. The *Country Dance*, for example, seems to owe more to the Polish mazurka than to the English maypole.

But these dances are attractive, and if nothing else may have been a powerful influence on Edward German as he worked on his own various sets of dances; and, through him, on Eric Coates as he composed his earliest suites. Is there an earlier example of the 'English 6/8' – so ridiculed by later critics – than Cowen's *Graceful Dance* (unless it be *Greensleeves*)?

Ex 7.3   Frederick Cowen: *Four English Dances in the Olden Style* (*Graceful Dance*)

In its obituary for Cowen in 1935, the *Musical Times* remarked how cruel fashion had been to him:

> … he lacked gusto … and came nearest to it in the first set of *Four English Dances* for orchestra, a suite that once had a vogue but lost ground when 'ye olde style', the bane of English music forty years ago, was superseded.[12]

But a study of Cowen's overture *The Butterfly's Ball* (1901) shows fashion, and the *Musical Times*, to be unjust. This is a waltz-overture owing something to Dvořák, but in the clarity, transparency and picturesque detail of its orchestration losing nothing in comparison with the Czech master. How such a fine work comes to be all but forgotten reflects a lack of confidence by today's promoters that any Victorian work could possibly rival a continental one.

Stanford, too, has had to wait until the last years of the twentieth century for any practical re-appraisal of his work, which, however, provides little that might reasonably be termed 'light' – although certain of the six Irish Rhapsodies might count. The seven symphonies, now recorded on the enterprising Chandos label, are entirely approachable, and as with Cowen and Mackenzie, render inexplicable a country which has neglected its musical heritage to such an extent. In mitigation, it may be that the weight of emphasis during his lifetime on the work of Elgar may have been partly responsible for this.

Elgar's background was, for his time, somewhat lower in status than was usual for a composer. His father was a piano tuner, organist and music shop proprietor, all three callings testifying to the spread in Worcester and its surrounding district of a music culture able to support them. The living was comfortable, but not so lavish as to be able to pay for a musical training for Edward – a training that would have caused little problem for the families of Parry or Delius. There would be no study at Leipzig for him, such as Cowen had enjoyed. Everything Elgar did as a young man, therefore, reflected the need to earn, while he had perforce to learn as he earned. Thus he served in the shop (no doubt perusing the books and scores when there were no customers), played the organ for services and the violin for the Three Choirs and other orchestras. 'For the sake of the fee', as he noted bitterly.

This is as good a way as any for a young musician to learn his craft, especially involving as it did much work with amateurs. But it left two legacies, one psychological and the other musical. For most of his life, he became subject to self-pity, to depression and to their concomitant physical debilitations. Musically, the lack of systematic training which would have subjected him to regular criticism, left the occasional stylistic weakness, of which the inordinate repetition of one rhythm within a melody is an example. Having said that, Elgar of course transcends all his petty faults to remain, with Delius, one of the two massive figures towering over the British musical landscape of their time.

Much of Elgar's light music – even that of ostensibly later date – originated in his early years. By this is meant up to his thirtieth year, for he had an inordinately long period of 'early years'. Some of it was a response to his needs as a violinist (and, indeed, the needs of his pupils), and of the professional orchestras in which he played, or the amateur ones he directed. Such pieces as *May Song*, *Chanson De Matin* and *Chanson De Nuit* (Op. 15,1 & 2) were conceived for violin and piano, and subsequently orchestrated. The limping beauty of *Carissima* (1914, but originating earlier) and *Serenade Lyrique* (1899), suggest a conception in Elgar idly fingering his violin. He would often improvise – both on violin and piano. The Serenade is an elegant slow waltz, as is the last orchestral work Elgar wrote, *Mina* (1933). Elgar's cairn terrier had this name, but the music sings nostalgically of past times.

Rosemary, too, started life first as a piano trio and then as a piano solo. Dating from 1882, when the twenty-five-year-old composer was visiting his friend Dr Charles Buck in Yorkshire, it is one of Elgar's earliest extant pieces. Buck played the cello, his mother the piano. With Elgar as violinist, they made the necessary trio. Thirty years later it was orchestrated, in which form it has most currency today. Throughout his life, Elgar retained not only an affection but almost a need for his early salon pieces, the ideas of which (as Michael Kennedy has pointed out)[13] often presage the ideas of his mature serious work – albeit in more sophisticated form. The point is readily apparent if, for example, *Rosemary* is taken note of before a hearing of the first movement of the Second Symphony.

This characteristically limping rhythm occurs elsewhere among Elgar's major works, most notably in the first movement of the Cello Concerto.

The Elgar miniatures are generally framed in a ternary (ABA) form, with the outer sections in a major key and the contrasting centre in the minor. All deliver the essential Elgar message of wistful melancholy. Of them, the two *Chansons* are surely as perfect miniatures as we are likely to hear. *Chanson De Nuit*, in particular,

Ex. 7.4   Elgar: (a) *Rosemary* (1882); (b) Symphony No. 2 (first movement) (1911)

a) Rosemary (1882)

b) Symphony No. 2 (first movement) (1911)

is a lament for transience to which Elgar returns again and again in the symphonies and concertos. One heretical thought is hard to banish. Are not the large-scale Elgar orchestral works in reality strings of intense moments of vision linked by passages which together give the music scale, but do not necessarily grow organically? In this view, Elgar becomes a master miniaturist, and the Variations on an Original Theme (*Enigma*) – a sequence of linked miniatures – his masterpiece.

In March 1888, Elgar conducted Stockley's orchestra at Birmingham in a *Suite in D*. It consisted of a *Mazurka*, *Serenade Mauresque* and *Contrasts* (which together were published as *Three Characteristic Pieces*, Op. 10, 1–3) and a march *Pas Redouble*, which was subsequently dropped. The *Mazurka*, though a sturdy and well-constructed dance, has little of Elgar's personality about it. The *Serenade Mauresque*, particularly in its contrasting interludes, is a different matter. After a nod in the direction of the harmonic minor scale, which along with everyone else he took to be vaguely oriental, the music offers fleeting glimpses of the intimate Elgar 'down by the river' – moments so precious in many a later work. *Contrasts: AD 1700 and 1900* is a clever trifle deriving from Elgar's visit to Leipzig in 1882. There he heard the Gewandhaus Orchestra, but found time also to visit the theatre. His fancy was taken by two dancers 'in antique dress dancing a gavotte; when they reached the footlights they suddenly turned round and appeared to be two very young and modern people, and danced a gay and lively measure. They had come down stage *backwards* and danced away with their (modern) faces towards us – when they reached the back of the stage they suddenly turned round and the old, decrepit couple danced gingerly to the old tune'.[14] All of this Elgar depicts quite graphically in his music. His 'decrepit old couple' dance in canon to a tune Elgar said came from Corelli. There is some academic counterpoint and even a piece of augmentation – all banished when it is the young couple's turn.

For *Sevillana* (Op. 17), Elgar also supplied a helpful note. This work dates from 1884, in which year it was conducted on 1 May in Worcester by the cathedral organist Dr Done. But its importance is that it was the first work of Elgar to be heard in London – eleven days after the Worcester performance when August Manns gave it at the Crystal Palace. 'It is', wrote Elgar 'an attempt to portray, in the compass of a few bars, the humours of a Spanish Fete'. He goes on, tongue in cheek: 'missiles are freely thrown, and at least one stiletto is drawn – but these are only modern Spaniards, and no tragic result follows … '.[15] Little of this can be inferred from what is basically a *valse* in the French ballet style of Delibes – as was also the *Mazurka* mentioned above. Neither Poland nor Spain exercised his deepest concerns; he never visited either country. But *Sevillana* demonstrates in its brass writing something of the swagger which would characterize his mature work.

Salut D'Amour (Op. 12, 1888) was originally written for piano and subsequently orchestrated. Elgar sold it outright to the publisher Schott who issued it not only in its original piano version, but also in twenty-four other versions, including mandoline and piano, two mandolines and guitar, and two cellos and piano. Its popularity was immediate, and the royalties on it, had Elgar received any, would have been enormous.

Elgar was never entirely happy writing for the piano, and it is possible to see in the layout of the original keyboard version the orchestral genius thinking in orchestral terms. The more obvious Elgarian fingerprints, such as the drooping intervals of a sixth are in place; but the climax – quite eruptive for such an unpretentious piece (see Ex. 7.5) – would, like *Rosemary*, be reworked years later to take its place in the resplendent closing pages of the Second Symphony.

Ex. 7.5   Elgar: *Salut D'Amour*. © Copyright 1899 by B. Schott's Söhne. Reproduced by
permission of Schott & Co. Ltd, London.

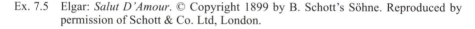

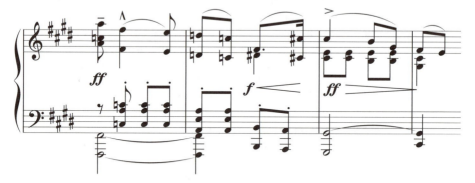

The *Three Bavarian Dances* (Op. 27), too, originated in another medium. They were taken from the Six Choral Songs *Scenes from the Bavarian Highlands* – originally written with piano accompaniment (1895) and a year later given an orchestral accompaniment. The three selected for purely orchestral treatment are: *The Dance (1)*, *Lullaby (3)* and *The Marksman (6)*. The point made above as regards thinking in orchestral terms is equally valid in *Lullaby*, where hardly any adjustment was necessary to translate from the voices-and-piano medium to that of the orchestra. Here, the main theme was already in the piano, and it fitted the orchestral violins well. The (alto) voice part was already in the middle of the harmony, and was well suited to the orchestral tenor instruments. Together with the bass, Elgar's favourite three-part texture was easily evolved (see Ex. 7.6).

Ex. 7.6   Elgar: *Scenes from the Bavarian Highlands* (*Lullaby*)

While the *Serenade in E minor for strings* (Op. 20, no. 1) was completed in 1892, it is believed[16] to have been a revision of three pieces for string orchestra originally performed by the Worcester Musical Union on 7 May 1888. If this is so, then the *Serenade* ranks with *Salut D'Amour* among the last Elgar instrumental works written before his marriage in 1889 to Caroline Alice Roberts. After that year, the main thrust of Elgar's work was directed into major choral and orchestral works. It cannot be coincidental that this focusing came with his marriage. Elgar was 32 in the year of his marriage, an age when most composers would expect to be established.

And so he was, in provincial Worcester. It would take another seven years to transform him from a provincial into a national figure. In this transformation, the *Serenade in E minor* may lay claim to be a first, if still transitional, masterpiece. It is the imprints of personal voice and style which distinguish an Elgar from a Cowen; imprints such as the containment of a melody within a minor seventh or a drooping sixth (see Ex. 7.7).

Ex. 7.7   Elgar: *Serenade in E minor*

a) 1st movement

b) 2nd movement

After his death, a reaction to Elgar set in which persisted for some decades. Since the most accessible of his works were the various manifestations of his patriotism, it was these that attracted the most criticism. At the end of the twentieth century, with Empire dissolved and monarchy precarious, it is possible to hear Elgar's magnificent marches (and, indeed, his otherwise neglected occasional regal and wartime choral work) for what they are: quite simply some of the finest work in their genre ever written.

His work in this field is both light and popular, for here he is the musical mouthpiece of his time. Except, perhaps, among a cynical intelligentsia, patriotism and pride in Empire went hand-in-hand. At the centre of this empire was its focal point: the monarchy. But since the death of her Prince Consort in 1861, the monarch had withdrawn from public life into a period of continuing mourning. The end of that mourning was effectively forced on Queen Victoria by the advent of her Diamond Jubilee in 1897. By then, the rampant growth of music publishing, of choirs, of orchestras and of music halls happily coincided with what was to be the first great explosion of royal adulation.

At the basement end of the festivities, Leslie Stuart responded with what became one of the most popular street songs, the already-mentioned *The Soldiers of the Queen*. This was one of a flood of songs, including *The Queen! God Bless Her* by

Myles B. Foster; and of cantatas, including G.F. Huntley's *Victoria, The Bard's Prophecy*, J.L. Roeckel's *The Victorian Age* and Frederick Bridge's *The Flag of England*. Only Stuart's song is remembered now.

For the Jubilee, Elgar wrote his first surviving march – the *Imperial March*, given its first performance by massed bands at the Crystal Palace in 1897. Four years earlier, Sullivan had written his own *Imperial March*, for the celebrations attending the opening of the Imperial Institute in South Kensington. Sullivan's march had been a brave effort by an exhausted man in decline. Its undistinguished material is subjected to inordinate repetition; its accompaniments are unimaginative. Elgar's march was at first criticized by Novellos – to whom the composer had submitted it – for melodic short-windedness. Couldn't there be some eight-bar phrases to relieve the preponderance of two-bar ones? Elgar revised his work, whereupon it was accepted for publication. Never one to miss a chance of royal favour – despite his lament in later years of the vulgarity of Court – he sought permission to dedicate it to the Queen. The arrogance of Elgar's public music-making manner and, in the trio, the intimacy of the private man are here side by side. While his true greatness would be confirmed two years later with the *Enigma* Variations, it was this march which first caught the imagination of the public, and symbolized the effective passing of the torch of laureateship from Sullivan to Elgar.

A year after the Diamond Jubilee, *Caractacus* was completed. In it the Romans unfortunately defeated the British. Elgar saw no reason in this why the work should not also be dedicated to the Queen, for the British Empire would inevitably eclipse that of Rome in magnificence. The work is included here because of its fine *Triumphal March*: a purple patch, the spectacular brass writing of which eclipses not only that of Sullivan's *Imperial March* but much of Elgar's own.

The projected coronation of Edward VII in 1902 looked set to outshine all previous celebrations, but the illness of the king forced its postponement. For it, Mackenzie, German and such lesser lights as Percy Pitt had all written marches, while Elgar had contributed the splendid *Coronation Ode* to words by Benson. A competition for a new coronation march had been held, with a prize of fifty guineas. It was won by a Canterbury musician, Percy Godfrey – a moment of glory for him before obscurity enveloped him again. From Cornwall, a Redruth composer of locally favoured Christmas carols sent in his entry. Although unsuccessful, Thomas Merritt's march was rediscovered years later – by no less a figure than Sir Malcolm Arnold. Living in Cornwall at the time (1966), Arnold organized and conducted an elaborate *Salute to Thomas Merritt* in Truro Cathedral. Merritt's Coronation March proved to be rather splendid. Certainly, it compared favourably with that commissioned by the makers of Bile Beans (a popular laxative) from one J. Michael Watson.

In 1911, it was coronation time again, as George V succeeded to the throne. Another prize for a march was offered; this time by the Musicians Company (since 1950 The Worshipful Company of Musicians). None of the entries was found to be good enough – even though there were two hundred of them. 'A fearful slight upon competitors', commented one disgruntled entrant. Another called it an injustice. She had 'submitted a bright and easy march, and yet no prize was awarded'. But the major figures were all in attendance. Along with Mackenzie, Parry, Stanford and German, Elgar made his contribution. His Coronation March (Op. 65) is a magnificent movement of almost symphonic proportions, but in its emotional implications too serious to rank here as light music.

No such reservation can apply to the *Pomp and Circumstance* marches, of which in the first decade of the new century there were to be four. Elgar told King Edward VII that he had carried the trio tune of No. 1 in D (1901) around for some twenty years. This would suggest that it was yet another idea to have been conceived while Elgar was working at the Powick asylum. Over the succeeding years since its appearance, an aura of jingo-ism (never expressed by the composer himself) has accreted to this fine march. But nothing could be further from its companion-piece, No. 2 in A minor (1901). If anything, there is in the trio a feeling of the German band, while in the outer sections the arrogant confidence of the *Triumphal March* has shrunk to the nervous manner remarked on by so many who observed or played under Elgar the conductor. No. 3 in C minor (1904) seems to have puzzled listeners and conductors alike, with the result that it is the least played of the set. Its trombone writing may also cause problems to all but virtuoso players. It is included here for completeness but is hardly light music. There is about it a prevailing black mood, perhaps reflecting the prolonged fit of depression to which he was subject over the winter of 1903–4.

In the Fourth March (in G, 1907), Elgar attempts a trio tune to equal that of No. 1. But, as he himself acknowledged, a tune such as the latter comes but rarely. No. 4's trio tune has a good enough basic idea; what is worrying is the repeated repetition of one rhythm in the outer sections of the march, bar after bar.

The March of the Mogul Emperors from the *Crown of India* Masque (1912: London Coliseum) is a march in triple time 'cooked up', in Elgar's own words, from earlier discarded sketches. *The Empire* march was written for the 1924 Wembley Exhibition. It had been blown up from a march originally written for piano trio. Elgar's last march was the *Pomp and Circumstance* No. 5 in C, Op. 39, completed in 1930. But this, too, had been sketched much earlier. It is a joyous piece, with little of either pomp or circumstance about it. Rather in its playfulness does it seem to have about it the manner of a Powick Lancers.

Autres temps, autre choses. The sort of march needed in the 1930s was altogether more swinging and loose-limbed than that of the grand Elgar set-piece. There would be no further coronation, where such a set-piece might be expected, until 1937. By that time, the young William Walton was ready to don the Elgar regalia with his *Crown Imperial* march. After 1911, too, the occasions for which marches might be commissioned changed in character. Football matches, futuristic films and political events were more likely to call for them than the big state events. In April 1914, Granville Bantock even produced one 'for the Coming-of-Age Conference of the Independent Labour Party'. Elgar would never have done that, supposing the strongly anti-socialist Caroline Alice had permitted it.

To a present-day observer, Elgar's relationship with his wife had more the appearance of son to mother than man to spouse. Certainly, the child was strong in him, and Lady Elgar indulged his 'japes', his kite-flying and his chemistry experiments. Musically, from about 1905 onwards, a growing element of nostalgia entered his work, this notwithstanding his comment about the Symphony No. 1 in A flat (1908) which, he said, reflected a 'massive hope in the future'.[17] Such nostalgia is there for all to hear in the slow movement of the Violin Concerto, in the *Falstaff* interludes, and in the sunset's dying radiance at the conclusion of the Symphony No. 2. But it is equally apparent in his slighter works, where the nostalgia so often manifests itself as an aching yearning for the lost innocence of an ever-faster receding childhood. The works concerned – *Dream Children* (1902), the two *Wand of Youth* suites (1907 and 1908 respectively), *Starlight Express* (1915; which itself included music from the *Wand of Youth* suites) and the *Nursery* suite (1931) – seem to hold for many listeners the essence of a tortured soul such as never achieved even the possibility of resolution or haven which was at least in prospect for his own Gerontius. His beliefs, he said, died after the experience of that oratorio. But the longing for long-lost halcyon days in Worcestershire (which may never have existed in reality) were never to leave him.

And so, with a charge of such intensity, it may reasonably be asked if these works are light music at all. But the nature of enjoyment – for many English people, at any rate – encompasses the pain of nostalgia.

* * *

The paths of Elgar and Frederick Delius crossed very seldom. Informed opinion at the time saw Delius and Elgar as the antithesis of each other. Today, at a distance of many decades, the contrast seems by no means as clear-cut. For, as with Elgar, Delius's music seems increasingly to look back, in this case to youth in Yorkshire, to early manhood in Florida and Paris, to friendships celebrated among the mountains of Norway. Delius rejected orthodox religion; Elgar may have done. Both wrote light music.

Delius's light music is in the main early work, dating from his days in Florida, Paris and Norway. As mentioned in Chapter 1, his earliest published work is the polka for piano, *Zum Carnival*: a suave salon piece, deriving from Johann Strauss rather than the Richard who was to be such a dominant influence a few years later. It makes credible the picture of the young and handsome violin teacher welcomed in all the soirées of Jacksonville.

Elgar quarried similar products of his teens and twenties, to be reprocessed later. Delius, too, would re-fashion anything he thought worthy, but he did not as a rule delve back as far as Elgar. He did, however, throughout his mature work attempt to recapture the essence of an experience. And so we have a fascinating situation whereby such early light pieces as *Sleigh Ride* (1887–88), *Marche Caprice* (1887–88), *Summer Evening* (1890), *Spring Morning* (1890) and the whole four-movement *Florida* suite (1887: revised 1889) were actually written at the time of the experiences the composer would later retrospectively distil in the music he is today remembered for. Delius set no store by this early work, and would probably have preferred it forgotten. However, together with such a contemporaneous operatic excerpt as the dance *La Calinda* (*Koanga*: 1895–97), all this music is attractive and has charm. Delius a charmer? Our mental picture of him is of later years – of James Gunn's forbidding portrait and of Eric Fenby's description of the irascible old man, racked by pain. But as a young man-about-town, he was noted for his charming personality. In 1887, for example, he took part in a concert at Harrogate, to celebrate Queen Victoria's Golden Jubilee. 'Mr Delius … charmed the audience with his violin solos', wrote the local paper.

But as with Elgar (and also just as with Delius, impossible at present to explain, only to conjecture about), at some point, a searing experience transformed his art.[18] The transformation can be heard most specifically if we compare the American Rhapsody for orchestra *Appalachia* (dating from 1896) with its reworking six years later as *Appalachia* for baritone solo, chorus and orchestra. Both versions picture scenes from Jacksonville life: the ballroom, the street marching band and other events. This is light music. But the later version is crowned with a choral passage of overwhelming intensity. As we know from Dr Fenby, it was a work for which Delius felt much affection. In it, the slave has passed down the river, never to return, and the artist himself has passed on, in lingering regret.

Apart from this early work, little else of Delius can be described as just light music. Always each experience is reviewed, as one which will never recur. The *Marche Caprice*, *Sleigh Ride* and the others of the charming young Englishman are exactly what they seem – unproblematic light music. But thereafter, as his faithful amanuensis Eric Fenby wrote:

> … he cannot exult, nor can he dance, and the faintest flicker of a smile never crosses his face.[19]

If for Delius, his light music was largely apprentice work on the way to mature mastery, for his contemporary Sir Edward German it proved to be his most enduring legacy. Those two symphonies he had heard performed by 1895 probably pointed the path he would have preferred to take, given the choice. But he is in some ways a transitional figure, presaging the advent of Eric Coates and other early twentieth-century composers who unashamedly set out to write specifically light music.

German's first purely light orchestral work (as distinct from theatre incidental music), was the *Gipsy* Suite, consisting of four characteristic dances. It is dedicated to Sir August Manns, who gave its first performance at the Crystal Palace in 1892. But it is thought to have been written in 1889, which puts its composition just after German's first engagement by Richard Mansfield for the Globe production of *Richard III*. It is difficult to see why a suite which contains a valse and a minuet should have anything to do with gipsies; it might indeed be more popular if renamed. The answer probably lies in the illusory perception of an increasingly convention-bound middle-class – 'getting and spending' – that the life of a Romany had a reckless, romantic freedom. German was not the only one to exploit this perception. Coates and Löhr pitched their lonely caravans, the poet W.H. Davies stood and stared, and even Vaughan Williams trod the open road. But the fact that the title *Gipsy* Suite belies the music need not detain us, for this music is well worth our attention. The opening valse is particularly elegant, and in style is a prototype of the Coates slow waltz – in particular of his waltz *Dancing Nights* (1931). The *Allegro di Bravura* has a wild abandon not usually to be found in German. The *Menuetto* seems to be more of a slow waltz than a minuet and seems a little out of place here. The closing *Tarantella* may be a response to Mendelssohn, but in its downward-spiralling chromatics oddly anticipates Rachmaninoff. Overall, the orchestration is masterly.

Masterly, too, is the *Welsh Rhapsody*. The work was first heard at the 1904 Cardiff Festival, and as it was based on Welsh airs culminating in *Men of Harlech*, its reception was predictably tumultuous. It is more sinfonietta than suite and its four movements run without a break. The opening *Allegro Risoluto* uses the tune of *Loudly Proclaim o'er Land and Sea*. There follows a *scherzando* treatment of *Hunting the Hare* and a slow movement on *David of the White Rock*. Perhaps Coleridge-Taylor remembered the latter when he came to write the first movement of his *Petite Suite de Concert* a few years later. The best is kept till last. The finale is a technical tour de force, in which German's *Men of Harlech* approach from the distant Welsh hills in an exhilarating march. It predates Respighi's legions marching to Rome (*The Pines of Rome*) and achieves a similar triumph while managing to avoid the Italian's vulgarity.

The *Coronation March and Hymn* were based on two themes from the incidental music he had written in 1892 for Irving's production of Henry VIII. The hymn was *Veni Creator Spiritus*. After the great event, and the performance of his music – at which German confessed he 'felt just a little moved' the new king sent him a medal. German wrote to his sister: 'I expect the others have had one too; still it is very nice of him, isn't it?'[20]

One more composer whose work was completed before the outbreak of the First World War must be considered here. This is Samuel Coleridge-Taylor (1875–1912) who, although as a student wrote much fine chamber music and as a young adult devoted most of his time to cantatas, nevertheless left a number of worthwhile light orchestral works. The *Four Characteristic Waltzes*, Op. 22, written for the 1898 season of Henry Wood Promenade Concerts, were early examples. The *Musical Times* liked them, as did Elgar, who had been sent a copy of the score by his friend A.J. Jaeger. These waltzes may seem today to lack the character and sparkle of the best waltzes of Percy Fletcher or Archibald Joyce – let alone of Eric Coates or Haydn Wood. But this may be because of the required somewhat staid nature of the late Victorian waltz. In any case, Coleridge-Taylor soon showed that he could do better. Elgar had been asked to provide a work for the 1898 Three Choirs Festival at Gloucester, but was under pressure to complete his cantata *Caractacus*. He had

7.1   Samuel Coleridge-Taylor

liked the waltzes; he now persuaded the festival committee to pass on the commission to his young colleague, who responded to it with the *Ballade in A minor*, Op. 33, 'dedicated to my friend A.J.J.'.

The *Ballade* is dramatic in style, simple in construction, and orchestrated with clarity and brilliance. The influence of Tschaikowsky is evident throughout; he clearly knew the *Romeo and Juliet* Fantasy-Overture and also *Francesca da Rimini*. *The Musical Times* immediately noticed the Tschaikowsky influence, but also commented on the work's 'barbaric moments' and 'crude feeling';[21] comments which would be echoed for at least a decade, and which reveal something of the perceptions with which, as a coloured man, he had to contend. In the high noon of Empire, it was clearly inconceivable that non-whites could be anything but 'barbaric', even if they boasted a Royal College of Music pedigree.

But for Coleridge-Taylor, who saw himself as an Englishman, an unending and unsolvable dilemma was posed. His instincts and training pointed him towards mainstream European tradition, but his colour created expectations – especially in the United States of America – that he would express the aspirations of his father's race. A tough but amiable man, he tried to satisfy both instincts and expectations. As far as his publisher was concerned, he could do no wrong after the overwhelming success of *Hiawatha*. Novello eagerly published everything he offered them. Mostly, he offered more cantatas, which went the rounds of the festivals and then the choral societies, without ever quite matching the success of *Hiawatha*. Nor did the overture *The Song of Hiawatha* (1899: Op. 30, No. 3), the *Scenes from an Everyday Romance* (1900: Op. 41, No. 1), the *Idyll* (1901: Op. 44), the scherzo *Hemo Dance* (1902: Op. 47, No. 2) and the *Four Novellettes* for strings and percussion (1903: Op. 52) long survive. The *Danse Negre* (*African* suite: Op. 35) fared better and in its various arrangements was at one time enormously popular.

But three later works have retained a precarious hold. They are the Rhapsodic Dance *The Bamboula* (1910: Op. 75), the *Three Dream Dances* (1911: from Op. 74) and the *Petite Suite de Concert* (1911: Op. 77). Their publication coincided with a partial transfer of allegiance from Novello to Hawkes, and they provide evidence that, in the last three years of his life, Coleridge-Taylor's muse, after a period of chronic overwork which for a while dimmed his creative sparkle, recovered her spirit.

He took *The Bamboula*, still unfinished, with him on his third and last visit to the USA in May 1910, orchestrating it on board ship. It was first performed at Carnegie Hall on 27 May 1910, by the then New York Philharmonic Orchestra under his direction. The piece is based on a mere snippet of Creole tune, taken from his own Twenty-Four Negro Melodies for piano (see Ex. 7.8).

All the ideas in the work are spun from this, to create an ingenious combination of variation and ternary forms.

The *Three Dream Dances* are delightful miniatures which are still given an occasional hearing in the remaining old-fashioned hotels, winter gardens and pump-rooms; the *Petite Suite de Concert* is rather more substantial. Hawkes thought

Ex. 7.8   Samuel Coleridge-Taylor: *The Bamboula*

sufficiently highly of it to publish it in full score. Thereafter, it was issued in innumerable versions from piano solo upwards. It is one of those rare works which will sound well in almost any version. One movement in particular – *Demande et Réponse* – achieved huge sales in its own right. Many a front-parlour piano re-sounded to it. Coleridge-Taylor never wasted material, and he was forever recycling his student work. For *Petite Suite*, he exhumed a very early unpublished work for reciter and piano trio, *The Clown and Columbine*. This title throws some light on the *Petite Suite*, for one of Coleridge-Taylor's favourite works as a student was Schumann's piano work *Carnaval*, among whose procession of fanciful characters are, of course, Harlequin and Columbine. *Petite Suite de Concert* predated Eric Coates's *Miniature Suite* (1911), by only a few months. The immediate popularity of Coleridge-Taylor's work probably encouraged Coates on his own succession of light orchestral suites, which owe much to it.

After his early death in 1912 at the age of thirty-six, Coleridge-Taylor's music declined in popularity. He was a musician who looked backwards; who never attempted to understand, much less absorb, the new styles of the twentieth century, which even in its first decade were already very evident. For a time, his publisher Hawkes attempted to squeeze a little more from the unpublished works, in particular from music he had written for a *Hiawatha* ballet in the hope that Diaghilev might take it up. Once again, the indispensable Percy Fletcher was summoned, to orchestrate first a suite from the *Hiawatha* ballet music (1919) and then in 1925 the 'last oozings' for the *Minnehaha* Suite. It seemed the public only wanted to hear anything connected with *Hiawatha*.

Shortly before Coleridge-Taylor died, the producer T.C. Fairbairn had discussed with him the possibility of dramatizing the *Hiawatha* trilogy but it was to be a further twelve years before Fairbairn could realize his dream. Using the Royal Albert Hall, and engaging the Royal Choral Society, with Eugene Goossens III, Albert Coates, Geoffrey Toye and Malcolm Sargent as conductors, he presented the work each year between 1924 and 1940. Thus the name of Coleridge-Taylor was kept alive. Thereafter, his reputation slipped even further, but in the last decades of the century, some fine recordings were issued, which have encouraged enthusiasts to listen again to the works of this splendid – even noble – musician.

Notes

1. Father of Sidney Jones, composer of *The Geisha* (see Chapter 3).
2. Mayhew, Henry (1861), *London Labour and the London Poor*.
3. R. Norman Concorde (concert agent) to Frederick Delius, 7 February 1900.
4. Holst, Imogen (1938), *Gustav Holst: A Biography*, Oxford University Press, p. 15.
5. Young, Kenneth (1968), *Music's Great Days in the Spas and Watering Places*, Macmillan, p. 52.
6. Ibid, p. 63.
7. A hypothesis that argues that operatives are promoted to the level of their own inefficiency.
8. With what wry thoughts, one wonders, would he have heard his protégé Eric Coates's *London Everyday* Suite in the last years of his long life? Was Coates alerted to the existence of the older man's work, and if so, was this a factor in Coates's decision to rename his work simply the *London* Suite?
9. Walker, Ernest (1907), *A History of Music in England*, Oxford University Press, p. 298. (How the insularity of the title must have irritated Mackenzie!)
10. Shaw, George Bernard (1932), *Music in London*, Vol. iii, 4.10.1893, London, p. 57.
11. Walker, Ernest (see n. 9), p. 296.
12. Scholes, Percy (1947), *The Mirror of Music*, Novello/Oxford University Press, p. 104.
13. Kennedy, Michael (1968), *Portrait of Elgar*, Oxford University Press, p. 213.
14. Elgar to A.J. Jaeger, 4 February 1899. Jaeger was dealing with the publication of the pieces at the time.
15. Elgar's programme note for the Worcester Amateur Orchestral Society, 9 April 1885.
16. Kennedy, Michael (see n. 13), p. 339.
17. Elgar to Walford Davies, 13 November 1908.
18. Tasmin Little, the eminent exponent of Delius's violin music, has researched the possibility that Delius had a liaison with a coloured woman at Solano Grove, who may have given birth to a son he never saw, advancing the idea that this might have been that transforming experience.
19. Fenby, Eric (1936), *Delius as I Knew Him*, London, p. 170.
20. 15 August 1911.
21. *Musical Times*, 1 October 1898.

CHAPTER EIGHT

Patriotism and War (1): 1914–1918

Until at least the 1930s, British colonies, dominions and protectorates were regarded in the United Kingdom as physical possessions, and the British Empire had
become a peerless example of mercantile theory. Throughout the nineteenth century it was seen of the greatest importance to defend and extend this empire.
Moreover, it seemed (at least to the English) to carry with it a duty of international
policing and punishment. The Empire thus acquired a moral validity far beyond its
economic function, and it was here that artists – and in particular musician-artists –
could assist by clothing it in its mystic glowing light. But by the beginning of our
chosen period, musical endeavour was increasingly at the beck and call of an
efficiently organized music industry. Commercialism was thus never too far away.

Throughout the period, the political hour would invariably call forth a musical
response; some responses being more ludicrous than others. An early example
occurred in 1876, when Turkish atrocities in putting down the Bulgarian Revolt
provoked Gladstone to promise to 'turn Turks out of Europe, bag and baggage'. It
inspired one Anselm Thenam to pen a *New Valse de Salon* 'founded on the notes
BAG BAGGAGE'. It even reached a second edition.

Pretexts were plenty in the 1880s. In 1882, Sir Garnet Wolseley was sent with
his troops to Egypt – to help the Khedive against his enemy, Arabi Pasha. His
efforts were celebrated by Mrs Mounsey Bartholomew, who dedicated her *Wolseley*
March to him. Three years later (1885), the death of Gordon prompted P.R. Barclay
to a *Gordon* March. Both marches trudged into oblivion.

The responses of music-hall were often much more significant. Indeed, they
brought the word 'jingoism' into the language. The Second Russo-Turkish War
(1877–78) provided the occasion for 'The Great McDermott'[1] to sing his *War Song*
around the halls. It was admonitory; it demonstrated a flexing of muscles to warn
Russia that its designs on Turkey would not be tolerated if they resulted in a
Russian challenge to British naval power in the Eastern Mediterranean:

> We don't want to fight, but by jingo if we do,
> We've got the ships, we've got the men, we've got the money too,
> We've fought the bear before, and while we're Britons true,
> The Russians will not have Constantinople.

The *Musical Times* commented: 'It is surprising how those people will shout for
war who have no intention of fighting themselves.'[2]

The subjects of such songs as these were probably not chosen to influence their
hearers, in the way that a modern tabloid newspaper might hope and intend to

influence its readership, although it is likely that the songs had some effect. Rather are they evidence of the concerns of the population; of what was being talked about in the clubs and pubs. As such, they might well have a reverse side. The *War Song*, for example, was open to parody – which it duly received from Herbert Campbell:

> I don't want to fight – I'll be slaughtered if I do;
> I'll change my togs, I'll sell my kit, and pop my rifle too;
> I don't like the war, I ain't a Briton true,
> And I'll let the Russians have Constantinople.

Clearly, the British stiff upper lip was by no means universal in late Victorian times. Even the new semi-amateur Territorial Army was not immune to playful humour, as the music-hall comic Little Tich (Harry Relph) demonstrated:

> *One of the Deathless Army*
> I'm a bolger sold – I mean I'm a soldier bold.
> I'm not so young as I used to be before I got so old.
> I'm a regular toff I am, I am, I say I am;
> But you can't tell what's inside the jar by the label on the jam.

> *Chorus*
> For I'm a soldier, a Territorial,
> The girls will say when I'm on parade
> "There's one of the boys of the Old Brigade"
> If I ever go to war, I'll drive the enemy barmy,
> Hi!Hi! Never say die!
> I'm one of the Deathless Army.

The tune for this dredges the depths of banality. But it hardly mattered, as Little Tich was in the habit of interrupting his songs with long stretches of patter.

When the South African Boers declared war on Great Britain in 1899, British prestige was clearly at stake. But at home, there was no danger of either invasion or bombardment. Nothing closed, and the vast majority of the population went about their business as usual. But as people congregated in the public houses, music halls and theatres, the war was the major matter of concern and discussion. Once it broke out, songs tended to come thick and fast. The most famous of the songs of the Boer War – *Goodbye, Dolly Gray* – was not, however, composed especially for it, but originated in the Spanish-American War (1898), which had ended too quickly for the song's publisher to exploit his asset.

Nearly half-a-million troops were dispatched to South Africa over the duration of the war. With numbers on this scale, dockside scenes of impassioned farewells, with much handkerchief- and hat-waving were a common event, which many families experienced. A 'Naval Fantasia' for piano: *Departure of a Troopship* by Fabian Scott was typical of a number of such works for the time (1900) which assisted the listener to imagine the scene with written captions every few bars:

> Infantry heard approaching in the distance,
> A mother's parting with her only son ... etc.

Leslie Stuart's *Soldiers of the Queen* now became a Boer War anthem. Each new event released an outpouring of material, culminating in Mafeking Night and a new song, *The Heroes of Mafeking*. The fact that Sir Redvers Buller had been dismissed for not relieving the town did not deter F.V. St Clair from reminding everyone (in *Cheer Up, Buller*) that 'this soldier saved Natal'. His successor, Lord Roberts, needed no defence:

> He's pals with Tommy Atkins, He's chums with all the nobs.
> He's Irish! He's British! And He's Dear Old Bobs.[3]

There were to be many other anthems and songs, some of which anticipated the end of the war well before it actually came. Sullivan was in his grave before his last work – a setting of the *Te Deum* – composed well in advance of the cessation of hostilities – took its place in the Peace Service (8 June 1902).

Writers always kept their eyes on events, ever ready to spot an opportunity. A not-too-obvious one occurred in Ireland, just before the outbreak of war in 1914. When the Liberal government brought in the Third Home Rule Bill, there were threats of civil war in Ireland, with the result that troops were sent over. J.E. Blakely half-rose to the occasion with his *Off To Ulster* march: a march more distinguished by the beauty of its cover than the originality of its music, the limpness of which is typical of many others of its time, and makes much more understandable the furore which a few years before had greeted such a real full-blooded march as Elgar's *Pomp and Circumstance*.

*　*　*

From the 1870s onwards, a new trend had been discernible. As Prussia – a half-century earlier an ally of Britain against Napoleonic France – began the process of German unification, the threat of growing Teutonic menace was ever more apparent, a threat in turn mirrored in the musical world. In an article in *The Musician* (25 August 1897), Nicholas Kilburn (choral conductor and dedicatee of Elgar's *The Music Makers*) had somewhat despairingly asked: 'Is Germany the leading musical nation?' For all the reasons discussed in the first chapter of the present book, it seemed that this was so. The campaign against things German, however, was to be articulated not by Kilburn's serious sector of the musical spectrum but by the music halls, with their usual sensitive fingers on the public pulse.

At first, such a song as *The Sea is England's Glory* (Stephen Glover & J.W. Lake: Ascherberg, Hopwood and Crewe) was content to assert to the world in general a somewhat bombastic view of British maritime rule – challenge who dare:

> The Sea is England's Glory
> The bounding wave her throne,
> For ages bright in story
> The ocean is her own[4]

But in 1891, exasperation with Germany – who did dare to challenge – found sarcastic voice in Charles Osborne's *The Naval Exhibition*:

And Nelson certainly fought in vain
To sweep the foreigners from our main;
For down at Chelsea I declare
There's swarms of foreigners everywhere;
There's German music to greet the ear,
There's German sausage and German beer
There's German yeast in English bread,
On German matches you're bound to tread.
In fact the management of the show
Prefers the foreigner, don't you know?
The work they didn't attempt to halve,
They hired Germans to wait and carve,
While English waiters are left to starve …

When in August 1914, war actually broke out, most musicians felt themselves to be in a precarious position, for it was feared there would be a total cessation of all musical activity. With the situation looking so grim for music, a meeting was held on 13 October 1914 in the Small Queen's Hall, London, with Sir Frederick Cowen in the chair. Not a lot was achieved beyond the adoption of the suggestion that a National Association for the Protection of British Interests in Music be formed; but the voicing, particularly by the representatives of orchestral and theatre musicians, of a host of complaints against foreign musicians in general and Austro-Hungarico-Germans in particular had the effect of lancing an especially virulent boil. Why did concert agents always prefer foreigners? Why did British musicians have to dress up as Hungarians or Viennese to get a job, and why did they have to promise not to divulge that they were British? Why were Belgian refugee musicians allowed to take their jobs? No satisfactory answers came.

More concrete results accrued from the 'Music in Wartime' committee (president: Sir Hubert Parry). Just before the end of the war, The *Musical Times* could report that this admirably business-like committee had given ten thousand engagements to musicians, and had helped nearly two hundred families of needy musicians by paying maternity home and school fees.

As is often the case, what actually happened as a result of the war was nowhere near as severe as had been feared. In the early years of hostilities, there was admittedly a falling-off in the number of recitals given, and a number of music festivals were either cancelled or postponed. But the Queen's Hall Proms continued, as did the Royal Philharmonic, London Symphony Orchestra and Bournemouth concerts. Even in the uncertain closing months of 1914, Brighton decided its November festival should go ahead, and it continued to maintain its thirty-two member orchestra. Harrogate even decided to allow its director of music (Julian Clifford) to spend £3,500 he had requested for music provision, a considerable sum for the time. For the spas and seaside resorts now realized that, with the curtailment of travel to European watering places, they all stood to gain an increased clientele.

The musical press recorded remorselessly every pro and anti Central Powers action – and even thought – some of which may strike us today as somewhat petty. The Guildhall School of Music, for example, dismissed all its professors of German, Austrian or Hungarian origin. Chappells (the publishers and concert promoters) decreed that no German pianos would be allowed in their Queen's Hall. They were, it must be said, piano manufacturers as well as music publishers; it perhaps shows remarkable tolerance that they had not insisted on this before. Schirmers published the complete national anthems of the Allies, arranged for school use by Dr Charles Vincent. The makers of Bovril also published them. On the back-wrapper, an advertisement for the product appeared:

A Requisition from the Front:
"Send me Bovril, urgently wanted"

Sir Henry Wood chafed at the chore of performing these anthems nightly at the Proms, a custom which continued right through 1915.

On the opposing side, Hans Richter, who had retired to Germany, gave all his British and Russian decorations to be sold for the benefit of Austrian wounded. At Cowen's meeting, it was sourly observed that he hadn't returned 'the filthy lucre which enabled him to retire to the Fatherland'.

The voice of reason was not altogether silenced. Even at Cowen's meeting, some brave artists ventured the unpopular view that 'Good music must not be tabooed or ignored, no matter from what country it may come'.[5] The eminent critic Robin Legge emphasized the point:

Do let us recognise that it is the music that is the thing, not the birthplace of the composer.[6]

The Royal Philharmonic Society, however, excluded Beethoven, Wagner and Brahms from its programmes until March 1918, when Sir Thomas Beecham, clearly making a point (for he didn't much care for the work) included the *Eroica* Symphony. There was one exception. In November 1916, Landon Ronald opened his Royal Philharmonic Society concert with Wagner's overture to *Die Meistersinger*. Some musicians adopted a compromise position. Henry Coward, the great trainer of choirs, opposed German music only; and then only that written after 1870, which conveniently allowed him to continue to perform the Brahms *Requiem* and much Wagner. Sir Henry Wood played the great Austrian classics and Wagner at the Proms, but did not programme works by living German composers. But one member of Parliament (Sir Arthur Markham) attacked the inclusion of any German music, while Hubert Bath (later to compose the *Cornish Rhapsody* for the film *Love Story*), who had been very vocal at Cowen's meeting, attempted to organize a boycott of it.

European romantic operetta and musical comedy ceased to be programmed. The music of our French and Russian allies benefited from all this, with composers such as Debussy, Balakirev, Borodin and Rimsky-Korsakov coming to the fore (particularly in Beecham programmes). Home-grown musicals such as *The Maid of the Mountains* and *Chu Chin Chow* did well, too. But above all, it was British orchestral and choral music that benefited most. Music by Ethel Smyth, Ralph Vaughan Williams, Balfour Gardiner, Bax and Bridge, that might otherwise have been given no hearing, was performed, not to speak of the consolidation of the public awareness of the major figures of Elgar and Delius.

Except insofar as parents and loved ones parted from their young sons and betrothed as they were dispatched abroad after volunteering for service, the effect on the civilian population was at first one of petty irritations rather than of major disruptions. There was at first no conscription; there was deemed to be little danger of invasion. There was coastal shelling but raids by zeppelins, while frightening, were limited in effect. But then the casualty lists from the front began to lengthen, and with their publication, civilians too found themselves at the centre of the war. The army grew, conscription came, and women took over the jobs of those who had gone to fight, not only in munitions factories, but in orchestras – on the pier, at the spa and in the theatres. The London Coliseum Orchestra – particularly admired by Elgar – eventually had only one male player: the timpanist.

The war had been confidently expected to end by Christmas 1914. By 1916, the realities of the situation could not be ignored. Beecham's Royal Philharmonic Society programme (26 February 1917) of Balakirev, Mozart and Franck found room for Clara Butt to sing Edward German's new song: *Have You News of My Boy Jack?* The title is a yardstick of the anxiety generated in two and a half years of a war that showed no signs of ending. It had been a very different story in 1914, when Alice Delysia encouraged the gentlemen in her audience:

> We don't want to lose you
> But we think you ought to go … (Paul Rubens)

Years before the war, Vesta Tilley, dressed as a male soldier, had reassured the faint-hearted with *The Army of Today's All Right*, and had conveyed a potent message to those who could construe, in *Jolly Good Luck to the Girl Who Loves a Sailor* and *All the Boys in Khaki Get the Nice Girls*. All's fair in love and war, perhaps.

Marie Lloyd personalized these sentiments in a song written for her by Charles Collins and Fred Leigh: *Now You've Got Yer Khaki On*:

> I do feel proud of you, I do honour bright.
> I'm going to give you an extra cuddle tonight.
> I didn't like yer much before yer joined the army, John
> But I do like yer, cocky, now you've got yer khaki on.

She sang this at one of the Sunday night concerts for the troops given at the Princes Theatre, Shaftsbury Avenue; generally, though, this song was not typical of those actually sung by troops in trenches, which differed again from those banalities on offer at home in England.

The most grave events and the most serious movements could be trivialized in a way which makes its own comment on society's attitudes in the early years of the twentieth century. Montague Ewing, for example (better known for *The Police-man's Holiday*) in 1915 penned a prancing military two-step *Somewhere in France*, its orange, sepia and black cover showing a line of artillery with officer, sword at the ready; an image contrasting surreally with the jolly music within. This was fairly typical, as was Jean Vernon's *VC March: 1915*, 'dedicated to the Gallant Heroes of the Great European War', also of appalling banality. But at least it had the intention of measuring up to its grave subject. Sadly, what it served to show was how little the realities of the war had as yet penetrated the consciousness of those at home.

The songs produced for home consumption in the first year of the war were marked by an almost unreal insouciance, which was to reappear a quarter of a century later in the opening stages of the Second World War. Typical of many were *When We've Wound Up the Watch on the Rhine* and *We Shall All Do the Goose-Step* (Mark/Darewski/Francis, Day, Hunter: both sung in the show *Business as Usual* (London Hippodrome, 16 November 1914). Others included songs which focused on the necessary hate-figure: the Kaiser. Typical of these were *I Want to Meet the Kaiser* (Ernest Shand: Francis, Day, Hunter), *I'm Giving Up My Job to the Kaiser* (Tom Costello) and *Kaiser Bill is a Merry Old Soul* (Ambrose Vink).

If the fighting men in the Flanders trenches sang anything at all, it would have been to the accompaniment of concertina or mouth-organ (mostly German-made in the early years of the war). Here the realities were ever-present. The war would obviously be long, and the sentiments of the lyrics, therefore, were nostalgic, anxious for faithfulness and for the preservation of everything as it had been.

If your company was trudging up to duty on the front line, it helped to have a good tune with a firm rhythm to which to march. *Tipperary*, which qualified both in its sentiments and in its march-tune, in some ways defines the perfect First World War tune. But it had been written before the war as a music-hall song, and fulfilled its destiny only after a *Daily Mail* war correspondent reported hearing it sung by some soldiers in France. This fact was then used by the publisher in a new campaign to boost its otherwise flagging sales. *Pack Up Your Troubles* was another marching song, a competition prize winner. The fortunes of winning entries in competitions has been, to say the least, variable, but *Pack Up Your Troubles* became almost as popular as *Tipperary*.

Of the nostalgic songs, Ivor Novello's *Keep the Home Fires Burning* was one of the best and certainly the most popular. Novello (1893–1951) had been one of three articled pupils of Sir Herbert Brewer at Gloucester Cathedral (the other two were Herbert Howells and Ivor Gurney). This song by a mere twenty-one-year-old when it was written (1914) presaged a brilliant career for Novello – not only as a composer, but as an actor, playwright and impresario. Its lyric was invested with a longing for faithfulness, for domesticity and normality, and it was set to an immediately memorable tune. It was taken by Lena Ashwell to France with one of her concert parties, and first sung at Rouen in 1915. This, and other popular songs, could now be commercially recorded. In his *Music on Record*,[7] Fred Gaisberg, the pioneering director of the HMV company, tells us that they were distributed in their thousands from early 1916, and that many portable gramophones were to be found in the trenches at the front. By 1918, the Zonophone company found that its increased production and sales enabled it to reduce the price of its product drastically – from two shillings and sixpence to one shilling and sixpence. Nor did Zonophone neglect the troops in its advertising:

> Don't forget our soldiers – especially the wounded. Where they have a talking instrument send them Zonophone records.[8]

Once the material was available, it could be parodied by bored yet inventive soldiers. If we needed any measure of the popularity of Herman Löhr's 1911 song *Little Grey Home in the West*, it would be provided by its front-line parody *Our Little Wet Trench in the West*. Hymn tunes, too, could be altered. Thus, *The Church's One Foundation* easily became *We Are Fred Karno's Army*, while the splendid tune of *What a Friend We Have in Jesus* fitted *When This Wretched War is Over* like a glove.

What is immediately striking is the absence during the war itself of vainglorious, aggressive music from the acknowledged 'great' composers of the day. During the pre-war build-up of international tensions, Elgar, Parry and the others had reflected in manner and style, if not in actual intention, the glory of the burgeoning imperial state. During the war itself, this aspect of their work fell strangely silent. Elgar – sadly misinterpreted in the coming 1920s and 30s – is a case in point. Works like *Carillon* (Op. 75: 1914), *Une Voix Dans le Desert* (Op. 77: 1915) and *Le Drapeau Belge* (Op. 79: 1917) – all settings (as recitation) of Cammaerts' words with orchestral accompaniment – said no more of British aspirations than did *Polonia* (Op. 76: 1915). Unless, that is, Elgar's complex psychology dictated that he could only face real horrors of war (as opposed to a game of soldiers, represented in their pomp and circumstance) by proxy, as it were. But even in the three fine choral settings of Laurence Binyon that comprise *The Spirit of England* (Op. 80: *The Fourth of August*, *To Women* and *For The Fallen*), there is no petty nationalism; rather an elegiac compassion and nobility: 'there is no music of his which is quite so incomparably noble'.[9]

This music is not, of course, in any sense light; but it was, at least in intention, popular in that it attempted to fulfil the function of an artist voicing the deepest feelings of an otherwise inarticulate populace. It nevertheless fell to Sir Hubert Parry to write the real national anthem – an anthem to express the aspirations of a people who could all too often be forgiven for seeing no point at all to the war; an anthem towering over the official one – itself a weak thing. In 1916, he set Blake's *Jerusalem* in tune so strong and with harmonies so stirring as to be incomparable. Thereafter, no one else has dared to set it. It was the finest anthem of the war.

A number of composers served in the armed forces and some – F.S. Kelly, Denis Browne and George Butterworth among them – died in it. Among those who served and survived were Ralph Vaughan Williams, Ivor Gurney, Arthur Bliss and E.J. Moeran, all of whom in its aftermath and in their various ways recorded in their music the psychological wounds with which it left them.

By ironic paradox, the most cataclysmic event caused and experienced by humanity in its recorded history up to that point was, in general, mirrored not in its serious but in its light music. As the war dragged on, such banalities as J.W. Cherry's *Britannia, The Pride of the Ocean* or G.H. Clutsam's *Who Sings for England* seemed increasingly hollow, when the tragedies came down, in the end, to suffering individuals. Thus, Theodore Bonheur's[10] *The King's Own* stresses valour, but against the backdrop of massive loss of life dwells on the death of one particular soldier. Haydn Wood's *Roses of Picardy* became a kind of allegorical requiem for those losses. The yearnings for home of those who survived were reflected in such songs as Percy Elliott's *Till I Come Back to You* (1916: with Teschemascher) and Hubert Bath's *Sweethearts and Wives* (1917).

In 1917, America entered the war and the increasing numbers of American troops sent to Britain over the early months of 1918 brought their own music with them. The visits some years before of J.P. Sousa and his superb band, and those of such groups as The Jubilee Singers, had already given us a taste, and a growing enthusiasm, for trans-Atlantic styles. They marched to George M. Cohan's *Over There*; they stimulated the spread here of ragtime, and showed, to those with ears to hear, what the popular music of the future might be.

Notes

1.   Pseudonym for G.H. Farrell.
2.   Lunn, H.C., ed., *Musical Times*, June 1878.
3.   *Dear Old Bobs* (1900), composer unknown.
4.   It is notable how much of this material speaks of England rather than of Great Britain.
5.   *The Musical Herald*, 1914, p. 403.
6.   Ibid. 1914, p. 428.
7.   Gaisberg, Fred, *Music On Record*, pp. 76–77.
8.   Zonophone advertisement, 1918.
9.   Young, Percy (1955), *Elgar O.M.*, Collins, p. 302.
10. Pseudonym for Alfred Rawlings.

CHAPTER NINE

The 1920s

The War to end war finally ended, with an armistice at the eleventh hour of the eleventh day of the eleventh month. At least, that was what the victors thought. They were not to know that it was merely half-time in a conflict that was to break out again with renewed ferocity two decades later. For, as Bernard Shaw observed, 'the dread of defeat, instead of being removed by victory, is merely transferred to the next war'.[1]

Naturally, a mood of cynicism regarding the possibility of any real security, and of disillusionment with the idea that any existing heads of state might be able to achieve it led in turn to a living for the moment; a discarding of all restraint. Again, Shaw put it uncomfortably:

> boys who for years did not believe they could escape death for many weeks more ...
> excited girls who could refuse these doomed boys nothing ... [2]

The habit, and expectation, was established as those who had fought and survived now returned home. Many were maimed. All had unspeakable memories. Naturally, they looked for their old jobs or better, and for their place in society for which they had fought. They were heroes, deserving the status of heroes.

They found that, in four years, it was the status of their womenfolk which had been enhanced. Women had taken their jobs, albeit sometimes unseemly ones. At the government's behest, they had driven vehicles and made shells. Their price for this was political and social emancipation. But many women had been widowed, or had lost their fiancés. There was now an imbalance of women over men, many of whom now had to continue providing for themselves, having lost their provider. They were not easily going to give up either their jobs or their newly-won freedoms.

What was true generally was true specifically of the music profession. There had always been an unwritten rule that women were not engaged in symphony orchestras unless they played the harp; a rule swept away, to his credit, by Sir Henry Wood. But from well before the end of the nineteenth century, women had formed their own ensembles, and during the 1914–18 war, these came into their own. Thus established, they were hardly going to disband when it ended. Catering firms such as Lyons employed them – at, for example, the *Maison Lyons* Marble Arch restaurant. Department stores such as Barkers in Kensington used them, to play in the restaurant at lunch and tea-times.

In the new post-war decade, women's dress reflected both their new status and the philosophy behind it. Gone were the long flowing skirts, the impossibly tiny waists and the emblem of womanhood: the bosom. Gone, too, were the long hairstyles – now trimmed to a shingle. The 'flapper' had arrived. She went to dances and she stayed out late. There was no longer any place for an illusory romanticism, only for a short-term cynicism. The world belonged to the Bright Young Things.

Last-century concepts of morality, of improvement and of deferred gratification crumbled. What now mattered was immediacy – particularly immediacy of enjoyment, carrying with it no philosophical baggage. An apparent (and illusory) prosperity for a while masked social ferment among the underclasses. These, in any case, would play but a vicarious part in the accompanying musical ferment of the decade. Their representatives might busk to those attending the theatre or nightclub. But as partakers, they would be excluded until they could afford a gramophone and records.

When there have been major changes of social and economic philosophy, musicians have usually matched the new thinking in appropriate sounds and rhythms. Late Romanticism had found its musical expression in the luxuriant textures, the lush harmonies and the soaring melodic lines of Strauss, Elgar, Delius and Rachmaninoff as they exploited, and revelled in, that great glory of their art: the full symphony orchestra. But in the cold and not-too-brave new world of the 1920s, their message and the sounds in which it had been expressed, seemed irrelevant. Osbert Sitwell has unforgettably illuminated the image of the elderly Elgar as he now appeared to the bright young things; an unalterable Edwardian figure, observed on a visit to Frank Schuster's house on the river at Bray:

> ... I seem to recall that we saw, from the edge of the river, on a smooth green lawn opposite, above an embankment, and through an hallucinatory mist born of the rain that had now ceased, the plump wraith of Sir Edward Elgar, who with his grey moustache, grey hair, grey top hat and frock-coat looked every inch a personification of Colonel Bogey ... [3]

Yet there was no one obvious direction in which musicians might go. It was a time for experiment; but in musical experiment, there lay always the danger of losing one's audience. This was for many years to be the fate of the atonalists and serialists. Others shied from anything so positive, and thought in terms of reaction or rejection. Anti-Romanticism looked for the antithesis of the lush, blended sounds of the full orchestra, for the opposite of the rich, exotic harmonies, and for an alternative to the hour-long symphony. The circus band offered itself as a model. Stravinsky adopted (and adapted) it for *L'Histoire du Soldat* and the *Circus Polka*. 'Wrong' harmonies proved to be a bracing antidote to the lush chords while short pieces which did not develop, but consisted of contrasted sections, satisfied the need to reject the Austro-German symphonic construction techniques.

In light music, the new influences from the United States of America, which had been growing in their effect throughout the previous decade, complemented these trends. As noted in the previous chapter, their force had been enhanced since 1917 with the ever-increasing American troops deployed in Europe. This infectious

American music offered a heady cocktail of spirituals, Sousa-style and New Orleans-style marches, ragtime and jazz. Its effects were felt not only in Britain, but all over Europe; even as far as revolutionary pre-Stalinist Russia.

Ragtime is simply the displacement of accent (usually in the melody) against a steady pulse in the bass. The technical term for this is syncopation. With its disruption of the traditional patterns of stress, it may not be too fanciful to see it as a neat metaphor mirroring the rapidly changing patterns of society itself, as the natural order was everywhere challenged and upset. Ragtime dated from long before the war, and its effective ambassador in Europe was Irving Berlin's *Alexander's Ragtime Band*. Berlin's popular piece is not, in fact, a particularly characteristic example of ragtime, nor were those rags in the 1912 London Hippodrome show *Hullo Ragtime* (23 December 1912) which ran for 451 performances. The more authentic work of Texas-born Scott Joplin (?1868–1917) made little impact here until long after the period, when some of it was used in the 1970s film *The Sting*. Exploration of Joplin's work then revealed that, far from always being a raucous razz-ma-tazz, ragime – at any rate in Joplin's hands – could be a sensitive medium, capable of expressing many moods. Back in 1918, most European composers were unaware of Joplin's work, but a few dabbled in the more superficial aspects of the style. Stravinsky was one, with his *Ragtime for Eleven Instruments* (1918) and *Piano-Rag Music* (1919); Bliss was another, with *Rout* trot (1923). The Cakewalk was another American import, of even earlier vintage.[4] Like ragtime, it, too, employed syncopation.

Both the Cakewalk and ragtime styles were often written down. Jazz – the third American import – was not. That is to say, it was not as practised in New Orleans, whence it originated in the later nineteenth century. Here and in the Southern states generally, it was improvised, and was peculiarly the music of coloured groups. The improvisations were on the basis of an agreed chord sequence, and the music proceeded by variation; each variation or 'break' featuring a different player in turn, with interjections, or counterpoints, by the others. The style was thus polyphonic and, to the extent that it was syncopated, it incorporated features of its ancestor: ragtime. Other elements feeding into it were West African rhythms, gospel song, Southern marching and funeral bands, and the Blues. Blues covered both an overall style and a specific technique. The style was an expression, again in the first place improvised, of depressed mental states, brought on by poverty, ill-treatment or rejection in love. The specific technique was that of the so-called 'blue notes' of the scale: degrees three and seven which, for example in the scale of C were played or sung at a point midway between E and E flat, and B and B flat respectively.[5]

Attempts by white groups to play jazz tended to be greeted with derision by coloured exponents. It was, nevertheless, from white musicians that Britain first became acquainted with what they took to be jazz styles, and there was much debate as to what was, and was not, true jazz. In November 1918, Irene Castle (of the authoritative dance team Vernon and Irene Castle) expressed her view that an authentic jazz band had yet to appear in Britain. It is doubtful if the earliest British groups, of which the British Syncopated Orchestra (appearing in October 1921 at the Kingsway Hall, London) was one, would have filled the role for her, proficient though they were.

One group purporting to be authentic did spend three months in London in the late summer of 1919. This was the Original (Dixieland) Jazz Band. But because this and other visiting bands tended to clown, to spar with their instruments and to wear silly hats, jazz was not at first taken seriously here. Nor was its cause helped when popular classics were syncopated. Herman Darewski, for one, proudly asserted that he had managed to produce syncopated versions of tunes from *Faust* (Gounod), *Il Trovatore* (Verdi) and *Peer Gynt* (Grieg), and, as his ultimate *tour de force*, Wagner's *Tannhaüser*.

The common perception of jazz among the academics of the time can be observed in the contemporary music dictionaries. The 1925 edition of one,[6] after dismissing a jazz band as a 'nigger orchestra', goes on to describe its constitution as 'Any band of noisy, nondescript instruments'. Sir Hugh Allen, addressing the 1922 conference of the Incorporated Society of Musicians, suggested that jazz was written/played from a low motive and a bad impulse. Sir Henry Coward, the distinguished choral conductor, saw in jazz nothing but a threat to everything he held sacred. 'We must ban jazz', he told the same society six years later in 1928. But, as the *Musical Standard* (30 June 1928) pointed out, if it had done nothing else, jazz had at least ousted the ballad.

Where ragtime had been largely centred around the piano, the jazz band usually consisted of all, or a selection from, trumpet (or cornet), trombone, clarinet, saxophone, banjo, bass, piano and percussion. The sound was therefore raw; raucous even. In Britain, the saxophone in particular brought a shudder to musical purists, despite the fact that such respectable musicians as Bizet had used it in their work. 'It is greatly abused in jazz-bands', said the same musical dictionary quoted above.[7] Good saxophonists were at first hard to find. Their rich, oily tones were much prized and highly rewarded in the night-clubs.

The tendency in London was to civilize the essentially rough expression of jazz, in order to turn it into a vehicle for society dancing. The dancers thereby missed the point – that a dance beat and a jazz rhythm are two quite different things. The civilizing tendency was given further force when the American white musician Paul Whiteman (1890–1967) brought over his big band in 1923, playing at the Kit-Kat Club. The Whiteman band, playing what he called symphonic jazz, looked in constitution more like a symphony orchestra than a jazz band; unsurprising when we remember Whiteman's background as a violist in the Denver and San Francisco Symphony Orchestras. With twenty-seven musicians, improvisation was, of course, unthinkable. What Whiteman played was 'symphonic syncopation', in orchestrations by his back-room genius Ferde Grofe.

The spurious nature of the 'Mickey Mouse' work of the Original Dixieland Jazz Band, and the sanitized work of Whiteman and others were revealed when records of such figures as Sidney Bechet, King Oliver and Louis Armstrong began to become widely available, showing how the real thing sounded. By then, serious composers had extracted what they needed from the styles. For them – Ravel, *Les Six*, Walton, Lambert and even Shostakovich – it was the jazz mutes, the trombone glissandi, the syncopation and the blue scale that they needed. In the 1920s, improvisation – the chief characteristic of jazz – was not the option for serious composers it was to become in the 1960s.

American singers did not, perhaps, have the same influence on British composers as they did on their fellow British singers. But one – the coloured blues singer Florence Mills and her accompanying group The Plantation Orchestra, who together appeared in London in 1923 and 1926 – had a profound effect on Constant Lambert. So profound that his friend the pianist Angus Morrison maintained that it was:

> One of the key experiences of his life … moving him in a far deeper way emotionally than any other music he had hitherto heard.[8]

For Spike Hughes, the chief impression was not so much of the singer, but of the 'remarkable technical precision' of the Plantation Orchestra, and its use of brass:

> Here was a band which used them for gay, farcical and sentimental purposes so that the lions we knew could roar as gently as any sucking dove.[9]

*   *   *

The decade of the 1920s was a crucible for light music, into which a number of ingredients were poured, to be mixed and mutated in the process. If American music was one such ingredient, it was certainly modified on reacting with the British ingredients, which included not only the music itself, but also the new sound technologies and even the indigenous British institutions. These institutions included the music halls, the hotels, the theatres, night clubs and restaurants. It was these that became the forcing grounds for light music in the 1920s. In an economic climate in which businesses either adapted to meet public taste and demand, or went under, most tried to adapt.

The music halls, as they had existed in Edwardian times, would not survive the decade. Their optimistic ethos and philosophy of acceptance of what is, now had no place. Silent films made remorseless inroads on their audiences. By the end of the war, cinema audiences were already to be counted in millions rather than hundreds of thousands. The spread of broadcasting in the new decade delivered the final blow.

Of the old stars, some, like Vesta Tilley, married their aristocratic suitors. Others, like Marie Lloyd or George Formby senior, died worn out. But some, such as George Robey or Harry Lauder, kept right on to the end of the road, and there were the new stars, such as Cicely Courtneidge, Jessie Matthews, Evelyn Laye, Jack Hulbert and above all, Gracie Fields, beginning to establish themselves. They diversified – into straight plays, cabaret, recording, revue and eventually film.

Although it had been in existence before the war, and was in essence a reinterpretation of Victorian Burlesque, revue became a 1920s' phenomenon. C.B. Cochran and André Charlot were its pioneers, although George Grossmith junior[10] claimed to have introduced revue to this country with the popular wartime *Bing Boys* shows. These featured such huge hit-songs as *If You Were the Only Girl in the World (The Bing Boys are Here)* and *Let the Great Big World Keep Turning (The Bing Girls Are There)* and were vehicles for Violet Loraine and George Robey.

Cochran overcame the shortages and stoppages of 1921 to put on the topically titled *League of Notions* (17 January 1921), turning the Oxford Music Hall into the New Oxford Theatre in which to present it. Seeing the new trend, the Palladium and the Victoria Palace, too, adopted revue. A succession of revues now followed. They proved to be surprisingly accommodating in the catholicity of what they might include. In 1925, for example, Cochran's revue *On With the Dance* (30 April 1925), which ran for 229 performances at the London Pavilion, featured 'A Hogarth Impression' *The Rake* with choreography by Leonide Massine and music by Roger Quilter. Given his sexual orientation, Quilter seems an odd choice to provide music for the drunken Rake's wanton women dancing erotically around him. But the pretext of the music is now forgotten, and we are left with an attractive suite. And the last movement *Midnight Revels* takes even Quilter beyond his usual cosy parameters, with a distinctly jazzy conclusion.

Revue established the careers of Beatrice Lillie, Gracie Fields, Jessie Matthews and many others. It also revealed, in Vivian Ellis (born 1904) a composer who, in any other country but England, would have long ago been accorded the status of a George Gershwin or a Richard Rodgers.

Ellis had been a pupil of the pianist Myra Hess, and had studied composition at the Royal Academy of Music. He was sufficiently accomplished as a pianist to be a recitalist. His misfortune was to be writing his songs in an age when the artist who sang them took all the glory. The composer took the royalty, but little else. A few titles, chosen at random, may serve to give some idea of his remarkable consistency:

Over My Shoulder (*Mercenary Mary* 1925. Perennially associated with Jessie
    Matthews – the essential flapper – although not originally sung by her)
Spread a Little Happiness (*Mr Cinders* 1929. Sung by Binnie Hale)
I'm on a See-saw (*Jill Darling* 1934. Sung by John Mills and Louise Brown)
She's My Lovely (*Hide and Seek* 1937. Sung by Bobby Howes)

And his greatest triumph was still many years off, as we shall see in Chapter 16.

Three of the songs in the above list were from musical comedy. Revue, like music hall, did not long survive the twin blows of the 1926 General Strike and the advent of 'talkies' in 1927–28. But its essentials were carried on in the variety shows promoted by George Black and the Moss Empire's chain of theatres.

Musicals (or musical comedy, musical play and operetta; the differences between them were so slight as to be merely ones of name) continued to be produced right through the decade, despite the enormous financial risks involved. Risky, because the public demanded ever more lavish spectacle, the cost of which had to

be balanced against rising theatre rents – which were inevitably reflected in esca-
lating seat prices. The story would be one of struggle by the home-grown musicals
to avoid being swamped by the tide of American and pseudo-Viennese ones.

The two big British successes of the war years had been *Chu Chin Chow* (31
August 1916) and *The Maid of the Mountains* (10 February 1917) with music by
Frederick Norton and Harold Fraser-Simpson respectively. *The Maid* had been a
vehicle for the musical comedy star Jose Collins (daughter of the music-hall veteran
Lotte Collins, who exhausted herself singing and dancing *Ta-Ra-Ra-Boom-Di-Ay*). It
ran for 1352 performances; *Chu Chin Chow* exceeded that figure by nine hundred.
But the formula then failed. Their successors, including Percy Fletcher's *Cairo* and
Ivan Caryll's *Kissing Time*, did not do as well, and the market for musicals was wide
open to American invasion. In the vanguard was Jerome Kern (1885–1945), followed
closely by Vincent Youmans, Rudolph Friml and Sigmund Romberg. (Friml and
Romberg were respectively Czech and Hungarian who, like so many European
musicians, emigrated as young men to the United States.)

Kern was a New Yorker who, like Gershwin a little later, started out as a Tin Pan
Alley song-plugger. As a young man, he was a frequent visitor to London. He first
made his mark here when, in 1914, he contributed to *The Girl From Utah* what was
to become one of the great 'standards': *They Didn't Believe Me*. In 1921, his show
Sally ran for nearly a year at the London Wintergarden. A rags-to-riches story, it
boasted another show-stopper in *Look For The Silver Lining*.

1925 saw the arrival of Friml's *Rose Marie* at Drury Lane, where it stayed for
two years. In the same year, Youman's *No No Nanette* was established at the Palace
Theatre, to run for 665 performances. Night after night, Binnie Hale and Seymour
Beard would bring the house down with *Tea For Two*. *No No Nanette* was the
quintessential flapper show. It had the pace which all too often eluded the home-
produced show. And, as *I Want to be Happy* showed, the Americans could syncopate
without self-consciousness.

Romberg's *The Student Prince* came to London in 1926 after a successful run on
Broadway, but withered in three months, to become fodder for the amateur circuit.
But when *Rose Marie* finally closed, Romberg's *The Desert Song* succeeded it
(1927), to become one of the biggest successes of the decade. A public intoxicated
with the recent and real exploits of Lawrence of Arabia on the one hand, and of
Rudolph Valentino's fictional sheik on the other, was ripe for the Red Shadow and
his North African outlaw riffs; there being little distinction in its mind between
Arabia and Morocco. It was all sandy.

Some promoters fondly remembered the profitability of Lehár's *The Merry
Widow* at Daly's Theatre in 1907. They tried reviving it, and Lehár himself had
written many successors. One of them – *Frasquita* – failed miserably in 1925,
despite having José Collins as its star:

> From the beginning, everything seemed to go wrong. And yet, ironically enough,
> here was a play steeped in the glamour and romance of Viennese light opera, with
> gorgeous music and with one song in particular, the Serenade, which I consider one

of the loveliest I have ever sung … How strange it is that the worst play so often contains the best song.[11]

Nor did other Viennese imports, such as *The Gipsy Princess* (1921: Emmerich Kalman) or *The Last Waltz* (1922: Oscar Strauss) do so well, when compared with the long runs in the previous decade of *The Maid of the Mountains* or *Chu Chin Chow*.[12] But *The Last Waltz* did achieve an historical footnote; it was the first musical to be broadcast; from Station 2LO at Marconi House.

In 1928, a work of seminal importance reached Drury Lane, London, from the United States. This was the Jerome Kern/Oscar Hammerstein II musical *Show Boat* (1927), which introduced to British audiences the young bass singer Paul Robeson. *Show Boat* demonstrated that the form of the musical was capable of dealing with a serious subject – and thus paved the way for such examples some sixteen years later as *Oklahoma*. But there was to be a home-grown attempt at an answer to it.

Towards the end of the decade in 1929, a British musical opened at His Majesty's Theatre, which seemed set to stem the alien tide. Noel Coward's *Bitter Sweet* reversed a recent trend in that it went on from London to Broadway, New York – as Gilbert and Sullivan and the pre-war British products had always done. It succeeded in reinterpreting the nineteenth-century Viennese operetta, down even to its waltz-song; although Coward's waltz-song *I'll See You Again* manages to seem not out-of-place in the spirit of the 1920s.

Sir Noël Coward (1899–1973) possessed what he modestly called 'a talent to amuse'. But this talent – approaching genius – was astonishingly versatile. He was a master of the 'patter-song', in which no-one excelled him in performance. Such examples as *Mad Dogs and Englishmen Go Out in the Mid-day Sun, Don't Put Your Daughter on the Stage, Mrs Worthington*, and *Don't Lets Be Beastly to the Germans* (banned in wartime for a while before its irony was grasped) show him in the tradition stemming from Sir William Gilbert through to Michael Flanders and Donald Swann. Coward's own clipped diction when he performed his own work would surely have won plaudits from Gilbert himself. But, Coward could as easily, as Gilbert could but rarely, touch a sensitive nerve in his public, with the cocooned cosiness of *A Room with a View*, or the sentiment of *London Pride*.

*　　*　　*

The restaurateurs soon realized that modern young things wanted more than a meal. They wanted an evening's entertainment, looked for dancing and, after that, a cabaret. An importation from New York, cabaret had first appeared there around 1915, opening at midnight when the crowds leaving the theatres were looking for further diversion. It reached London over the 1921–22 season, coinciding with the passion of night-owls for dancing.

The dance enthusiasms of the 1920s reflected the dismantling of the barriers between the sexes, which now seemed to have little point or justification. Of the pre-war dances, the close-contact ones still had some life in them. The waltz was one, but it was now considerably faster. The difference can be heard by comparing

9.1   Noël Coward and Beverley Nichols

one of Coleridge-Taylor's *Characteristic Walzes* with, say, Coates's fine example in his *Summer Days* Suite.

The tango was another. First danced in Britain in 1912 by George Grossmith junior and Phyllis Dare in the musical comedy *The Sunshine Girl*, its continued popularity was confirmed by the number of specialist tango bands in the period. But the Boston – a predecessor of the foxtrot – had lost its popularity long before the war was over. Apart from the foxtrot, other post-war dances included the Quickstep – a speeded-up version of the foxtrot – and, of course, the Charleston. This syncopated dance enjoyed two years or so of frenetic popularity and an equal measure of disapproval from the self-appointed guardians of morality, who were to be punished when it was displaced in public favour by the even more disreputable Black Bottom.

The craze for dancing in the clubs and restaurants suggested that the 1920s would be years of plenty for performing musicians, for the demand for dance bands seemed to be insatiable. These bands catered, of course, for the top strata of society; strata that could easily afford the expensive style of nightly dining out and dancing in town. One of the earliest bands was that of Jack Hylton at the Kit-Kat Club.

In 1925, Hylton advertised for an arranger. His advertisement was answered by Joseph Holbrooke, the composer of tone poems who we noted in Chapter 4 writing music-hall songs. Holbrooke had already written a number of foxtrots, and now orchestrated for Hylton. The echoes of the equally impecunious Elgar writing lancers for the asylum resonate clearly. Lancashire-born Hylton (1892–1965) started in the profession as second pianist for a Rhyl concert party. He was then just thirteen. Out of a job when the summer season was over, he went on stage calling himself 'The Singing Mill-Boy'. Such resource and toughness indicated a man who would climb, and thereby employ one of his other attributes, an unusually sharp business brain. By the 1940s, Hylton had outgrown the band-world to become an impresario, promoting tours by the London Philharmonic Orchestra, a music festival at Harringay and even shows by The Crazy Gang.

Other famous bands of the 1920s included those of Jack Payne, Debroy Somers at the Savoy, of Carroll Gibbons following him there, of Harry Roy and Bert Ambrose. The last-named – soon to drop the proletarian 'Bert' for professional purposes – demonstrates just how lucrative band work in the 1920s could be. In 1927, the Mayfair Hotel thought it well worth its while to pay him the record salary (for the time) of £10,000 per annum to front the band there.[13] Many *cognoscenti* of the dance-band world would award Ambrose the palm as the finest of all band-leaders. Certainly, his extant recordings reveal a tightness of ensemble worthy of a Toscanini, and an ear for the blending of sound approaching that of a Stokowski.

Ambrose became a high-society icon, as did Debroy Somers. Somers' debonair appearance belied his nature, which was happiest when he was in the background as an arranger and orchestrator. The Savoy Hotel management asked him to form an orchestra of the highest quality. This he did, bringing to it his own preferences for a sweet orchestral, rather than a blatant jazz sound. He gathered together a splendid group of eleven musicians – at first mainly Americans. He had, however, to be pressed hard before he would front his new creation; The Savoy Orpheans. Nor did he stay long with them. In 1923, he organized his own orchestra which, after its debut at the London Hippodrome, toured the country appearing in shows produced by George Black or Firth Shephard. Thereby he blazed a trail, which would be followed by many other band-leaders.

*   *   *

The inventive geniuses of the late nineteenth century had concerned themselves with sound and visual image. With regard to sound, they devised ways of transmitting it and of preserving it. Images, too, they preserved; on film, then on moving film and finally on moving film complemented by sounds. The transmitting of sounds (broadcasting) and the concept of the sound movie belong more properly to a later chapter since their effects were in the 1930s rather than in the 1920s. Here we are concerned with preserved sound and with silent film.

Preserving sound by means of the player-piano and its accompanying rolls may at first seem to be a spurious way of doing it. It is the piano, after all, that is making the sounds, operated by whoever is at the keyboard controls, with the artist nowhere in prospect. And yet a player-piano may give a more accurate and faithful reproduction of how a pianist actually sounded than an early recording might do. This is because the piano-roll process was a complex one, in which each note played was subject to a number of modifications, making for some parallels to the contemporary digital mastering techniques.

Great pianists such as Percy Grainger, Josef Hofmann and Leopold Godowsky made rolls, as did composers such as George Gershwin, Gustav Mahler, Claude Debussy and Sergei Rachmaninoff. But by the 1920s, the piano-roll catalogues carried an ever-increasing number of light music items.

The player-piano was also, perhaps, a manifestation of a less reputable trend, a siren call to those who wished to take the waiting and practice drudgery out of learning to play. You were at least sitting at the instrument to operate it – and were more likely to 'astound your friends', as the press advertisements for rapid correspondence tuition in playing put it, than by your efforts to 'play in one month'. And the player-piano – or pianola – did play all the notes as written. Learning by correspondence, or with Miss Smith in the next street, you would aspire only to the 'easy' arrangements now widely available – hardly to the original.

By the beginning of the decade, recording was growing out of its mere novelty status, and was being taken seriously by musicians and public alike. Even by 1911, at least a dozen records of Sousa's band had been available. By 1915, no less a distinguished conductor than Arthur Nikisch had given the medium his *imprimatur* by recording Beethoven's Fifth Symphony. The process, however, was still an acoustic one, in which the performers crowded round the recording horn as best they could. Some instruments recorded better than others; those others were often replaced by instruments that retained more definition on wax. Voices seemed to preserve their quality more than instruments. Strings fared worst of all – with the result that much early recording sounds predominantly brassy. Since in the first days of recording it was necessary to call on an existing repertoire, music was mercilessly butchered and cut to size in order to fit the time available on the side of the record.

The process of electrical recording had been technically possible, and available from the beginning of the 1920s. The Armistice Day Service in 1920 was recorded electrically. But at first, the new process made slow progress, because both manufacturers and dealers still had enormous stocks of acoustic records to sell. There was, too, opposition from the music profession itself, which saw a threat to its livelihood. But in 1924 came the first British recording of a major classic work: the Symphony No. 4 in F Minor by Tschaikowsky. From then on, the recording industry firmly established itself. At HMV, Fred Gaisberg set about recording all the major Elgar works with the composer conducting (and re-recording those previously done acoustically). The rival company Columbia had recorded Gustav Holst conducting his suite *The Planets*. For the first time, it was possible for a composer not just to leave the imperfect code of notation to indicate his intentions. He could now present the work himself in living sound for all posterity.

Recording companies proliferated, featuring labels such as Zonophone, Homophone and Brunswick. But the classical market was dominated by His Master's Voice and Columbia (which were subsequently to merge). By 1923, sales of records had reached a point which justified a periodical devoted to recorded music. The magazine *The Gramophone* was founded. Discs standardized at twelve inch and ten inch, revolving at 78 rpm. The two classical companies marketed their records at two levels of price, determined by the celebrity and fees of the artists involved.

Composers now began to see their income derive more from record royalties and less from sheet music sales, which declined by some 50 per cent over an eight-year period from 1925 to 1933. Naturally therefore, and especially in light music, they began to shape their music, in size and in instrumentation, to the needs of the industry. Ballads enjoyed a brief revival, and 'novelty' numbers flourished. Then, as now, the income from popular music and the negligible costs involved in its production could offset the huge outlay necessary to record the serious orchestral repertoire.

Silent film attained its peak of popularity in the 1920s. Variously called picture-palaces, kinemas or biographs, their numbers in Britain reached a total of over three thousand in that decade. There had been a huge building programme, funded by massive investment. Musicians benefited, for though the films were silent, entertainment soon withers in a climate of silence. Before the 1914–18 war, the films were more often than not accompanied by a pianist, playing whatever seemed most suitable from his or her repertoire. Later, there might be a small orchestra of up to a dozen players, but after the war, an ensemble of two violins, cello, horn, piano and drums was usually to be found.

The post-war publishers now identified a new market need. In 1919, Novellos published folios of music specially written to accompany film. Boosey followed with Frederick Curzon's *Kinema Kameos*. There were twelve of the latter, with titles such as *Aspiration* (for a passionate scene) and *Perplexity* (depicting indecision). They would have been useful to the many silent-film musicians who had no talent for improvisation.

For a particularly important feature film, the promoters would make a special effort. The silent version of *The Three Musketeers* justified the engagement of Eugene Goossens III conducting the London Symphony Orchestra to accompany it. By 1928, the use of mood-music, as it was now beginning to be called, justified the British Screen Music Society that year in publishing a guide to it. By then, it has been calculated, some three-quarters of the instrumental music profession in the country were employed playing in the picture-houses. Clearly, the regular employment of a symphony orchestra was impracticable, but the small ensemble could often give a good account of itself. Thus, towards the end of the decade, a band interlude might provide a contrasting item in a film-show, and in the larger cinemas, the orchestra might boast an independent reputation. At the Astoria, Brixton, in 1929, for example, Fred Kitchen conducted an orchestra of some seventeen players. A year later, Lazell's Picture House in Birmingham was still employing an orchestra good enough to broadcast, and big enough to play Coleridge-Taylor's *Hiawatha* ballet music.

Sound film had been available in crude form since 1923, but it was an expensive process in which producers were loath to invest while silent films were doing so well. But once early sound films such as *The Jazz Singer* (1927) and *Hell's Angels* (1930) had demonstrated its possibilities, silents inevitably became redundant. So, too, did the thousands of musicians who had enlivened them. Music's live function shrank to providing music to accompany the ice-cream girl in the interval between features. And the number of performers was in any case reduced to one – the organist, who confined his efforts to the interval.

Since the installation of the first cinema organ, believed to have been at the Palace, Accrington, organs had been fitted in many cinemas, each one displacing a number of instrumentalists. Organs by Wurlitzer, Compton and others, their consoles arising in a glory of kaleidoscopic lighting from the bowels of the theatre, became commonplace. In turn, they stimulated a new generation of virtuoso performers; such players as Reginald Dixon, Robinson Cleaver, Frederic Bayco, Fela Sowande and Reginald Foort, to name but a few, became household names. At a more humble level, many of those presiding at the cinema organ console doubled as church organists. The traditional extemporizing skills of the church musician came in useful in the secular sphere.

It would take a few more years, but by the middle of the 1930s, the considerable power of music subtly composed to influence and enhance the effect of a sequence of filmed images had been grasped. A new profession, that of composer of film background music, was about to arrive.

Notes

1. To an American journalist, quoted in Holroyd, Michael (1991) *Bernard Shaw*, vol 3, Chatto & Windus, p. 34.
2. Ibid., p. 35
3. Sitwell, Osbert (1949), *Laughter in the Next Room*, Macmillan, p. 192.
4. The Cakewalk was a parody by coloured folk of white dancing styles. It was itself parodied by Debussy in his *Gollywog's Cakewalk* (*Children's Corner* Suite: 1906–8).
5. On the piano, the effect is achieved by playing the notes almost simultaneously.
6. Dunstan, Ralph (1927), *Cyclopaedic Dictionary of Music*, Curwen/Kegan Paul.
7. Ibid.
8. Shead, Richard (1973), *Constant Lambert*, Simon, p. 38.
9. Hughes, Spike (1946), *Opening Bars*, Pilot, p. 307.
10. Son of George Grossmith, the Gilbert and Sullivan star.
11. Collins, José (1932), *The Maid of the Mountains: Her Story*, Hutchinson, p. 246.
12. Although it must be said that the star of *The Last Waltz* – again José Collins – had a succeeding engagement awaiting her in the play *Catherine*.
13. Even if, as seems likely, he had to pay the orchestra's wages out of this, the salary is still strikingly generous.

CHAPTER TEN

Instrumental Music (2): the Second Wave

The composers discussed in Chapter 7 were born in the period spanning 1840 to 1870. Such figures as Sullivan, Parry, Stanford and Cowen grew to maturity and produced the bulk of their work in a period of relative stability. Even Elgar, Delius, German and Bantock had written most of their best work before the convulsions of 1914–18. But for those born in the period 1870–1900, their studenthood, and the time in which they had produced their early work, was one of musical transition while their mature work came at a time when the various social and media changes reviewed in the previous chapter were taking place.

Some of the young men of the new generation still looked back to a musical world already fast receding. They would be left high and dry. Others of this generation would exhibit a capacity for fearless exploration hardly suspected when they were students. But all were subject to a European music dominated by the legacy of Wagner – 'The Music of the Future', which they could either embrace or reject.

By the end of the first decade of the new century, Straussian orchestral polyphony had grown exuberantly from its Wagnerian roots, like an exotic creeper out of control in the hothouse. In their respective ways, Delius and Elgar made responses to both Wagner and Strauss. And, by 1908, the work of all four was readily available to the newly emerging young men. In very general terms, the melodic and textural influence of Elgar is often apparent on them – particularly his three-part textures of melody, bass, and independent free part in the middle. This can be heard most readily in the work of Eric Coates who, along with Haydn Wood, also shows how Straussian orchestral practice could be reinterpreted. Delian harmony entered the system like a drug; in so many of his imitators, the moment the pace slackened, the basses and the inner harmonies would droop semitonally. What is not often so apparent is any specific influence of the work of the principal teachers of composition themselves, that is to say, of Charles Stanford and Frederick Corder.

For some, a cleansing antidote seemed necessary, and one presented itself with the rediscovery – perhaps just in time – of a rapidly disappearing heritage of folk-music. But, as noted in the previous chapter, the 1914–18 war had swept away futile (as it seemed) Romanticism, doing much of the necessary cleansing for them.

In this rapidly changing artistic climate, composers could adapt or cease. Most would-be composers going up to study at their colleges probably saw themselves in the tradition of the great masters, writing their symphonies and concertos that nobody now wanted. But a few perceived a future as writers of light music in its own right, rather than as something to be indulged in as just a relaxation after the last symphony.

While the composition student of the 1880s and 1890s could still study abroad (and a number did) the choice at home broadened when the Royal Academy of Music was joined by other institutions, chief of which was (for composition) the Royal College of Music – transformed in 1883 from the National Training School of Music. But some still looked across the channel. In the past, those opting for a continental music training had favoured Leipzig. The new generation of the 1870s and 1880s looked to Frankfurt when they wished to study abroad, and if they had the funds for it. Here, Iwan Knorr (1853–1916) held sway as principal teacher of composition at the Conservatorium. Norman O'Neill, Balfour Gardiner, Roger Quilter and Cyril Scott all had a background of some wealth, and could well afford to go there. Percy Grainger was less financially well-endowed but for a short while, he, too, joined the others under Knorr's direction.

As noted in Chapter 5, O'Neill (1875–1934), the oldest of the so-called 'Frankfurt' gang, devoted much of his creative energy to theatre music. But throughout his life, he also wrote orchestral music, much of it light in character and much of which could provide rich pickings for an adventurous recording company. Sadly, the bulk of it was left in manuscript, needing research to ferret out what still remains. But the following works were published:

Hornpipe (1916) Op. 48: Bosworth
Punch and Judy (1924): Ascherberg, Hopwood and Crewe
Festal Prelude (1927): Bosworth
Two Shakespearean Sketches (1928): Cramer

Henry Balfour Gardiner (1877–1950) suffered from a lack of creative confidence, which grew ever more apparent as he grew older. In any case, he held that musical creativity flickered out 'at a certain age', and when he reached what he deemed to be that age, other interests such as architecture and forestry claimed more of his attention. The result is that his catalogue is littered with unfinished projects and destroyed manuscripts. He was a wealthy man, and is remembered today for such acts of generosity as paying for the Queen's Hall Orchestra and Adrian Boult in 1918 to play to Gustav Holst his Suite: *The Planets*, and for buying Delius's house at Grez-sur-Loing in order that the financially embarrassed composer might continue to live in it. But two accessible works by Balfour Gardiner come within the scope of this book. One is *Overture to a Comedy*. Written in 1906 and dedicated to York Bowen (revised a few years later), this work was often programmed by Landon Ronald. But Gardiner's dismissal of it was typical of him: 'I've always hated this work'.[1] The other is the still popular *Shepherd Fennel's Dance*. Written in 1910 and dedicated to Sir Henry Wood, it rapidly achieved enormous popularity, especially as its dedicatee lost no opportunity in conducting it. It even spawned progeny – such as Quilter's *Midnight Revels (The Rake)* and

David Moule-Evans's *Old Tupper's Dance*. Perhaps it influenced, too, the idea at least of the finale to Eldridge Newman's *Dorset Suite*, entitled *The Old Josser's Dance* (Newman was conductor of the Folkestone Municipal Orchestra 1928–39). Suggested by the character in Hardy's *The Three Strangers*, Gardiner's infectious minor masterpiece features one of those 'once-heard, never forgotten' tunes (see Ex. 10.1), and is further distinguished by the exemplary clarity of its construction and orchestration.

Ex. 10.1   Balfour Gardiner: *Shepherd Fennel's Dance*. © Copyright 1912 by Hawkes & Son (London) Ltd. Reproduced by permission of Boosey & Hawkes Music Publishers Ltd.

A tenuous link between the Frankfurt Gang was the influence, either as exemplar or as friend, of Delius. His work was known and admired on the continent well before it made any progress in England. When that progress began, the pioneering work, promoted by both Beecham and Wood, was *Brigg Fair* – which in fact revealed only one facet of the cosmopolitan master. It was the langorous episode for solo horn in that work which created an English summer mood, a mood which others tried to capture. Balfour Gardiner was one, Moeran another. Gardiner's mediant-dominated melody at the heart of *Shepherd Fennel's Dance* echoed that of Delius, as do its semitonal downward-drooping harmonies.

Roger Quilter (1877–1953) is remembered by posterity more for his exquisite songs than for his orchestral music – some of which he did not himself orchestrate. The *Three English Dances* (Op. 11: 1910) were orchestrated by that unsung work-horse of English music Percy Fletcher (1879–1932). First performed on 30 June 1910 at the Queen's Hall, these dances depend heavily on the sequential style so familiar from Elgar and German. Little disturbs their sunny Englishness. The *Four Country Pieces* (Op. 27: 1923) were arranged for orchestra as recently as 1991 by Ernest Tomlinson, in a graphic colouring that is probably nearer to what Quilter himself might have approved, in preference to the 'fail-safe' approach of Fletcher. As Tim McDonald has pointed out,[2] Numbers 1 and 3 (*Shepherd's Song* and *Forest Lullaby*) suggest a kind of 'Quilterian Song without Words'. Movements 2 and 4 (*Goblins* and *Pipe and Tabor*) are rather more exotic, especially in Tomlinson's orchestral colouring. The 'chopsticks' of *Pipe and Tabor* seem to nod in the direction of Ravel's *Laideronette, Imperatrice des Pagodes (Ma Mère L'Oye)*. Quilter shared with Ravel certain child-like qualities which manifest themselves in the subjects of their music. He needed words to focus his general amiability, and certainly the durability of his most popular work without them – *A Children's Overture* (Op. 17: sketched 1911, completed 1919) – is due in part to the sharply defined character of its nursery tunes, which have been known to most since early childhood. The overture is little more than a medley of the well-loved tunes, but it needs to be no more than this. The orchestration here is Quilter's own, and shows complete mastery in its vivid colours.

Like so many of the composers discussed in this study, Quilter wrote an opera. But how often are British operas remembered only by an extract – most usually a waltz? That had been the fate of German's *Tom Jones*. So it was also with Quilter's light opera *Julia* (1936). The work failed at the Royal Opera House, Covent Garden, and no complete score was published. But extracts were subsequently issued, one of which was a fine *Concert Waltz*. It is as good as the best Eric Coates waltzes, which is saying a great deal.

Cyril Scott (1879–1970) is mentioned here merely for completeness, since his light music, although once frequently heard in ensemble arrangements, was mainly for piano, and as such will be considered in Chapter 11. His work suffered a massive decline in reputation in the 1930s, from which it is only now recovering, as re-evaluation takes place.

Much of the lesser known work of Percy Grainger (1882–1961) is also being re-evaluated and recorded, but a small core of his light work has never lost its place in the repertory. Delius met him in April 1907, while on a visit to London: 'A most charming young man, and more gifted than Scott, and less affected'.[3] And indeed, of all the 'gang', Grainger now appears to have been not only the most original and creative, but also the least susceptible to the influence of Knorr, with whom he studied for only three months. An Australian who served as a band instructor with the American armed forces in the 1914–18 war, and who in 1918 became an American citizen, he qualifies nevertheless as a British composer of light music because it was in this country that most of it was written. Both as a man and as an artist he was a true original of the early twentieth century, who could provide enough discussion material to keep a psychiatrists's convention fully occupied.

Throughout Grainger's life, the dominant figure in it was his mother. After only three months of formal schooling in Melbourne, Percy was educated by Rose Grainger herself; she fed him 'on the Icelandic Sagas, the Anglo-Saxon Chronicles, and Rose's bigoted feelings against brown-eyed and dark-haired people'.[4] Thereafter, he sought out Nordic types (and, after Rose's death, married one) and rejected Jewish ones, as he rejected all Roman and Greek influences. This in turn led him to create his own idiosyncratic style of English, from which all 'impurities' were ejected. Thus 'baton-wielder' for the Latin-derived 'conductor' seems reasonable; 'a chance for all ye' for the Greek-derived 'democratic' seems funny. A man of awesome energy, he rejoiced in putting his body through extremes of physical endurance, and was a sexual masochist from a very early age.

He became one of the great virtuoso pianists of his time, an acknowledged exponent of Chopin, Schumann and Grieg. The elderly Norwegian composer befriended the young Grainger, who became a peerless interpreter of the A minor Piano Concerto. Grieg's work was a major influence on that of Grainger, as it was at first on that of Delius. Did Delius, in his turn, have much influence on Grainger? This is arguable – and it may in any case have been reciprocal. A study of Grainger's arrangement of the Lincolnshire folk-song *Brigg Fair* for tenor and chorus (1906) suggests that Delius may have received more than just the tune for his English Rhapsody of 1907. Indeed, he appropriated more than just the tune when he used Grieg's *In Ola Valley* for his miniature, *On Hearing the First Cuckoo in Spring*.

Grainger's search for racially artistic purity resulted in his rejection of the sonata principle (which he saw as representing an Austro-German tradition) in favour of short constructions which used either a variation or a passacaglia technique. That search led him, too, in the direction of folk-song, which he considered the most basic musical expression. There was always a thread of logic in Grainger's thought-processes, and the concept of direct musical expression dictated two further aspects of his work: (a) the importance of the chord – used not so much structurally as a great classicist might use it, but for its emotional 'heart-tugging' capacity, and (b) the eventual jettisoning of the whole inherited baggage of notation and its associated musical impedimenta, in favour of 'free music' – randomly derived – to which he devoted the last two decades of his life.

In Grainger, the dividing line between what is light and what is not can be obscure. Certainly, the succession of short works he wrote in the seven years 1905–12 appear to be light music of the highest quality. Disconcertingly, we have to take into account Grainger's own jarring comment on them:

> … there is so little gaiety and fun in them. Where other composers would have been jolly in setting such dance tunes, I have been sad or furious. My dance settings are energetic rather than gay.[5]

These dance settings are all 'rambles' through chosen folk, or traditional, tunes (and in one instance a Handel one; although that, too, may have had a traditional origin). But in no case is there a definitive version, since Grainger used what he called an 'elastic' scoring for his 'room-music', 'dishing it up' in various costumes. This habit was, perhaps, another manifestation of his rejection of the Austro-German tradition, that aspect of Romanticism which saw the artist's utterances as sacrosanct, and their notation and precise execution as unalterable. Thus, in the following pieces, there can be up to eight valid versions, without taking into account the versions the conductor Leopold Stokowski made for his own recordings.

Of the pieces selected here, the passacaglia *Green Bushes* is the earliest, dating from 1905–6. It is a remarkable example of Grainger's inexhaustible repertoire of patterns: derived from the old tune, superimposed on it, or combined with one another. It is a technical tour-de-force which will reward study by any budding composer. Grainger followed it in 1907 with *Molly on the Shore*, based on two Irish reels. Again, the approach is linear; and the 'a-chance-for-all-of-ye' in Grainger's outlook meant that he naturally distributed the ideas around all the instruments, so that it would be a delight to play.

The piano piece *Country Gardens* was 'rough-sketched for room-music about 1908'. Rather as the Prelude in C sharp minor and *Land of Hope and Glory* pursued their respective composers around the world, so did *Country Gardens* pursue Grainger. No one played it with quite such rhythmic verve as he did, but Artok's orchestral version is also very colourful. The basis of the work in the Berkshire tune *The Vicar of Bray* may seem far-fetched, but is nevertheless there. The Morris dance fiddlers who played it over the years simply edged farther and farther away from their starting-point, until only a skeletal connection remained. From the same year came *Shepherd's Hey* its tune also filtered through Morris dance; in this case the Tyneside *Keel Row*. *Mock Morris* itself followed in 1911.

Neither Grainger nor the folk of Derry would have been much amused by Eric Coates's feat of turning *The Londonderry Air* into a minuet.[6] Grainger respected the beauty of the melody, and left his well-known arrangement in versions for chorus, piano, strings, wind, orchestra and 'large room-music'. But there is also a completely different working for harmonium, optional female chorus, optional unison men's chorus and 'elastic scoring from 3 bass parts up to full orchestra'. This version is a technical experiment, with chromaticism which some might think excessive.

The last of these pieces is *Handel in the Strand* (1911–12), a kind of miniature concerto movement for piano and strings. Its ostinato figure seems to have been suggested by Handel's *Harmonious Blacksmith* tune from his E major Harpsichord Suite, but it is a matter for conjecture whether or not the tune was Handel's own. Clearly, Grainger's title alludes to the fact that Handel resided for a while at Burlington House. This is an infectiously joyous piece, inspired, he said, by his delight in the pure sea air of the Dutch coast. But there may have been another inspiration. One wonders if he was confusing *Mock Morris* with *Handel in the Strand* when he claimed the former was connected with an old music-hall ditty *Always Merry and Bright*. Perusal of *Mock Morris* suggests no connection at all. *Handel in the Strand*, however, does yield a number of phrases suggestive at least, of the word rhythms of Alfred Lester's famous song in *The Arcadians*.[7]

*   *   *

For those who could not afford to study abroad, there were the London Conservatories which in the last quarter of the nineteenth century had multiplied. Failing that, it was a question of self-tuition, or a hard progress climbing the ladder from a few humble violin or piano lessons. The principal centres for composition (*pace* Trinity College of Music, Guildhall School of Music, London College of Music and others) were the Royal College of Music and the Royal Academy of Music. A distinctive 'house style' in their respective alumni was (and is) discernible.

When the RCM opened in 1883, Charles Villiers Stanford was appointed Professor of Composition. As a disciple himself of Brahms, his pupils were put to writing sonatas, quartets, concertos and symphonies. This predisposed them inevitably towards serious music, with the result that when they wrote light music (which most of them eventually did) it was almost as a by-product, a relaxation or quite simply to make some money. The earliest RCM pupils of note were Ralph Vaughan Williams (1872–1958), Landon Ronald (1873–1938), Gustav Holst (1874–1934), Samuel Coleridge-Taylor (1875–1912), William Hurlstone (1876–1906), Thomas Dunhill (1877–1946), John Ireland (1879–1962) and Haydn Wood (1882–1959).

Coleridge-Taylor and Hurlstone, their work completed before the outbreak of the First World War, have been discussed in Chapter 7. Thomas Dunhill was their fellow student at the RCM but compared to them has been seen as a minor talent. Beside chamber works and operettas, he did leave a number of light orchestral suites. Like so many, he himself survived the currency of his music, but at least he had the pleasure of hearing his overture *Maytime* warmly received at a 1946 Promenade Concert, shortly before he died.

Sir Landon Ronald was a fine conductor, especially of Elgar (although he professed not to understand *Falstaff*, the work Elgar dedicated to him). What little time he had was subsumed in administration, as principal of the Guildhall School of Music (1910–38) and a host of other time-consuming responsibilities. His music awaits re-appraisal, but despite his ballads and incidental music, he does not appear to have been a significant composer. Having said that, his *Birthday* overture would surely merit an occasional hearing.

Vaughan Williams and Holst, two mutual soul-mates, first met at the RCM in 1895, when the former re-entered it after his studies at Trinity College, Cambridge; Holst had been at the RCM since 1893. Thereafter, they showed each other their work, knowing that the resulting reciprocal criticisms would be frank and impartial. At the time of their meeting, Holst had adopted some aspects of socialism, and in particular the ideas of William Morris, who advocated the concept of the socially responsible artist-craftsman serving the community. It is likely that these ideas left their mark, too, on Vaughan Williams.

While neither Holst nor Vaughan Williams were inherently light composers, both were innovators, not perhaps as wholesale as the dodecaphonists or the later aleatorists but in their own way as fearless and questing. But music which is to serve a community must make some concessions if it is to be effective. Thus, side by side with his major utterances of warning, such as the Fourth and Sixth Symphonies, Vaughan Williams wrote hymn tunes and edited hymn books, an exercise of craft akin to a carpenter fashioning a simple, sturdy chair. With a service philosophy of this order, it comes as no surprise to find that he wrote music for Women's Institute choirs, and even an instrumental *Concerto Grosso* (1950) for the Rural Music Schools, incorporating a part 'for those who prefer to use only open strings'.

So, too, was it with Holst. Against *The Planets* (popular but weighty), *The Hymn of Jesus* and the *Choral Symphony* must be set such light works as the suite *Beni Mora* (1910) and the *Suite in E Flat* (1900). While Vaughan Williams enjoyed a private income, Holst was less fortunate. In order to support himself at the Royal College of Music, he played his trombone in the theatres and halls. Musicians tend to have musical sponges for minds; anything can be grist to the mill. It may not be too fanciful, therefore, to hear the styles of music he would have had to play (see Chapter 4) reflected in the *Suite in E Flat* in *The Perfect Fool* ballet music, and even in *Jupiter* (*The Planets*), where at least one tune would have made an effective song for Marie Lloyd, given suitable (for her) words. Such adoption of vulgar styles would be seen frequently in the early years of the twentieth century – in the work of Stravinsky, Bliss and *Les Six*; it can also be found in Joseph Holbrooke (a one-time music-hall pianist) and even in Vaughan Williams. An instance is his Symphony No 2 (*London*) where, in the first movement, one of the second subject ideas would not disgrace the great Marie, not to speak of the onomatopoeic overtones of the 'squeeze-box' concertina in the scherzo.

Neither Vaughan Williams nor Holst would have followed William Morris too far in his conscious medievalism, but they certainly offer a parallel with the unsophisticated approach by Morris to his work, in their adoption of folk-song; both as such and, in Vaughan Williams's case, as a factor in shaping his own ideas. Both Vaughan Williams and Holst kept close to their amateurs and pupils: Holst with his Whitsuntide Singers, and his orchestra of Paulinas, Vaughan Williams with his Leith Hill Festival. Works such as Holst's *St Paul's* and *Brook Green* Suites, and Vaughan Williams's *Partita* (1948) and the above-mentioned *Concerto Grosso*, all seem to meet the requirements of the best light music, albeit in a different world to that of German and Grainger.

There are other parallels between Holst and Vaughan Williams, such as their work for military and brass bands. Vaughan Williams's *English Folk Song* Suite for military band (1923; also for orchestra) and Holst's *Moorside* Suite for brass (1928) both needed to appeal to those who were to play them. Here, perhaps, is the difference between the light music of German and Coates, and that of Vaughan Williams and Holst. The former aim at the audience, the latter – in their light music – at the performer. A pointer to the difference in approach between the two friends can be heard in their respective approaches to a shared tune: *Greensleeves*. Vaughan Williams, finding it apposite for his opera *Sir John in Love*, sets it simply as the gravely beautiful melody it is, giving it a dream-like introduction in a similar mood to that invoked by Delius at the opening of *Brigg Fair*.[8] Holst's approach, in the last movement of the *St Paul's Suite*, is more intellectual. He has observed that *Greensleeves*, notated in triple time, will fit the compound-time sixteenth-century tune *Dargason* in double counterpoint, setting up all manner of rhythmic tensions on the way (Ex. 10.2).

Ultimately, Frank Bridge proved also to be fearless and questing. Much of his early career was devoted to chamber music (he was a violist) and conducting. Only a small part of his orchestral output can be termed light, and much of that dates from the first half of his composing career. It includes a *Coronation March* (1901), the *Suite for Strings* (1909–10), and arrangements of the tunes *Sir Roger de Coverley*

Ex. 10.2   Holst: *St Paul's Suite* (fourth movement)

and *Cherry Ripe*. Some of his light piano music was also subsequently arranged for orchestra. The popular *Rosemary* (from Three Sketches: 1906) is the most well-known example of these arrangements. The four-movement *Suite for Strings* has the quality which should have assured it the popularity accorded Elgar's *Serenade* or Holst's *St Paul's Suite*. But there is a reticence and introspection about its *Prelude* and *Nocturne* which do not reach out to the listener, who must make an effort. Since light music should require little effort, it probably doesn't qualify.

Playing the viola – and therefore hearing music from the inside – conveys an unparalleled advantage to a composer; thus blessed, he will know how to make his music fun to play. The truth of this is testified by *Cherry Ripe* (1916) and *Sir Roger de Coverley* (1922). Along with *Sally in our Alley* (1916), these were written for string quartet, but sound superb in their versions for string orchestra. *Sir Roger de Coverley* nonchalantly restructures the old dance tune in lyrical style to serve as its own contrasting subject. Bridge subtitled his arrangement 'A Christmas Dance' and thought that anticipations of the New Year sufficient reason to hint at *Auld Lang Syne* in the last bars. *Cherry Ripe* is almost two pieces, running simultaneously: the old tune and a contrasting but close-fitting dance. Both are show-pieces, not only for the players but also for Bridge's inventive skills, and for his enviable capacity to create textures in which everything sounds to best advantage.

Bridge was a pacifist, who suffered as much mental anguish as those directly involved in the 1914–18 war. After it, a certain bleakness entered his work; at its most acute, a cold withdrawal, akin to that of Holst in, say, *Egdon Heath*. After a period of neglect, the post-war Bridge is now being re-evaluated, to reveal a major master. But the world of his light music had been left for good.

John Ireland – an exact contemporary of Frank Bridge – wrote little orchestral light music, but we do have the splendid *Comedy* overture for brass band (1934), arranged as *A London Overture* in 1936 for full orchestra. In the main, his light work went into his exquisitely wrought piano music, to be considered in Chapter 11. But a case could be made out that he is an illustration of the point made in Chapter 1: namely, that most English music has tended to be light. Thus, such imposing works as *Mai-Dun* and *The Forgotten Rite* are approachable and immediately enjoyable, not to speak of the *Epic March*, the overture *Satyricon* or the *Concertino Pastorale* for strings. The Piano Concerto in E flat (1930) is, too, a rare twentieth-century example of an unpretentious work for piano and orchestra giving pure enjoyment at a first hearing. Until very recently, no Prom series was complete without it.

Haydn Wood (1882–1959) thought so highly of his teacher Stanford that he wrote a Stanford Rhapsody *Westward Ho*. In one of his articles for *The Musical Opinion*, the composer Havergal Brian (quoting another RCM pupil, the Spanish musician Pedro Morales (1879–1938)) pinpointed Wood as: 'a composer of dual personality: Dr Jekyll, who writes serious, large scale works, and Mr Hyde, who writes popular ballads and orchestral music'.[9] The analogy will not stand further pursuit, for Hyde's enthusiasm for low life has no counterpart in Wood, whose music is ever civilized in intention and fastidious in craft. But it is true that throughout his life, popular ballads and light orchestral music alternated, Jekyll and Hyde fashion, with more serious work. The latter included a Phantasy Quartet for strings which won second prize in the first Cobbett chamber music competition (1905), and a set of Variations on an Original Theme (1903), the Violin Concerto in B minor (1932), the Philharmonic Variations for cello and orchestra (1939) and the Piano Concerto in D minor (1947). Such works betray a hankering for what he would have perceived as artistic respectability.

He had, of course, made a considerable fortune from his ballads, but in the 1930s, he seemed to follow Eric Coates and others along the path of light orchestral music. For this, he was particularly well equipped; he was as skilled in counterpoint as Coates, and was, if anything, even more enterprising in orchestration. If there is such a thing as a light music tone poem, *Mannin Veen* comes near to it. Dating from 1932, it attempts to suggest in sound the Isle of Man in which Wood grew to maturity. The suite *London Cameos* appeared as late as 1957 in its entirety, but according to Tim McDonald,[10] it is likely to have been written in 1942. If it is indebted to Eric Coates, this in no way diminishes its magnificence. Wood's first movement (*The City*) is somewhat to the east of Coates's *Covent Garden* (*London* Suite), and his last movement (*A State Ball at Buckingham Palace*) lacks Coates's light touches in waltzes, but approaches those of Tschaikowsky in its splendour. In the intermission, *St James' Park in Spring*, there is a sustained glow to the violin writing, an almost seamless unwinding of melody, illustrating that 'sense of flow' said by Delius, whose influence is apparent, to be all a composer needed.

There is a patrician aspect to much of Wood's orchestral music; he would only go so far in pursuing popularity. But such a miniature as the late *Sketch of a Dandy* (1950) shows that he could, and did, adapt his style so as not to be outshone by some of the emerging post-war new men.

With the remaining Royal College of Music composers born in the period 1870–1900, we approach those figures whose principal work appeared after the 1914–18 war. The first of them was a holder of the Mendelssohn Scholarship who, after teaching at various public schools, went on to become a distinguished director of the RCM itself, Sir George Dyson (1883–1964). As with so many other RCM composers, Dyson would probably not have seen himself as a light composer, and indeed had a symphony and a violin concerto to his credit. He is mentioned here for his overture *At The Tabard Inn*, a prelude to the cantata *The Canterbury Pilgrims*.

How many remember that Geoffrey Toye (1889–1942) conducted the first performance of Vaughan Williams's *London* Symphony? Toye was, indeed, primarily a conductor, for the Beecham Opera, D'Oyly Carte and Sadler's Wells companies. But he wrote a symphony, two operas and other works, all now forgotten. He has become one of the legion of one-work composers, and even that work – the ballet *The Haunted Ballroom* (1935), which in the event Diaghilev declined – is remembered only for its familiar waltz. Was it, perhaps, a response to Ravel's ghostly nightmare *La Valse* (1920)? Toye's work has not Ravel's savage power, but does have an atmosphere which still draws its devotees.

From the mid-1930s onwards, and especially after the death of his son Michael in 1937, the work of Herbert Howells (1892–1983) became ever more thoughtful and profound, as he worked on two of the peaks of British music: the *Hymnus Paradisi* and the *Missa Sabrinensis*. But his earlier output included a few orchestral works which are authentic light music: *Puck's Minuet* and *Merry-Eye* (1917–20), *Procession* (1922) and the suite *Pageantry* (1934) for brass band. The two pieces *Puck's Minuet* and *Merry-Eye* were written for Sir Herbert Brewer and Sir Henry Wood respectively. As noted in Chapter 7, Howells had been an articled pupil of Brewer, who had founded an amateur orchestra in Gloucester. It is possible to imagine *Puck's Minuet* being played satisfactorily by the amateurs of the time, but not *Merry-Eye*, whose delicacy and transparent textures need playing of the highest order, not to speak of its mercurial changes of mood, which range from the lightest scherzando to a dream-like contemplation. The scoring includes a concertante part for piano, as other composers of the time were starting to do, having no doubt learned from Stravinsky just how effective the instrument could be in defining and clarifying patterns within an orchestral context.

Howells was a popular and effective festival adjudicator, who knew what was wanted when in 1934 he was commissioned to write a test piece for the Belle Vue Open Championship. *Pageantry* was the result. But by 1937 and his bereavement, his thoughts were already turning towards the great choral masterpieces which were to crown his later years, and for the Coronation of that year, he could only offer an arrangement for full orchestra of *King's Herald* from the *Pageantry* Suite. Similarly eleven years later (1948), when the BBC asked him, Michael Tippett and Gordon Jacob to write *Music for a Prince*, he went through his catalogue, to find the 1914 work, *The Three Bs*. From it, two movements were salvaged and re-named *Corydon's Dance* and *Scherzo in Arden*. As Christopher Palmer has revealed,[11] *Scherzo in Arden* was originally called *Blissy*. Thus does Sir Arthur Bliss find his way into our account, even if his own early work is too sardonic to be considered light music.

Like Howells, Armstrong Gibbs (1889–1960) was a much loved festival adjudicator. Known today by his songs and one other work, he had nevertheless written five operas, three symphonies and an oboe concerto, all forgotten. The other work was the suite *Fancy Dress* (1935), and even that is remembered only for its bitter-sweet waltz, *Dusk*. This nostalgic piece, curiously reminiscent of Coleridge-Taylor's *Valse de la Reine* (Four Characteristic Waltzes) enjoyed a spell of popularity for a few years after the Second World War.

This remarkable tally of composers trained at the Royal College of Music concludes with two figures of talent and one – arguably – of genius. Arthur Benjamin, like Percy Grainger, originated from Australia and, like him, wrote much of his music in the United Kingdom. In the tradition of most of the other RCM composers, he wrote major serious works: in his case, operas, a symphony and a violin concerto. They surface but rarely. What is still heard is the piquant *Jamaican Rumba*, together with other West Indian arrangements, which were the fruit of his examining tours for the Associated Board of the Royal Schools of Music. These include *Jamaicalypso*, *San Domingo* and *Caribbean Dance*. Such was the publicity Jamaica received from the popularity of these arrangements that Benjamin received an annual barrel of rum from that grateful country.

Perhaps the popularity of *Jamaican Rumba* overshadowed Benjamin's other light music: the *Cotillon* Suite, for example, or *A Light Music Suite*, *North American Square Dance Suite*, *Red River Jig*, *Prelude to Holiday Rondo* and the *Overture to an Italian Comedy*. *Cotillon* is based on English dance tunes collected by Playford in his *The Dancing Master*. The *Overture to an Italian Comedy* is basically a tarantella. But this 1937 work wickedly apes some Italian vulgarities, such as trumpets made to sound like cornets, and stentorian tenor 'Sorrento-isms'. Rossinian in its agile woodwind writing, it anticipates by a few years Walton's own Italianate overture, *Scapino*.

Gordon Jacob (Ex. 10.3) has fared rather better than some of the more unfortunate composers in the foregoing, who seem to be condemned to be remembered by only one or two works. Rarely making a big impact, his music is nevertheless widely played and sung – by amateurs, wind groups and bands. He never seemed to be at a loss when challenged by the most formidable commissions for the most unlikely forces. His work is, in a word, useful. While rarely subject to what Elgar used to call 'the divine afflatus', he was capable of a sunny lyricism when it was needed. The *Sinfonietta* shows this:

Ex. 10.3   Gordon Jacob: *Sinfonietta* (first movement)

Clarinet

Like Benjamin and Walton, he, too, wrote an Italian overture, *The Barber of Seville Goes to the Devil*. (While on the subject, Eric Fenby's *Rossini on Ilkla Moor* Overture (1938) ought not to be forgotten.) The general public would first have heard Jacob's light music without necessarily registering his name. Over the period 1942–48, he contributed some twenty-five arrangements of popular and traditional tunes to the BBC radio comedy series *It's That Man Again*, starring the comedian Tommy Handley. Typical of them was *The Galloping Major*, with its cascading chromatic scales for woodwind, so unerringly placed. Jacob's profound understanding of the orchestra has always tended to overshadow other aspects of his work, but it has also enabled him to write precisely to a required level of technical difficulty. The *Denbigh* Suite for strings is a fine example, as is the noble *Fantasia on the Alleluia Hymn* for full orchestra. Jacob was really a latter-day Kapellmeister, a more effective exponent of *gebrauchsmusik* than ever Paul Hindemith proved to be.

Like Jacob, E.J. Moeran (1894–1950) served in the army in the 1914–18 war. Both became second lieutenants. Jacob was taken prisoner; Moeran was so severely wounded that a metal plate had to be fitted into his skull. There any parallels ended, for while Jacob had diligence and reliability, the more erratic Moeran was touched by genius. The mess of his personal life resulted partly from the injury, and partly from his association in the 1920s with Peter Warlock (q.v.). This was certainly the view of Herbert Howells:[12]

> ... one of the things I never forgive Warlock for was that he really debauched one of the nicest creatures God ever made, called E.J. Moeran. When Moeran came down from his public school, when I first came across him ... he was one of the gentlest, nicest people ... and a *very* promising composer. And then he got in with the Heseltine clan, took to drink ... (H.H. talking to Richard Walker and Robert Spearing, 1 April 1971)

The son of an English mother and an Irish clergyman, Moeran was educated at Uppingham and at the Royal College of Music, where he studied with Stanford's pupil John Ireland. At various stages in his life, he absorbed transient influences like a sponge: those of Ireland himself, Ravel, Delius, Elgar and a number of others. But one general influence that remained was that of folk-music. He was, in his early days, an avid collector, particularly in East Anglia. After some early piano music and songs, Moeran followed the example of the other Royal College student composers by producing chamber music – a string quartet, a piano trio and a sonata for violin and piano. In his maturity, he produced a handful of major works: the magnificent requiem-like Symphony in G minor, the lyrical Violin Concerto, the Cello Concerto, and the Sonata for Cello and Piano, and it is on these that his reputation will ultimately rest. He was not, therefore, a 'light' man, but in the 1940s he did contribute two indisputably light orchestral works. These are the *Overture for a Masque* (1944), and the *Serenade in G* (1948). Some might also include the *Sinfonietta* (1944), but the diminutive of the title belies the substance and rigorous thinking of this fine work.

The overture was written in response to a wartime commission from Walter Legge (at the time working for ENSA) to Moeran, Bax and Rawsthorne for a work from each which would be suitable for concerts given to the troops. Moeran found it difficult to get going on his commission; this may explain why he opened his overture with a fanfare he was writing almost simultaneously for a Red Army Day concert in February 1944. The overture turned out to be bright in style and robust in construction. But a bright mood was not one that Moeran could maintain for long, and at its heart is a wistfully sad episode in F sharp minor.

Most of the Royal College composers seem to have written at least one light overture, and that of Moeran is among the best, even if it owes something to Balfour Gardiner's *Overture to a Comedy*.

Ex. 10.4   (a) Balfour Gardiner: *Overture to a Comedy*; (b) E.J. Moeran: *Overture for a Masque*

a) Balfour Gardiner: Overture to a comedy

b) E. J. Moeran: Overture for a masque

(as accompanying figure to clarinet subject.)

Moeran had first attempted a light orchestral suite in 1932, with a work called *Farrago*. This was withdrawn, and it was not until sixteen years later that he tried again. For the new work – *Serenade in G* – he salvaged some material from the earlier one. (He had done something similar with his Symphony in G minor (completed in 1937) which used material from an unfinished one of 1924). Basil Cameron conducted a first performance of the *Serenade* at a Promenade Concert on 28 September 1948. On that occasion, there were eight movements, but the first published score omitted two of them: the *Intermezzo* and the *Forlana*. These movements were restored in the new edition which the publisher Novello brought out in 1996. As it stands, therefore, the work consists of an *Intermezzo*, *Air*, *Galop*, *Minuet*, *Forlana* and *Rigadoon*, framed by a *Prologue* and an *Epilogue*. This delightful work has echoes of Warlock's *Capriol* Suite. More distant, but still audible, are hints of Ravel's *Tombeau de Couperin*.

* * *

At the Royal Academy of Music, Frederick Corder taught composition from 1888, joined in 1898 by John McEwen. Unlike Stanford, Corder (1852–1932) was not an enthusiastic Brahmin; he was a Wagnerite. He had been a student at the Royal Academy of Music and had also studied at Cologne, where his teacher had been Ferdinand Hiller. While much of Stanford's own creative work is remembered and is being enthusiastically re-assessed, Corder is still thought of only as the mentor of others. An impression of Corder's teaching has been left by Eric Coates,[13] who forgot neither the huge quantities of work Corder insisted on – a fugue every week – nor the cynical reception of the offerings of some of the more avant-garde pupils. For neither Corder nor the RAM principal Sir Alexander Mackenzie could tolerate modernisms. And since Sir Alexander conducted the First Orchestra, a try-out of any student work which was unduly adventurous was assured of excoriating criticism.

Among the composers born within the period under consideration who trained at the Royal Academy of Music were Sir Granville Bantock (1868–1946), Joseph Holbrooke (1878–1958), Sir Arnold Bax (1883–1953), Hubert Bath (1883–1945), York Bowen (1884–1961), Benjamin Dale (1885–1943), Montague Phillips (1885–1969), Eric Coates (1886–1957), Alec Rowley (1892–1958) and Dorothy Howell (1898–1982). This is by no means a complete list, but it is immediately apparent from it that a large proportion of them distinguished themselves principally in light music.

Bantock, Holbrooke and Bax are the main exceptions to this. Even with his prodigious energy, Bantock's administrative work on the one hand and the preoccupation in his creative work with the Orient on the other, left him little time for light music. But there is the dream-like overture, *The Pierrot of the Minute* (1908) – light in style if not in intention. Holbrooke's experience as a music-hall pianist (see Chapter 4) informed even his serious work – possibly to its disadvantage with a public which likes things nicely pigeon-holed.

Bax, after a succession of symphonic tone poems, went on in the 1920s and 1930s to write the series of seven symphonies which are arguably his life's main achievement. But despite the encrusted detail and sophisticated orchestration, his thought is essentially quite simple and well suited to light music, which makes it a matter of lamentation that he left such a pitiful handful of it: for orchestra, only *Mediterranean*, *Overture to a Picaresque Comedy* and *Maytime in Sussex*.

Mediterranean was arranged for orchestra from its original piano solo, and was first heard in this version on 13 November 1922 in a concert conducted by Eugene Goossens. Were it not for the touches of castanets in the colourful scoring, one might be tempted to see this delicious titbit as a particularly lilting waltz. It does not, though, go as far in belying its name as does the *Overture to a Picaresque Comedy* (1930). Where are the rogues, pirates and brigands in this exuberant, shamelessly enjoyable piece of pastiche? For in it, 'Bax consciously parodies Richard Strauss, waltz and all – apparently to win a bet that he could not do it'.[14]

The role of Master of the King's Music sat uneasily on Bax's shoulders. *What is it Like to be Young and Fair?* – his choral contribution to the offering in 1953 to the new and young monarch, *Garland for the Queen* – had nostalgic resonances for the rapidly ageing composer. His march for the 1953 coronation was eclipsed by Walton's march, *Orb and Sceptre*. But the music written a few years before to celebrate the approaching twenty-first birthday of the then Princess Elizabeth is an unpretentious jewel of light music. *Maytime in Sussex* (1946) is written for piano and small orchestra, and is set out in the style of a one-movement concertino, with a very undemanding solo part. Did he consciously have in mind Liza Lehmann's song *Myself When Young* when he started it?[15] An evocative musical ramble through the Sussex Weald, it is among the most attractive works of Bax's declining years. It is the work of a relaxed man working well within his own limitations, a man who had at last focused and disciplined his inspiration.

York Bowen, Benjamin Dale and Dorothy Howell fail to yield much for the trawler of light orchestral music, although Bowen and Howell come into their own with music for piano. Bowen's three piano concertos – tuneful and lushly romantic – might surprise those who don't know them. But the remaining RAM composers of this generation have been remembered only for their light music – when, that is, they have been remembered at all.

Hubert Bath scored an early success with his cantata *The Wedding of Shon Maclean*, and his work still raises a resounding tinkle in the brass-band world from time to time. His career as an unspectacular but reliable jobbing composer gave no hint of the success which would be his in 1944. But this success belongs more properly to Chapter 14.

Alec Rowley has much to offer us. His output was considerable, much of it being written for teaching purposes. But he performed a signal service with his attractive Miniature Concerto for piano and orchestra. Youth and amateur orchestras today are far too sophisticated to play the unpretentious music of Rowley, preferring the more heady challenges of Walton and Stravinsky. But in its time (1947), when the technique of amateur orchestral players was not as comprehensive as it is now, this work enabled the average player to experience the joys of concerto-playing.

Rowley was a highly successful practitioner; he was, perhaps, the RAM equivalent of Gordon Jacob from the RCM – both having Kapellmeister characteristics. Of the two remaining composers from the RAM, Montague Phillips was to some extent a transitional figure, with a firm footing in both light and serious camps. At the RAM, he had covered himself with academic glory, winning the Henry Smart and Macfarren scholarships, the Battison Haynes prize (for an organ prelude and fugue) and the Lucas Memorial Medal (for an orchestral scherzo). In due course, he became a Professor, Examiner and a Fellow of the RAM. His serious music, such as his two piano concertos, the Symphony in C minor and the *Heroic* Overture, were all assiduously programmed by Sir Dan Godfrey at Bournemouth, and other works such as the *Charles II* overture and *A Moorland Idyll* were played by the BBC Symphony Orchestra. But the general public saw him as the composer of the songs *Sing, Joyous Bird* (written, like many of a hundred or so others for his wife, the soprano Clara Butterworth) and *The Fisherman of England* (from the operetta *The Rebel Maid* (1921); cut short on its run at the Empire Theatre by the Coal Strike, but subsequently taken up enthusiastically by amateur societies).

While Phillips saw the growing need in the 1920s and 1930s for 'middle-brow' orchestral music and attempted to meet it in innumerable suites and sketches, he – like Haydn Wood – was never quite able to bring himself down into the market-place; the role of follower of fashion was not for him. This Handelian quality was a prime characteristic of 'the uncrowned king of Light Music', Eric Coates, who managed to mould his work to whatever tastes were fashionable, without in any way compromising his standards. Coates would not have thought of himself as a pioneer, but such he was. Right from his first appearance before Corder at the RAM, he made it clear that he aimed to write attractive and successful light music. In 1906, it was by no means certain that he could earn a living by writing, and so he worked equally hard at his viola; in due course becoming second only to his teacher Lionel Tertis as a virtuoso of the instrument. For some years, he played in the London orchestras, rising eventually to lead his section in Sir Henry Wood's Queen's Hall Orchestra of 1913–19. During this time, he wrote assiduously. His success with the ballad *Stonecracker John* has already been noted; his first great orchestral success came with the *Miniature* Suite. It was dedicated to Wood, who had to encore its waltz when he conducted a first performance at the Promenade Concerts in 1911.

In 1919, Wood terminated Coates's engagement as principal viola. For Wood, music was a sacred art; Coates was perhaps rather more relaxed in his attitude to it. He put the viola away, never to touch it again until, in the Second World War, he gave it to a London Philharmonic player who had lost his own in the bombing of the Queen's Hall.

The abiding popularity of Coates's music over half a century was due not only to his innate creative genius, but also to his ability to recognize and absorb changing trends and influences. Thus, while the *Miniature* Suite and other early works owe a debt to Arthur Sullivan and Edward German, in the 1920s, Coates became sensitive to the new influences spreading from the USA. While in no sense a jazz composer – all his work is precisely notated, with no element of improvisation – he did for a decade or so adopt rhythmic syncopation. This was no mere theoretical exercise. As modern young things, typical of their time, Coates and his wife were enthusiastic – even fanatic – dancers, who haunted Jack Hylton's Kit Kat Club. But such were the compartmentalizing tendencies of the music establishment that he was never again treated as a serious composer (as opposed to a composer of serious music) by the critics.

The fruits of his 'up-to-date' style in the 1920s can be heard in the Two Light Syncopated Pieces (1924: *Moon Magic* and *Rose of Samarkand*), *The Selfish Giant* (1925) and *The Three Bears* (1926). The last two of these are Phantasies, the nearest Coates comes to the symphonic poems of Richard Strauss, which as an

10.1   Eric Coates

orchestral violist he knew literally inside out. *The Three Bears* is perhaps Coates's equivalent of *Till Eulenspiegel*. It is here that all the investment in rigorous early training paid its dividends. The counterpoint and even a fugue are effortlessly there, but they are applied with the lightest of touches.

From the 1920s onwards, Coates's work was dictated not only by the needs of the seaside and spa orchestra, but also by the requirements of his contract with his publisher Chappell. This stipulated that he produce each year one fifteen-minute and one five-minute orchestral work, together with three ballads. The contract itself was a reflection of the needs of the burgeoning recording industry and in particular of what could be accommodated on a 78 rpm record.

Thus it was that Coates wrote a succession of suites, individual marches and waltzes. The astonishing thing is that the succession is of such consistently high standard. First came the suite *Summer Days* (1919), which Elgar admired so much that he soon wore out his recording of it. Then followed the suites *Joyous Youth* (1927), *Four Ways* (1927), *From Meadow to Mayfair* (1931), and *London* (1932: originally called *London Everyday*, and probably altered to avoid confusion with Mackenzie's *London Day by Day*). With the *London* Suite, a new factor entered the financial equation when its concluding march – the superb *Knightsbridge* – was adopted by the BBC as the signature tune for its weekly radio programme *In Town Tonight*. Coates had been a founder-member of the Performing Right Society, and was one of the first composers to generate his income more from performance fees than from sheet music sales. The process accelerated when the Valse-Serenade *By the Sleepy Lagoon* (1930) and the march *Calling All Workers* (1940) were also used by BBC Radio; for its programmes *Desert Island Discs* and *Music While You Work* respectively.

The succession of suites had continued with *The Three Men* (1935), *London Again* (1936), *Springtime* (1937) and *Four Centuries* (1941). The Fourth Century – the twentieth – is entitled Rhythm. By the time it was written, the musical world had abandoned plain syncopation for Swing. And so, Coates's Rhythm movement looks back to the 1920s affectionately and nostalgically, its saxophones indelibly fixing the era.

Although the waltz which concludes the *Miniature* Suite was his earliest popular orchestral success, it did not prove to be the model for the host of fine waltzes that followed, any more than did the delicious valsette *Woodnymphs* (1917). The former still trailed a certain primness befitting pre-emancipation days, while the latter was very much *scherzando*. The waltzes of the 1920s and 1930s followed the example of *At The Dance* from the 1919 suite *Summer Days*, which had a certain erotic glamour to it. But, rather like the mazurka in the hands of Chopin, the waltz (Coates actually preferred the French *valse*) was a malleable style, well able to encompass music as diverse as that depicting the fun-loving teenager of *Sweet Seventeen* (1954) and the bitter-sweet autumn of *Dancing Nights* (1931).

Nor did Coates's first march (*Northwards* from the *Four Ways* Suite (1927)) become a prototype for the many that followed, fine though it is. *Knightsbridge*

(*London* Suite: 1932) is more typical; Elgar-in-procession would not do for the 1930s. Coates's people walk briskly rather than march, along a crowded but friendly thoroughfare. It is the work of a man writing in the context of his times, but technically, the racy effect is achieved by developing and emphasizing the off-beat rhythms.

Coates had his emotional and expressive limitations. He was, as his son Austin would point out, essentially a 'light' man. He appeared (one must emphasize 'appeared') to be untouched by either of the wars through which he lived. Rarely does his music resonate with passion, only with sentiment. His one attempt to measure up to the expression of a national emotion in his *Song of Loyalty* (to King George V) is a lamentable exercise. Nor did he really share the passion of his fellow serious composers for English pastorality. He was a townsman, who might take day-trips 'to the country' but whose musical pastoral scenes tend to be picture postcards, from which anything earthy has either been excised or sterilized. As Ernest Tomlinson wrote: 'In light music, tunes follow tunes, each one self-contained and contrasting'.[16]

Within the terms of this dictum, Coates's stature among light music composers must be dominant, for as a tune-smith, he was second to none. But he was more than a mere creator of melody, for his technique, both in construction and orchestration, was so effortless that we may tend to take for granted the myriad details of counterpoint and texture in which even the slightest Coates score abounds. And beyond that, and probably having no idea that it would be so, Coates more than any other composer of his time fixes in sounds the very essence of his times.

* * *

Neither the Guildhall School of Music nor Trinity College of Music, at the time under consideration, produced such strings of distinguished composers as the RCM or the RAM, but three figures deserve mention. Unfortunately, two of them have proved to be 'one work' composers, as far as the public is concerned. Both John Ansell (1874–1948) and Herman Finck (1872–1939) trained at the Guildhall School of Music, and both became theatre music directors, whose orchestras worked to a high standard in a field where standards were often variable. Ansell's Alhambra orchestra attracted the praise of such a distinguished conductor as Ernest Ansermet, and both Ansell and Finck (the Palace Theatre) made a number of recordings with their players.

In his compositions, Ansell tapped into the voracious demand for exotic and oriental subjects; his catalogue included *A Street in Algiers*, *Arab Dance*, *Egyptian Dance*, *In a Japanese Garden*, *The Indian Juggler* and many others. His considerable output also included a number of suites, three operettas, and such overtures as *The Windjammer* and *To an Irish Comedy*. Out of it all, only the overture *Plymouth Hoe* established any kind of currency.

Herman Finck wrote marches, suites, and, of course, many theatre shows of an ephemeral nature. He also claimed to have invented the Musical Switch – 'a potpourri of musical airs'[17] – for the first Royal Command performance, when King George V came to the Palace Theatre in 1912. There were one hundred musical references within its fifteen minutes. The idea was tried by many others, among whom Kenneth Alford was particularly successful. Today, Finck is remembered by one work, a trifle that achieved phenomenal popularity: the dance *In The Shadows* (Ex. 10.5). Finck had thought of the tune in 1908 but it came into its own two years later, when John Tillet asked Finck for a 'skipping-rope dance', as a routine he had devised for the dancing troupe of Palace Girls. Hawkes was reluctant to publish it, telling the composer he would have to be content with a twopence-per-copy royalty instead of his usual threepence. But over a million copies were sold at the time; ever afterwards, Finck lamented the loss of one million pennies. Under the title of *Danse des Ombres*, it sold widely in France, but as Finck was not a member of the *Société des Auteurs* he lost out here as well. It was pirated, errand-boys whistled it, and friends sent postcards to tell the haunted perpetrator that they had heard it in Russia, Japan, Scandinavia, China and Australia. It was inescapable:

Ex. 10.5   Herman Finck: *In the Shadows*. © Copyright 1911 by Hawkes & Son (London) Ltd. Reproduced by permission of Boosey & Hawkes Music Publishers Ltd.

Allegretto grazioso

Typical of a number who tried to imitate it was Percy Elliott, with *Dancing Sunbeams* (*Sunbeams and Moonbeams*: 1919). Finck himself wrote successors, including *On the Road to Zag-a-Zig*, the delightful *Pirouette* and the intermezzo *Laughing Eyes*. They are probably as good as *In The Shadows*, but never had the same acclaim. The public tends to be fickle in its tastes.

The third figure was one of the giants of the world of light music. Albert Ketèlbey (1875–1959) was a child prodigy. Philip Scowcroft[18] tells us that, as an eleven-year-old, Ketèlbey had a piano sonata performed at Worcester, and that the work was admired by Elgar. This must have also been galling for Elgar, who was the elder by some eighteen years, and who at that time had not even a *Salut D'Amour* to show for his pains. In 1888, Ketèlbey proceeded by scholarship to Trinity College of Music. Already a good pianist and organist, he now mastered the cello, clarinet, oboe and horn. Like Finck and Ansell, he went into the theatre world, becoming music director of the Vaudeville Theatre in 1897. A pioneer of recording, he was making organ records as early as 1909, and was for a time musical adviser to the Columbia company. Two early comic operas (*A Good Time*, 1896, and *The Wonder Worker*, 1900) point to his aspirations as a young man, while his occasional use of pseudonym (Anton Vodorinski and William Aston) suggest the shame feared by too close an association with light music.

Technically, Ketèlbey was comprehensively equipped. He knew the instruments, the public for which he catered, the infant recording industry, and the job of conductor. It yet comes as a surprise to discover how long it was before he perceived his true path, the path which led to the light music which would make him a rich man. The work that made him famous was *In a Monastery Garden*, and he was forty in 1915 when he wrote it. By that time, Elgar had overtaken him, and had written most of the music by which he is remembered.

Ketèlbey's work makes an interesting comparison with that of Coates, more especially as the period of their greatest popularity overlapped. Both clearly saw the gramophone as a prime medium for their work, but Ketèlbey additionally kept in mind the needs of cinema musicians during the two decades of silent films. Although Coates occasionally employed saxophones and jazz mutes, he basically thought of his music in terms of the traditional symphony orchestra. Ketèlbey indulged more in effects, such as bells, where it was feasible to use them – obviously in *Bells Across the Meadows* (1921), but also in the march *With Honour Crowned*. He was always unlikely to have resisted birdsong in the monastery garden, or the chance of the monks chanting their *Kyrie Eleison*. Coates would have been too fastidious for this, and would never have had a male chorus imitate a rabble begging for baksheesh (*In A Persian Market*: 1920) or joining in the fun of the fair at *'Appy 'Ampstead* (*Cockney* Suite: 1925). It was once cruelly said of the composer Joseph Holbrooke that he was a cockney Wagner. Ketèlbey may not have been a cockney Coates, but he does seem to have aimed his sentiment at a lower target than that of Coates. While Ketèlbey's strength is the sentimental singing melody, Coates's work is rooted in the more robust dance.

At his best, Ketèlbey exhibits a directness and simplicity which in its time hit home. His music, too, could dance, as we can hear in *'Appy 'Ampstead*. The same piece also shows, with almost contemptuous ease, how he could produce a *quodlibet* in which half-a-dozen tunes ranging from *Tell Me the Old, Old Story* and *There is a Tavern in the Town* to Rossini's *Semiramide* are paraded, with the bonus of some cockney spoons and a mouth-organ added to the *mélange*.

The old Birmingham Midland Institute, with Granville Bantock at its head, produced at least one composer of note. This was Julius Harrison (1885–1963), who receives a mention here for one work, the *Worcestershire* Suite. Harrison destroyed most of his early orchestral tone poems, and even his well-received Variations on *Down Among The Dead Men*. His years between 1915 and 1940 were occupied mostly in conducting: for the Scottish Orchestra, for Beecham's various operatic ventures, and (for ten years) as director of the Hastings Municipal Orchestra. In later years, he came to regret bitterly the time he spent conducting, years in which he could have been writing music. Ironically, it was the onset of deafness in the late 1930s which brought his conducting career to an end, thus releasing him for creative work. Much of the time left to him was devoted to the completion of what were to become his two monuments: the *Mass in C* and the *Requiem*. But in 1919, he had written the *Worcestershire* Suite, the titles of its four movements crystallizing boyhood memories of the county in which he grew up:

The Shrawley Round
Redstone Rock
Pershore Plums
The Ledbury Parson

The suite gave Harrison his most popular orchestral success. It was much admired by Elgar, who sent Harrison an old engraving of Stourport (Harrison's birthplace), as a token of appreciation. Stanley Baldwin, who came from the adjoining Bewdley, liked it too, and tried to play it on the piano. But it was, he wrote, 'a bit beyond my fingers'.[19]

We come now to those composers who climbed other ladders than those provided by the music colleges and conservatoires. The first group, born within a decade of one another, comprise Archibald Joyce (1873–1963), Sydney Baynes (1879–1938), Percy Fletcher (1879–1932), Charles Ancliffe (1880–1952) and Kenneth Alford (1881–1945). The first four are remembered for their waltzes; the last one for his marches. Coates had excelled at both, but his work retained its capacity to be heard primarily as written – in concert hall and on record. While he loved dancing, he would have expected his music to be listened to, rather than danced to.

In contrast, the work of these five was more likely to be experienced on the dance floor or parade ground. With some of them there was, as with Sullivan, a background of military bands. This was true of Joyce, whose father was a band sergeant in the Grenadier Guards. Joyce came up the hard way, playing in dance bands, music-hall and for dancing teachers. While he wrote a large number of marches, he was primarily considered to be the English master of the waltz. He wrote many of them, but attention centred overwhelmingly on one: *Dreaming* (1911).

> … although waltzes flowed from Joyce's pen until almost mid-century, he was essentially an Edwardian.[20]

The ladders available to Sydney Baynes led to the organ loft, to accompaniment (of Edward Lloyd and Ben Davies among others) and to theatre conducting. A thorough professional, he carried out much lowly but expert arrangement for the increasingly voracious BBC. Of his many waltzes (the names of which ended in Y: *Ecstasy*, *Flattery*, *Modesty*, etc.) one in particular is remembered: *Destiny*. The many others are scarcely inferior and should be heard from time to time.

Percy Fletcher's name has already appeared, like a shadow, throughout this book. Like Joyce and Baynes, he was a theatre musician. He did so much arranging of other people's work that it is little short of astounding that he found time for so much of his own, which is to be found in almost every field. In one corner of that field stands his corpus of work for brass band – including the tone poem *Labour and Love* (1913) and *An Epic Symphony* (1926). It is, moreover, the brass-band world we have to thank for keeping these and other works of his alive. He wrote even more orchestral suites than Coates, not to speak of much piano music. His waltz *Bal Masqué* (Parisian Sketches: 1914) shows him effortlessly solving the waltz problem – that of ensuring that the melody flies untrammelled over the basic triple rhythm.

Ex. 10.6   Percy Fletcher: *Bal Masqué*. © Copyright 1913 by Hawkes & Son (London) Ltd. Reproduced by permission of Boosey & Hawkes Music Publishers Ltd.

Like Joyce, Charles Ancliffe was the son of a bandmaster, and became a bandsman himself. His own once popular waltz *Nights of Gladness* uses a similar figure to that of Fletcher, but just as *Bal Masqué* skilfully conceals the downbeat, Ancliffe's waltz as surely emphasizes it.

Ex. 10.7   Charles Ancliffe: *Nights of Gladness*. © Copyright 1912 by Hawkes & Son (London) Ltd. Reproduced by permission of Boosey & Hawkes Music Publishers Ltd.

Of his many marches for band, *The Liberators* is best known.

Ancliffe was a worthy figure but among his contemporaries, his waltzes were excelled by Joyce, Fletcher and Baynes, and his marches by those of Kenneth Alford. Alford (born Frederick Ricketts) also trained in the band world, went to Kneller Hall, and took up an appointment as bandmaster to the Second Argyll and Sutherland Highlanders. Over a period of some thirty years, he wrote eighteen marches, of which two may stand as representative of their respective types. *Colonel Bogey*[21] (1914: subsequently used in the David Lean film, *The Bridge on the River Kwai* is in straightforward simple time. *On the Quarter Deck* (1917), however, is in compound time, reflecting the characteristic rhythms of the marches of the American John Philip Sousa.

One isolated and indeed still obscure figure was John Foulds (1880–1939), the son of a bassoonist and himself a cellist who for a few years played in Richter's Hallé Orchestra. Writing in the *Musical Opinion* in May 1939 on the occasion of

Fould's death from cholera in Calcutta, Havergal Brian – Foulds's strongest advocate at the time – opined that it was the failure of his vast concert opera *Vision of Dante* (1908) to secure a performance that caused Foulds to turn to light music. Lance Tufnell comments on Foulds's music generally:

> Perhaps the most immediately noticeable attribute
> of Foulds' music is that it contains a large number
> of good tunes.[22]

This assertion is confirmed in Foulds's *Keltic* Suite for orchestra, which gave its composer a few years of popular acceptance, and is still the most accessible of his light works. It caught the tide of popular Celticism, of which the phenomenal success of Rutland Boughton's *The Immortal Hour* was the most noted example. Foulds's work was in fact a light manifestation of that 'outer fringe' culture which on a more serious level promoted such otherwise disparate works as Holbrooke's *Children of Don* trilogy and Vaughan Williams's *Riders to the Sea*. Of its three movements, the *Keltic Lament* is simple in expression and was once played everywhere, and by every possible combination of performers. In the two outer movements, the Celtic feeling is less marked. The first movement, indeed, bears marks of Russian influence.

But while the *Keltic* Suite was justly popular, and can still give pleasure today, it is by no means typical of Foulds. Nor can it give any idea of the range of his work, encompassing as it did experiments in rhythm and in micro-tonality, and including as it did the *World Requiem*, the Cello Concerto and a String Quartet. In a letter to Adrian Boult (16 August 1933), Foulds mentions 'a dozen or so' of his light works as 'continually broadcast'. Would that we could hear some of them again now.

As Elgar found, the path was incomparably harder for those making their way without recourse to a college or conservatoire. The handful of remaining composers born in the last quarter of the nineteenth century belong in this group. Arthur Wood (1875–1953) was primarily a flautist who played in Godfrey's Bournemouth Orchestra, before being appointed Music Director at Terry's Theatre in 1903. Subsequently at the Adelphi Theatre, he conducted performances of Lionel Monckton's *The Arcadians*. Thereafter, like Percy Fletcher and so many others, he undertook whatever hack-work came to hand, no matter what drudgery it involved. His reward came when a BBC producer, looking through a pile of records in search of something to introduce a new radio series, came across his orchestral suite, *My Native Heath*. Since that time, the last movement *Barwick Green* has regularly introduced *The Archers*, generating huge royalties which Wood, at the end of an otherwise humdrum career, never lived to enjoy.

One more figure just slips into the last days of the nineteenth century: Frederick Curzon (1899–1973). For him, the times were perhaps out of joint. Active from the age of sixteen in the theatres and silent cinemas, he became in due course head of Messrs Boosey and Hawkes' Light Music Department. His own orchestral music at first made slow progress, of which Dan Godfrey and the Bournemouth Orchestra are witnesses. It was 1933 before he conducted any of his work there. Coates, Haydn Wood and Ketèlbey had been well established in the 1920s, and in consequence were better placed to survive the contraction in the market for light music which ensued as an effect of the Second World War. Curzon hardly came to the fore until those difficult post-war days – when the demands of the musical world were changing fast.

Much of his music is in short individual movements. These include such piquant 'characteristic intermezzi' as *The Dance of an Ostracised Imp* and *The Boulevardier*, both of which attained enormous popularity. It may be that the latter proved to be a model for Haydn Wood's *Sketch of a Dandy*. Of Curzon's suites, *In Malaga* and *Robin Hood* are the best known and probably the most rewarding. From the latter, *The March of the Bowmen* is particularly impressive.

*   *   *

At the outset of this chapter, it was stated that the generation of the last quarter of the nineteenth century would be working in times of war, change and upheaval. In retrospect, what is apparent now is how little these light music composers allowed the more unpleasant aspects of these characteristics of our century anywhere near their music. This holds true, too, of serious composers when wearing their light music hats. That is, perhaps, a mark of the highest professionalism, one which has no exact counterpart in France or Germany which suffered similar trauma. French light music rarely came untrammelled by any emotional baggage. The work of *Les Six*, for example, was rooted in a cynicism to be found in Britain in early Bliss, Berners and Walton, but avoided by the bona fide Light Music School. In Germany, too, it is difficult to find an equivalent. Composers such as Weill exhibited all the external trappings of a kind of light music, but were in fact mirroring their depressed, drab post-First World War world.

The British musicians were escapist, a fact underlined by the titles and subjects of their work. There were countless country scenes, mostly written by composers who never went down a country lane if they could avoid it. There were even more oriental ones, written by composers whose working chores and commitments would hardly allow them further east than Dover. And there was a love of the infantile. If someone else had already written a *Teddy Bear's Picnic*, you could at least hope to find room for *The Panda's Party*, and if there was already a *Butterfly's Ball*, there might still be space for *The Gnat's Wedding*. Very often, the title itself would make the difference between success and failure. Coates himself has testified to the difficulty of thinking of a title, and to his gratitude to a clergyman who suggested what proved to be the best idea he was ever given – that for the suite *The Three Elizabeths*.

The whole orchestral light music industry was, and is, market-driven, just as the madrigal industry and the nineteenth-century religious music industry had been before it. The light music market derived from an increasingly wealthy middle class, which demanded seaside entertainment, theatres, concert-halls and bandstands. And as recording and broadcasting became technically feasible, these, too, were exploited. As with any market, a large quantity of dross was produced. But once we have discounted the mass of musical rubbish, the fact remains that the composers mentioned in this chapter between them produced a body of work which in quality was unmatched elsewhere.

Notes

1. Gardiner to Grainger, 21 December 1924. Quoted in Stephen Lloyd (1984), *H. Balfour Gardiner*, CUP, p. 51.
2. Quoted in Tim McDonald (1992), music notes for CD 8.223444, *Roger Quilter*, Marco Polo.
3. Delius to Jelka Delius, 21 April 1907. Quoted in Lionel Carley (1983) *Delius: A Life in Letters 1862–1908*, Scolar Press, p. 287.
4. Bird, John (1982), *Grainger, 1882–1961*, Schott & Co., p. 6.
5. Bird, John (1982), *Grainger*, Faber & Faber, p. 62.
6. Self, Geoffrey (1926), *In Town Tonight*, Thames Publishing, pp. 20–21.
7. Produced at the old Shaftesbury Theatre, 28 April 1909 (see Chapter 3).
8. Vaughan Williams subsequently made other arrangements of *Greensleeves*, adding the Norfolk folk-song *Lovely Joan* as a contrasting idea.
9. *Musical Opinion*, May 1937, p. 699.
10. CD note: Marco Polo 8.223402.
11. Palmer, Christopher (1992), *Herbert Howells: A Centenary Celebration*, Thames Publishing, p. 25.
12. Ibid., p. 335.
13. Coates, Eric (1953), *Suite in Four Movements*, Heinemann, pp. 61–63.
14. Foreman, Lewis (1983), *Bax: A Composer and His Times*, Scolar Press, p. 266.
15. Bax's autobiography is significantly called *Farewell My Youth*.
16. Ernest Tomlinson, in his foreword to Scowcroft, Philip L. (1997), *British Light Music*, Thames Publishing, p. 9.
17. Finck, Herman (1937), *My Melodious Memories*, Hutchinson, p. 227.
18. Scowcroft, Philip L. (1997), *British Light Music*, Thames Publishing, p. 59.
19. Stanley Baldwin to Julius Harrison, 25 February 1927.
20. Scowcroft, op. cit., p. 57.
21. Reflecting the origin of the march on the golf course. Instead of calling 'fore', Alford's partner would whistle the falling interval C–A.
22. Tufnell, Lance (1988), 'John Foulds (1880–1939): An Appreciation', *British Music Society Journal*, 10, p. 47.

CHAPTER ELEVEN

Piano Music

Although ballads had been associated with favourite professional artists, the wider popularity of balladry had been among amateurs. A major factor in this was the spread, particularly in middle-class homes, of piano ownership. But when it came to what piano solos an amateur might play, there were problems. While the classic piano repertoire was readily available in a range of moderately priced editions, much of it was beyond a moderate technique. Certainly, in the first half of the nineteenth century, composers had poured out works for piano in almost unparalleled richness. Beginning with Beethoven and Schubert, however, and progressing through Weber, Schumann, Liszt, Mendelssohn and Chopin, those who wrote for the piano were either pianists themselves or (in the case of Schumann) had a wife who fulfilled the virtuoso role. Some of them came to Britain. Chopin was probably too ill to be more than a pale shadow of his earlier glory as a performer, but in 1840 Liszt made a gruelling tour of the country. It was only too apparent to his listeners that his music, and much of that of the others was not for amateurs to attempt.

It was this realization that enhanced the appeal of such a collection as Schumann's *Album for the Young* (Op. 68) and, later, Grieg's *Lyric Pieces*. This was music for domestic rather than recital purposes. But neither these nor any other collections matched the popularity of Mendelssohn's eight sets of *Songs without Words*, published at intervals over the period 1829–45. These had currency for the rest of the century. No home with musical pretensions was without a copy of the collected edition. While some of the pieces are tricky to play, most present few problems to a pianist of moderate technique. Other continental figures produced graded work which would help to develop that technique: Czerny, Kullak and Thumer among them. In addition, there were such specialists in the piano miniature as Cornelius Gurlitt, Stephen Heller and Johann Burgmuller. Any back-wrapper of an original Augener Edition will reveal many more. The market for piano music in Britain throughout the nineteenth century was thus dominated by European composers. And when the so-called Second Renaissance of English music began in the 1870s, it took some time to encompass piano music.

Sullivan had written nothing for the instrument after *The Princess of Wales' March* (1863) – and even that piece, although published for piano, was really for military band. Stanford's keyboard output favoured the organ rather than the piano, although between 1913 and his death in 1924, there appeared the *Six Characteristic Pieces* (Op. 132). The dedication to Moritz Rosenthal signified that they were not intended for the amateur market. *Five Caprices* (Op. 136) and a fine *Ballade* (Op. 170) may also be mentioned. The *Ballade* owes something to those of Chopin – particularly to the ones in a A flat and F minor. But the Op. 132 pieces are, as we might expect, a response to Brahms, especially noticeable in the concluding *Toccata*. And does not the idea of ending one's life's work with short piano pieces seem entirely fitting for a Brahmin such as Stanford, whose hero did much the same?

With Stanford, as with Parry and so many others, the creative eyes were fixed on the requirements of the great choirs and festivals, and on the need to secure the prime novelty commissions at the latter. Parry nevertheless found time to write piano music, and some of that may be classed 'light'. Observing the popularity of Mendelssohn's *Songs Without Words*, he produced three sets of his own between 1868 and 1877. He also wrote at least one piano masterpiece and that too is little known: the *Shulbrede Tunes* (1914).

Shulbrede is a major work, some forty-three pages of piano score. It is a reinter-pretation of Schumann's concept of a number of short pieces in which the whole is greater than the sum of its parts. Sometimes on paper, the music even looks like that of Schumann. These new scenes from an English childhood reveal Parry himself as a gentle elderly man, emerging at last from behind the façade of his public music-making, which had all too often obscured his warm humanity. This is real light music, which needs to make no patronizing concessions:

Ex. 11.1   Hubert Parry: *Shulbrede Tunes*, No. 5 (*Matthew*)

Allegretto amabile

Of the succeeding generation of composers – Elgar, Delius, German and Coleridge-Taylor – none was especially distinguished by his piano music. Although each had a working knowledge of the piano, they were primarily violinists. The piano is a difficult instrument for which to write effectively, and musical history has shown that the most successful composers for it have always themselves been pianists.

Much of Elgar's meagre output for the piano was immediately arranged for a variety of other instrumental combinations; indeed, it often gains thereby, as there is little specifically pianistic about it. But such pieces as *Skizze* (1903) and *In Smyrna* (1905) were not so treated, and stand as examples of his light piano style. Most idiomatic of all are the two pieces published by Keith Prowse in 1932 but written much earlier: the *Sonatina* and *Serenade*. (The *Concert Allegro*, Op. 46, written for Fanny Davies and mislaid for many years, is not light music.)

Similarly, the piano music of Delius amounted to an insignificant part of his work. There were a few early pieces, of which one – *Zum Carnival* – was published. This polka, dating from 1885, when Delius was a popular and charming young guest in the exclusive Jacksonville salons, is interesting in that it points the extent of the journey the composer had to make before he could write such a work as *The Song of the High Hills*. It would be thirty-four years before he would again write for the solo keyboard. Then, in 1919, it was for harpsichord rather than for piano. The *Dance* for harpsichord – a gavotte – was written for Violet Gordon-Woodhouse. It sounds at least as effective on the piano as it does on the instrument for which it was intended, but because of its complex chording, it presents a small-handed player with formidable problems.

Between the years 1922 and 1923, Delius produced his only other keyboard solos, the *Five Piano Pieces* and the *Three Preludes*. These, together with the harpiscord dance, are all authentic light music. Delius – a hard man – is in rare sentimental mood in the *Five Pieces*. They consist of a Mazurka and Waltz for a little girl, a Lullaby for a modern baby, a second Waltz which is probably best forgotten[1] and a final Toccata, which presents a few unrewarding difficulties. The set is dedicated to the pianist Evlyn Howard-Jones. Some of the orchestral pieces that were arranged for piano are effective. That of the Serenade from *Hassan* is one, and that, by Eric Fenby, of the *Air and Dance*, written for strings (1915) and subsequently dedicated to the National Institute for the Blind, is another.

Coleridge-Taylor had to study the piano at the Royal College of Music before he could be admitted to the presence of Stanford. He mastered it sufficiently for working purposes, but his music for it does not suggest, as does that of Liszt, Chopin or Rachmaninoff, that it could have been written for no other medium. Indeed, much of it was made available by the publishers in arrangements or orchestrations. It happens, though, that one work written originally for orchestra – *Petite Suite De Concert* (see Chapter 7) does make a more effective piano work than much of his music actually written by him for the instrument.

The nature and the titles of Coleridge-Taylor's keyboard music, as with the two albums of piano music by Edward German, indicate the perceived taste at the turn of the century. There is a movement away from sonatas and other serious forms towards short salon pieces, often in collections, and often with fanciful descriptive titles. Coleridge-Taylor yields, for example:

1897: *Two Moorish Tone Pictures*
1899: *African Suite*
1900: *Nourmahal's Song and Dance*
1904: *Moorish Dance*
        Three Silhouettes
        Three Cameos
1908: *Papillon*

This is a random selection. German's albums include *Graceful Dance*, *Valse Fantastique*, *Reverie*, *Abendlied* and *Columbine*. Here were two of the most distinguished composers of the period attempting to tap an obviously rich source of income. Others did the same. A little younger than the foregoing, Frank Bridge (1879–1941), Cyril Scott (1879–1970), Arnold Bax (1883–1953) and York Bowen (1884–1961) all wrote light piano music in their early years.

Bridge was one string player who successfully mastered the hazards of writing for the piano, in a number of miniatures, improvisations, sketches and characteristic pieces in the amiable romantic style of pre-1914 England. Some of them – such as *April* or *Rosemary* – still have currency as examination or festival fodder, but none gives warning, except in its technical mastery, of the fearless and disturbing work (anything but light) to come from Bridge's pen after the 1914–18 war.

Cyril Scott, too, was well known for such early salon works as *Lotus Land* and *Two Pierrot Pieces*, which are hardly representative of the main body of his work. A superficial resemblance of his harmonic language to that of the French Impressionists led to him being dubbed for a while 'The English Debussy', which did no favours to either composer. But strings of unresolved minor sevenths do not a Debussy make; rather does Scott's idiom (especially his melodic idiom) suggest the Ivor Novello and Noel Coward to come two decades later. Scott progressed from this, and his manifold interests – from the occult to naturopathy – left their mark on later work still largely unknown to the general public.

Bowen and Bax, both fine pianists, showed the influence of Russian music early in their careers. In Bowen's case, it seems to be that of Rachmaninoff, who had first appeared as a pianist in London in April 1899, and whose own early piano music was known here in the first years of the new century.

Bowen made an early impact with his piano music – such as the two sets of Preludes (Op. 81 and Op. 102), the three Piano Suites, the set of Two Part Inventions and the collections of light Miniatures, Novelettes, Sketches, and the Three Serious Dances. He was prolific, and at least one fellow composer – Sorabji – considered him to be one of the most important of his time. Posterity did not agree, and by the late 1930s interest in his work had faded. But it does have effortless flow, and in performance seems to fit the fingers like a glove. The Russian influence can be heard in the splendid Second Suite, where the *Intermezzo* lays out its melody between right and left-hand thumbs after the manner of Rubinstein's *Melody in F*, and the finale *A Romp* owes something to the Rachmaninoff of the Second Piano Concerto.

The Russian Romantics did not generally prove to be a fruitful quarry for British composers, although Percy Whitlock found them nourishing for his organ work, and Addinsell, Bath and others would find some meat left on the bone in the 1940s. But Bax visited Russia, and Russian influence can be heard in some of his early piano music – light music if sophisticated in manner. Of these, *Two Russian Tone Pictures* and *In A Vodka Shop* hold the most obvious Russian memories. A succession of short pieces followed, often dedicated to the young female pianists of the day, Myra Hess, Irene Scharrer and Harriet Cohen – the last-named disguised by the name 'Tania' which Bax affectionately used for her. They include *The Maiden With The Daffodil*, *Apple-Blossom Time* and *A Mountain Mood* (all 1915). Piano pieces continued to appear over the next five years, culminating in 1920 when seven were written. By that year, Bax's latent Celticism had become a potent force in his music. He was also increasingly occupied with large-scale work. The piquancy and fascination of his music for piano derives from the contrast between its essentially diatonically simple melody and its exotically chromatic setting, and complex texture:

Ex. 11.2   Arnold Bax: *Country Tune*

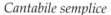

Cantabile semplice

The composers mentioned so far in this chapter have been judged by posterity to be the commanding figures of their time. But it was the lesser lights who provided the bulk and the quantity; who flooded the market with innocuous pieces, often similar to one another in style, and often requiring only a moderate technique. Their rustic titles occur again and again. Very often, the title will have the diminutory 'miniature' added to it; as in *Six Miniature Preludes* (Richard Walthew) or *Miniature Dance Suite* (Alec Rowley). How often, too, was the diminutive of the titular noun used, as in 'valsette', 'scherzino' or 'sonatina'. Perhaps this habit was an unconscious reaction to the giganticism of the recent pre-war Austro-German music. More likely it was a defence mechanism against possible charges of pretentiousness.

The period in which much of this material appeared cannot be defined with any precision, but appears to cover the first two decades of the twentieth century. Musicians have not, as a rule, initiated aesthetic movements but they have reflected them, albeit some years late. The spread of suburban railways and then of bus routes out of London and a few other cities enabled their citizens for a few precious years before ribbon development engulfed the broad acres, to 'have a day out in the country', as the transport companies in their advertising exhorted them to do. This 'country' was not the profound rurality of Somerset or Hereford, but sufficiently sylvan to generate a new experience for the emerging lower middle classes beginning to enjoy a little financial ease. The Amberley Wild Brooks and Darkened Valleys and countless other rural pictures now being celebrated in music would find a ready market. For those who would probe a little deeper, the stream of rural novels by Thomas Hardy from 1870 onwards presented an alternative image of country life. Into this was injected an element of fey supernaturalism – given focus in 1904 by the appearance of James Barrie's *Peter Pan*. Barrie's boy who never grew up may have had little to do with the imagined rural Arcadian paradise, but the pedigree of his name had descended from every (literally in meaning) wild and wandering unearthly forest and mountain creature.

On a prosaic level, Monckton's *The Arcadians* tapped the possibilities of this mood, as did the supernatural element of Barrie's own *Mary Rose*, in 1920 at the end of our two decades. But it was the composers of the hundreds of short piano pieces who reflected the woodland aspect of pantheism. Not that we may expect from them the profound subtlety and psychological insight of a Debussy. These 'tone pictures', 'fancies' and 'impressions' – the list of subtitles is extensive – are not impressionist in any sense that an impressionist painter would have understood. They are usually dance-style pieces to which a title has been added. Typical are Pierre Lescaut's[2] Four Tone Pictures *In Arcady* (1912):

1. *A Song of Twilight*
2. *Dianeme*
3. *Golden Youth*
4. *Zephyr*

Lescaut followed that up a year later with *Scènes Pittoresques*:

1. *Mid the Hush of the Corn*
2. *By the Murmuring Stream*
3. *Where Fairies Rove*
4. *Into the Crimson West*

Such pieces are these rarely showed much individuality, and indeed often bore a family resemblance to one another. They were usually presented in suites of four movements, in which the one common movement was often a waltz. Within the liberal constraints of the form, composers such as Percy Elliott disported themselves with movements entitled *Dancing Sunbeams* and *Moonrise o'er the Lake*

(Suite: *Sunbeams and Moonbeams*: 1919); Montague Ewing with *Dance of the Butterflies* (*Four Miniature Dances*: 1925); Maurice Winlaw with *Battle of the Flowers* (*Four Southern Sketches*: 1918); and Noel Norman with *Phantom Shadows* (*Four Night Fancies*: 1919). Among the best of these usually well-written and always professionally produced albums were those of the sadly underrated Percy Fletcher. His *Sylvan Scenes* (1921), with pastel-shaded cover illustrating a shepherd with his flock, is typical of, but better than, many (see Ex. 11.3). There is a balletic element to the four movements (*In Beauty's Bower*, *Sylvia Dances*, *The Pool of Narcissus*, *Cupid's Carnival*), all of which reflect the day-tripper's vision of a sanitized rural-tania in which damsels dance in the cornfield, and where there is neither abattoir nor any muck-spreading.

Ex. 11.3   Percy Fletcher: *Sylvan Scenes*, No. 2 (*Sylvia Dances*). © Copyright by Hawkes & Son (London) Ltd. Reproduced by permission of Boosey & Hawkes Music Publishers Ltd.

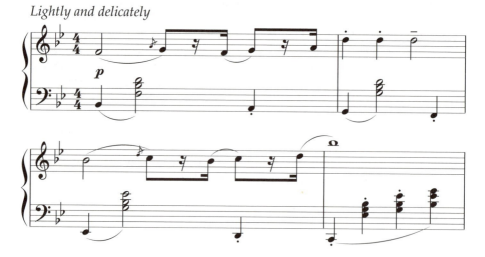

There were hosts of 'woodland' pieces, prevalent especially in the two or three years after 1918. It may be that the recurring photographic images from the Western Front of war-torn vistas with hundreds of tree-stumps standing like ghostly sentinels prompted some primeval urge to expunge their memory in music of which Norman O'Neill's *In The Branches* (1919) or G.H. Clutsam's *Woodland Song* (1921) are representative.

Beyond the hundreds of suites were the thousands of individual pieces; intermezzi no longer in the middle of anything, preludes leading to nothing, and humoresques with little humour about them. Seeking inspiration for these, a composer would often range farther afield, as Haydon Augarde did for his 1913 sketch *Egyptiana*, or as John Neat did (even farther) for his Japanese intermezzo *Almond*

Blossom. Augarde, who, according to his publisher, had already 'given the world another wonderful success' with his *A Hindu's Paradise*, regaled his devotees with *A Ride to the Pyramids*, which doesn't seem too far in musical spirit from the many rides down an English country lane that so many of his colleagues were offering.

While few of the above-mentioned pieces, and others like them, required an extensive technique to do them justice, they had not been written primarily as teaching material. Educational piano music became a separate and extensive market in its own right. At the most elementary level, the work of Walter Carroll (1869–1955) in his widely used *Scenes at a Farm* represented some of the best. The Local Examination Boards for music, of which the Associated Board of the Royal Schools of Music is an example, took teaching material a stage further when, as their own publishers, they classified material into carefully graded standards, often commissioning new music where nothing appropriate already existed.

In the early 1920s, a number of publishers attempted to establish catalogues of piano music of quality, music specifically written for the instrument and only rarely to be arranged for other media. Often, this meant gazing into the crystal ball in an attempt to forecast the successful composers of the future. Anglo-French backed Dorothy Howell, with her attractive *Humoresque* (1919), and John McEwen with his *Three Preludes* (1920). Sadly, posterity has not endorsed their judgement. Augener with John Ireland, Schott with E.J. Moeran and Novello with Herbert Howells all did better.

An important impetus came in 1924 when Oxford University Press established its music department, with Hubert Foss (1899–1953) at its head. An able pianist himself, Foss set about establishing a strong family of composers for his instrument. His early captures included Vaughan Williams's *The Lake in the Mountains*. (Vaughan Williams wrote little piano music but in 1921, Stainer and Bell had already brought out his *Suite of Short Pieces*, a beautifully crafted work, much of which is well within the capacity of, say, a grade VI–VII player.) Alan Rawsthorne's *Bagatelles* and Constant Lambert's *Elegy* followed later. Foss also found a place for the delightful *Duets for Children* by the young William Walton.

Vaughan Williams was already a major figure; the others would become so. But some of Foss's protégés did not achieve the same luminous distinction. Composers such as Herbert Murrill (*Suite Francaise*), Walter Leigh (*Eclogue*), Thomas Pitfield (*Two Russian Tunes*) and Robin Milford (*Jennifer's Jingle*), however, produced authentic light work which is still rewarding to play. Sometimes, Foss missed the mark just as Anglo-French had. Bernard Van Dieren's *Netherlands Melodies* seem quite crude in their treatment today. But then he would make amends by finding Alan Richardson's *The Dreaming Spires*. Richardson is remembered for this, if for little else.

The need, for the purposes of this book, to establish what is, and what is not, light piano music is bound at best to be a subjective exercise. The first three piano sonatas of Arnold Bax, for example, are clearly music of the most serious import; the fourth may not be. All the massive keyboard works of Sorabji are not music to trifle with, or which trifles with us. All? Does, maybe, his *In the Hothouse* reveal the master in a significantly lighter frame of mind? These examples of doubt serve to justify what may seem in the following to be an arbitrary selection.

The earliest piano music of John Ireland (1879–1962) had appeared before the First World War, and indeed, one of his most accessible pieces – *The Holy Boy* – dates from 1913. Ireland was a superb pianist, and his practical experience of the keyboard is reflected in the subtle textures and in the chordal lay-out of his music. It also sadly determines that much of his work is not within the scope of players of limited technique. His reputation as a composer for the piano was established with the three London pieces: *Chelsea Reach, Ragamuffin* and *Soho Forenoons* (1917). For twenty-two years (1904–26), Ireland was organist of St Lukes, Chelsea, and London was for long the focus of his musical thoughts. But there were to be other stimuli. A love of the Channel Islands bore fruit in the magnificent Island Sequence *Sarnia*, and a love of rural Sussex, where he subsequently lived, generated a response to its mystic antiquities: 'burial mounds and so-forth'. His rural piano pieces, such as *The Towing Path, Amberley Wild Brooks* or *The Darkened Valley*, are nevertheless those of a city-dweller, viewing the scene but not of it. As with Bax, the melodic idiom is, if not diatonic, essentially quite simple, set within a texture of often extreme chromaticism, further encrusted with many added notes.

Ireland had been a pupil of Stanford. So, too, after a period of articled studentship to Herbert Brewer at Gloucester, was Herbert Howells. It is a testimony to Stanford's teaching that his many pupils show such a diversity of style. The one trait shared by him with them, as indeed they share with each other, is solid craftsmanship. As suggested in the previous chapter, Howells' ultimate stature will be determined by his sacred music – both for organ and for voices. But this should not blind us to the quality of his handful of pieces for the solo keyboard. Of these, only a few qualify as light music, and of those, the most substantial are not for piano but for clavichord. The best of the authentic light piano music is often to be found in arrangements, such as *Triumph Tune* (1934), or the *Slow Dance* and *Cobblers' Hornpipe* (1926), both founded on tunes from Playford's *The Dancing Master*. Easier examples may be found in *Country Pageant* and *A Little Book of Dances* (1928), both now published in one volume (Associated Board).

In these early works, Howells's style is retrained – fastidious almost – although, as *Triumph Tune* shows, he can produce a swinging march if need be. The harmony in his early keyboard work is diatonic but not exclusively so, with the result that the occasional purple chords are the more effective. Melodically, his fancy will take flight in exotic arabesques. But there is a suggestion also of the phrases and textures of the Elizabethan keyboard masters. Certain of the *Country Pageant* and the *Little Book of Dances* could indeed be as effective played on a spinet or clavichord. Paradoxically, the two collections specifically written for the latter delicate instrument sound at least as effective when played on the piano. These are *Lambert's Clavichord* (Op. 41, twelve pieces written 1926–1927), and *Howells's*

Clavichord (Started1941. Published 1961. Two volumes; twenty pieces in all). The former had been published in a signed limited edition by Oxford University Press. It was a prestige publication of great beauty, as indeed was its successor (Novello). In these two collections, each piece is short and each is dedicated to a particular friend. Although he came from a rural background and might have been expected to reflect this in his work, he is not wholly of the English pastoral school. Much of his work is inspired by people or the memory of them. His titles invest his friends with an Elizabethan persona; by his own testimony, he would have liked to have lived in Tudor times.

The thirty-two clavichord pieces of the two collections cover an astonishing range of mood, emotion and wit. From *Lambert's Clavichord*, *Sargent's Fantastic Sprite* takes a kinder view of the conductor Malcolm Sargent than his later critics did. From *Howells's Clavichord*, the wit of the quotation from the march *Crown Imperial* in *Walton's Toye* is a delicious tribute to a composer Howells much admired. The decades that elapsed between the two sets saw Howells's style deepen in sophistication and linear complexity. Movements such as *Bliss's Ballet* and *Berkeley's Hunt* are still superb light music. But *Finzi's Rest* ('For Gerald: on the morrow of 27th September, 1956') is the *Nimrod* of this later-day *Enigma*.

If Alec Rowley is included as a major writer for piano, this should be qualified here. He was in no sense a great composer but he was a prolific one, and also an influential one in that huge numbers of budding pianists were fed his work. And this was no bad thing. His *Twelve Little Fantasy Studies* were often the first real music a child learner experienced; working within a limited range, Rowley's work had quality. For those a few months further on, his *Five Miniature Preludes and Fugues* (1946) painlessly introduced the principles of contrapuntal playing. Like so many others, Rowley went through his oriental phase: with, for example, the *Oriental Valse* (1919), *The Pagoda* (1920; admittedly in this case via Kew Gardens), the unfortunately named *Chinese Junk* (1926) and *A Chinese Suite* (1917). Rowley loved the French Impressionists, and in the last-named suite had caught up with them – at least as they were at the turn of the century. Sometimes, as for example in the four sets of *Poetical Studies* (Op. 41: 1920), Rowley's harmony seems more appropriate to musical comedy than to piano music. But it is a matter of individual taste. Some may well prefer the less exotic Rowley, to be found in the witty *The Rambling Sailor* (1928).

The Anglo-Irish E.J. Moeran responded readily to music that he loved: Vaughan Williams, Delius, Elgar, Sibelius, Ravel – all were grist to his mill. But in his piano music, it is the work of his teacher John Ireland that is the most obvious influence. Happiest as a solitary man amid Nature, much of Moeran's work reflects the rural ambience of East Anglia, the Welsh Marches and south-west Ireland, together with their folk-music. All this may suggest a composer with little distinctive personality of his own. Not so. Moeran's own character transcends the superficial similarities and the various influences; he may even use specific works by others as points of reference when it suits his purpose.

Among his earliest extant piano music are the Three Pieces dating from 1919 (*The Lake Island, Autumn Woods, At the Horse Fair*), *On A May Morning* (1921) and the Three Fancies of 1922: *Windmills, Elegy* and *Burlesque*. These titles may be reminiscent of hundreds of others of a kind already mentioned, but such pieces as these, together with *Stalham River* (1921) and *Summer Valley* (1925) represent his deepest response to such scenes. Are they light music? They certainly are immediately attractive. If there are doubts about their inclusion here, there can be none about *Bank Holiday* (1925); this exuberant, splashy piece is representative of the other, boisterous Moeran almost brought to destruction by his years of carousing with Warlock (see Herbert Howells's comment, quoted in Chapter 10.)

None of the Moeran works mentioned above are easy. But a good introduction for a pianist of moderate technique might be *The White Mountain*, an arrangement of the traditional Irish folk-song – easy, but lacking none of Moeran's quality.

If music is thought of as a spectrum with light music as its central point, that centre may be approached from either left or right. Thus, Andrew Lloyd Webber writes a Requiem, and pop composer Paul McCartney an oratorio, while symphonist William Walton indulges in the syncopations of *Façade*. Lloyd Webber and McCartney are moving to the right, while Walton is moving from the right towards the left. The composers mentioned so far in this chapter have approached light piano music from a position right of centre. But some approached from the left. Billy Mayerl (1902–59) poured out a profusion of dazzling syncopated pieces over the 1920s and 1930s. His work signalled an end to the woodland reveries and fields of corn. His titles were pert and snappy: *Bats In The Belfry, Honkytonk, Penny Whistle* and *All of a Twist* are a few of them. But there were still many flower titles: *Green Tulips, Autumn Crocus, Honeysuckle* and, the most popular of all his works, *Marigold*. Mayerl's strong melodic gift is heard in this as is a poetic quality which enables him to turn what is, on the face of it, an intractable syncopated style into a malleable vehicle for his thoughts which allows for much diversity. Mayerl ran a correspondence course: Learn How to Play Like Billy. But the truth is, no-one could play like him. His technique as a pianist was inimitable, particularly in the accuracy of his left-hand skips. As a twelve-year-old, he had in 1914 played the Grieg Piano Concerto at the Queen's Hall. Scowcroft[3] credits him with the first London concert performance (28 October 1925) of Gershwin's *Rhapsody in Blue*, although Andrew Youdell states that the British premiere was given by Arthur Benjamin. The two claims need not be mutually exclusive. Mayerl had his imitators, among whom was Charlie Kunz. But Kunz had little creative talent, applying the style only to medleys and arrangements, which did well enough in the variety halls.

In the years after 1945, the work of Mayerl and Kunz seemed dated and it lost currency. Indeed, British light piano music itself went into decline, relieved only by the work of a few composers such as Lennox Berkeley, Madeleine Dring and Richard Rodney Bennett. Music 'from the right' virtually ceased, since recitalists never included it; not even, as they might have done between the wars, as encores.

From the left, it continued for a while in the hands of such fine artists as George Shearing, Monia Liter and Semprini. But the piano itself was gradually superceded by the electric organ and electronic keyboards, the synthesizer and then the digital piano. They were cheaper to buy, and didn't need so much maintenance.

Notes

1. Why did he include this clumsily written piece, started in 1891, and apparently finished 31 years later in 1922?
2. Real name Frederic Mullen. Mullen also published under other pseudonyms, including Gustav Lind, Jean Morel and Philippe Carton. See article by A.J. Nosnikrap (pseudonym for J.A. Parkinson) in *Musical Times*, April 1985.
3. Scowcroft, Philip L., 'British Light Music', p. 67, and Youdell, Andrew (1996), 'Storm Clouds', *British Music*, 18, p. 19.

CHAPTER TWELVE

Sweet Singing in the Choir

Chapter 3 mentioned one of the dilemmas facing British composers in the post-Sullivan musical world of the first years of the twentieth century. Should they follow their public into the anaemic simplistic theatre of musical comedy? Should they try to establish a British National Opera? Should they abandon musical theatre altogether, and look for salvation elsewhere?

Some sought their crock of gold in an unsatisfactory dramatic substitute: the secular cantata. There was a strong demand for it in Britain at the turn of the century because of the vibrant amateur choral movement. This movement – a child of the aspirations of the newly emergent middle classes in the burgeoning Midland and Northern industrial cities – led to the great provincial music festivals: Birmingham, Leeds, Norwich and others. In marked contrast to today, when a new choral work is a sure guarantee – both in the choir and in the audience – of rows of empty seats – the late nineteenth- and early twentieth-century music festival made an important feature of novelties. The commissioning and composition of them provided a considerable proportion of a composer's income in the days before the existence of the Performing Right Society, especially when he could earn an additional fee for conducting his own work.

When this circumstance is added to the weak operatic tradition and to the strong non-conformist one to be found in Britain, the importance of the secular cantata in the choral festival movement is underlined.

Although Mendelssohn's *Elijah* (written for the 1846 Birmingham Festival) is termed an oratorio, it is a dramatic work which, with the excision of some 'commenting' items such as *O Rest in the Lord*, has been successfully staged. This would be neither possible nor desirable in examples by Parry on a high moral plane, or Stanford on a more earthly one. But it was to prove possible with Coleridge-Taylor, and it was to be he and Elgar who devoted, and perhaps wasted, years of their creative lives on the dramatic cantata. Wasted, because these works were so much at the mercy of their books. So, one might argue, is an opera. But certainly on the continent, and to a lesser extent in Britain, there was a tradition of professional opera librettists hardly to be found in cantata, which often made do with adapted poems, at best by distinguished poets (Longfellow was favoured) but more often by unsettable poetasters.

While he was not formally trained, and while in his early days he had written many a set of quadrilles and lancers, Elgar was very much in the 'schooled' serious music camp. He aspired to 'something great', an aspiration to be reinforced after his marriage to Caroline Alice. But given his background as a master of light orchestral music, it comes as no surprise to find that his choral music is not exclusively serious in purpose. His festival cantatas, while both lengthy and virtuosic in their choral and orchestral demands, are nevertheless often light in the sense that their subjects are not profound. The point can be illustrated if such works as *The Black Knight* (Longfellow/ H.A. Ackworth: 1896), *The Banner of St George* (Shapcott Wensley: 1897) or *Caractacus* (H.A. Ackworth: 1898) are compared with *The Music Makers* (Arthur O'Shaughnessy: 1912), for while the last-named is, like the first three, a loose secular cantata, unlike them it is clearly profound in both intention and effect.

These cantatas by Parry, Stanford, Elgar, Coleridge-Taylor and others were intended to appeal not only to the audiences who listened to them but also to those who performed them: the amateur choralists. It was these Elgar had in mind when, for example, he wrote the solidly singable opening chorus of *The Black Knight*, or the massive choral onslaught of *I Am the God Thor* from *King Olaf*.[1] Amateur singers relished such choruses as these.

But the dramatic cantata had inherent drawbacks which were difficult to overcome. In *Caractacus*, for example, Elgar's chorus of Celts have, at the conclusion of the cantata, to leap forward in time several hundred years to luxuriate in praise of Victorian Crown and Empire. But, moments before that even, they had been triumphant Romans. This is admittedly an extreme example of incongruity but it illustrates the challenge to credulity in cantata as opposed to opera, where at least the costumes help to show who is who. Despite their absurdities, however, the Elgar cantatas are wonderfully worthwhile, containing as they do such a flood of inspired music hardly paralleled by his contemporaries.

Some eighteen years Elgar's junior, Samuel Coleridge-Taylor often seemed to be trying to emulate his colleague's success, and followed the similar path of the festival circuit. But for him, it was to become a treadmill. His early success with the dramatic cantata *Hiawatha's Wedding Feast* (Longfellow: 1898) set him on this path for much of the rest of his short life. This cantata blew great gusts of fresh air through the dusty tradition of English choral music. The work dispensed with the formal counterpoint and fugal entries which, as Elgar said so apologetically, he and others thought to be expected of them. Coleridge-Taylor used his voices imaginatively, quite often separately rather than as a four-part group. Altos might sing alone and sopranos might be divided. As for the orchestra, instead of merely strengthening the voice leads, it has patterns of its own and often works against the choir, rather than being merely subordinate to it. Coleridge-Taylor's construction techniques owe much to the thematic transformation methods of Liszt and Wagner, and are handled with subtlety and certainty. It may not, for example, be immediately apparent that the brightly rhythmic opening idea of the cantata also suggests, after adjustments of interval, time and tempo, the love-song *Onaway, Awake, Beloved*, which forms the core of the cantata (see Ex. 12.1).

The work became so popular – in due course, the world over – that performances of it alone outnumbered for a few years those of cantatas by all of Coleridge-

Ex. 12.1   Samuel Coleridge-Taylor: *Hiawatha's Wedding Feast* (cf. Ex. 6.1)

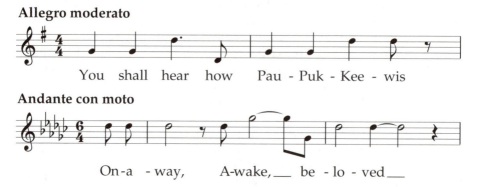

Taylor's leading colleagues. As a result of its success, he was inundated with commissions for choral works.

There were to be two sequels to *Hiawatha's Wedding Feast*; these are *The Death of Minnehaha* and *Hiawatha's Departure*. The complete trilogy makes up an evening's programme. The sequel cantatas, too, were performed everywhere, but never achieved the same acceptance as the *Wedding Feast*. Nor did such later cantatas as *The Blind Girl of Castel-Cuillé, Meg Blane, Kubla Khan* or *A Tale of Old Japan*. All fell into obscurity after the composer's death in 1912. Yet, with the possible exception of *The Blind Girl*, all contain much fine music. They were the attempts of a gentle, timid man to meet a demand.

They were nevertheless opera substitutes. He did write an authentic opera (*Thelma*), lavishing on it years of time he could ill afford. While concert organizers flocked to give his cantatas, he never secured a performance of his opera. It may have been destroyed; certainly it is now lost.

Both Elgar and Coleridge-Taylor tried their hand at the choral suite – settings of groups of poems on related subjects, which had the advantage of being free of any unwanted dramatic baggage. Curiously enough, few British composers had been attracted to this form in choral music, although the orchestrally accompanied song-cycle had a full pedigree.

Elgar's attempts to find vocal outlets for his work encompassed both instrumentally accompanied choral suite and song-cycle. The *Three Bavarian Dances* for orchestra have already been mentioned (Chapter 7). They had originated in *From the Bavarian Highlands* (Op. 27: 1895), a collection of six part-songs, with piano-duet and later orchestral accompaniment, to pastiche Bavarian folk poems by his wife Alice. At a time when European travel still had some novelty, these are musical picture-postcards, treating their subjects with a light touch, where others had celebrated their visits with substantial symphonies.

The song cycle *Sea Pictures* (Op. 37: 1899) for contralto and orchestra also had words by Alice, among others. These again are light songs; the work of a man landlocked in Worcestershire, but one who crossed the sea on occasion to Europe or America, and who reflected something of its power in his Second Symphony, when he experienced it at Tintagel.

Sir Hubert Parry – an ocean-going yachtsman – might have been expected to derive inspiration from the sea, but rarely did so. Sir Charles Stanford, however, may have noted the success of Elgar's *Sea Pictures* when he came to write his *Songs of the Sea* (1904) and then the *Songs of the Fleet* (1910). Coleridge-Taylor made his contribution to the choral suite with *Bon-Bon Suite* (Op. 68: 1908, Thomas Moore). This attractive work surely does not deserve the neglect into which it has fallen.

All these are light music of high quality; but few followed their example. Those few included Arthur Bliss (*Pastoral: Lie Strewn the White Flocks*: 1928) and Vaughan Williams (*Five Tudor Portraits*: 1935).

During the 1914–18 war, those choral societies which remained active suffered a decline which continued into the post-war world. The festivals they supported withered, and so therefore did the market for the dramatic cantata. The surviving choirs were smaller and had not the same enthusiasm for exploring new music. To tempt them, some composers sought out lighter subjects. Among them was Constant Lambert, whose setting of Sacheverell Sitwell's *The Rio Grande* (1927) embraced the rhythms and harmonies of the Jazz Age, and Herbert Howells's *A Kent Yeoman's Wooing Song* (1935), which attempted to bring sophistication to an essentially earthy text. But these demanded a virtuoso choir and orchestra. Closer to the needs of amateurs was Sir George Dyson, with such settings for chorus and orchestra as *The Canterbury Pilgrims* (Chaucer: 1929–31) and *In Honour of the City* (Dunbar: 1928) – arguably superior to William Walton's 1937 setting, and certainly easier. Is Walton's *Belshazzar's Feast* (1930–31) light music? Many will be scandalized by such an impious thought. And yet … does not the composer relish the pagan bits, where he can join Lambert in indulging in godless jazz, and where he can mock Handel as his Babylonians march to a grotesque distortion of *His Yoke is Easy*? Does he not relish these more than praising the True God?

While the scarcity of male singers – especially tenors – made it increasingly difficult to present a large four-part mixed chorus with anything like adequate balance, small and often very accomplished choirs did proliferate and flourish. A stimulating factor here was the life work of the Rev. E.H. Fellowes (1870–1951) in making available, in scholarly editions in modern notation, sixteenth- and seventeenth-century madrigals, motets, ayres and balletts, a vast repertory which was eagerly explored. Many of the madrigals and balletts are light music, setting light lyric poetry. That the exquisite pleasure they offer is more apparent within the table around which they are sung than to the listener outside does not gainsay the point. They could be sung with one voice only to a part. They needed no expensive orchestra (although instruments could replace missing voices), and that fact alone meant that the huge late nineteenth-century cohorts of singers were no longer necessary to punch through the dense wall of orchestral sound.

Our interest in them here is that such small groups needed variety, and therefore also proved a platform for the modern unaccompanied part-song. This, too, set lyric poetry – often of the Elizabethan and Jacobean periods – but it was audience orientated. Here again, Parry and Stanford had been leaders with such settings as *Since Thou, O Fondest* (Parry/Bridges), and the impressionist vocal tone poem *The Blue Bird* (Stanford/Mary Coleridge). Elgar, too, had found a ready market for his part-songs. Even today, such songs of his as *My Love Dwelt in a Northern Land* and *Weary Wind of the West* reappear regularly on the prospecti of competitive music festivals.

The early years of the twentieth century saw the folk-song movement in full spate. Stanford had occasionally set an Irish traditional melody, but the English folk-song revival had come too late for the main part-song activity of Parry and Elgar. Asked to comment on it, the latter had famously declared that he was English folk-song. Arrogant he may have been, but he had a point.

Led by Cecil Sharp (1859–1924), with Vaughan Williams, Grainger, Butterworth, Holst, Moeran and others in train, the collectors systematically explored each rural county, in the hope of rescuing songs before their last exponents died taking word and tune with them to the grave. They were part of a European-wide movement, and they went to considerable trouble to secure authenticity in recording each step of a dance, each nuance in melody and each variant in words.

Paradoxically, because Sharp's creative talents were limited, his own presentations of folk-songs he had collected allowed the tune and the words to speak for themselves, with the lightest of accompaniments. Others, arranging the tunes for SATB chorus, or into orchestral rhapsodies, would sometimes use them as pegs on which to hang their own elaborate pictures.

Vaughan Williams's four-part arrangement of *Just as the Tide Was Flowing* exploited the virtuosity of his chosen singers, giving them sophisticated fun far removed from the rural turnip field. Such brilliance needs no defence, any more than does Holst, enhancing the tragedy inherent in the Cornish folk-song *I Love my Love*. Grainger too, saw no reason why the whole force of his harmonic arsenal should not be deployed to intensify the essentially modal *Brigg Fair*.

Behind the feverish rescue of folk-songs lay William Morris-style socialism, to which the arguably middle-class art of music and its practitioners attempted to accommodate. This process was fed by the breakdown of class structures engendered by the 1914–18 war. Death appeared not to discriminate between classes.

And yet there is something wryly amusing about Cecil Sharp and his acolytes, decorously and gingerly dancing steps which would have come naturally to their original rough and ready creators. Nor did the trained singer feel inclined to modify his carefully nurtured vowels to enhance the earthy realism of raw folk-song.

One further manifestation of folk art remains to be considered. Such a great occasion for rejoicing as the anniversary of the birth of Christ naturally prompted Christmas songs and wassails, the origins of which are lost in time. In the nineteenth century, composers wrote Christmas hymns and the Christmas celebration gained further focus when Bishop Benson arranged the Service of Nine Lessons with Carols for use in the new Truro Cathedral, Cornwall. Neither the traditional carols and wassails nor the nineteenth-century Christmas hymns are light music, of course, but the tradition they represent did lead in the twentieth century to the Christmas concert by the town choral society. This fitted into the calendar well; a choir could give its main concert in early November and have a few weeks left over to learn its carol concert. The demand for new Christmas songs now proved to be very lucrative, and publishers could afford to try out young unknown composers without too much risk, where they had become increasingly reluctant to invest in printing large-scale scores.

The demand was such that general collections of carols and Christmas music began to appear. Down-market was the *News Chronicle*'s *Christmastide Melodies* (*c.* 1930) – with foreword by Dr Malcolm Sargent, in the hope, perhaps, of thereby investing it with musical respectability. Up-market was the influential *Oxford Carol Book*, which served choirs well for many years.

By the 1960s, the need for a new approach to carols, which would reflect contemporary styles had become apparent. OUP's first volume of *Carols for Choirs* appeared in 1961, to be followed at intervals by three additional volumes. Edited at first by Reginald Jacques and David Willcocks, they were marked by the sheer spread and variety of what they offered.

The difficulties of mixed-voice choirs and choral societies had been exacerbated still further in the 1914–18 war when the newly founded Women's Institute movement and other women-only movements began to form a host of SA and SSA choirs. But these created a new market which publishers and composers were quick to exploit. Such choirs, unhampered by often slow-learning male choristers, could sometimes achieve astounding virtuosity. Evidence of this can be seen in Julius Harrison's a cappella setting of *The Blessed Damozel* (D.G. Rossetti: 1928), written as a competition piece for the Blackpool Music Festival. Running to eleven real parts, the work explores every conceivable difficulty.

Although SATB had their problems, composers seemed reluctant to contemplate writing for a mixed-voice choir with only one male voice line, SAB, in which the B represented middle of the road baritone. But they would happily adapt their work so that it could be sung by women's voices. Vaughan Williams proved particularly amenable, consistently adopting a flexible approach in his requirements, whether in the voices or in the accompaniment. Having fashioned an SATB cantata (*In Windsor Forest*) from his opera *Sir John in Love*, he then adapted the cantata so that it could be performed with women's voices only. Subsequently, he wrote for the National Federation of Women's Institutes his *Folk Songs of the Four Seasons*.

It had been the gathering together, as a social event, of women in each town and village, caused by the creation of Townswomen's Guilds and Women's Institutes that had prompted the singing. Men had congregated for far longer in their workplaces, and so male voice choirs had had a correspondingly longer history. But they had been content to sing a restricted repertoire, and had been reluctant to learn new material. Their insistence on everlastingly *Climbing Jacob's Ladder* and on waiting for the *Sweet Chariot* to carry them home has meant that they have provided less stimulation to composers than have the women's and mixed-voice choirs.

But the biggest gatherings of all – at football matches – were male-dominated. Here, men would sing uninhibitedly, and were thus in the forefront of the community singing phenomenon of the 1920s and 1930s. Elgar, with little evidence of enjoyment, conducted them in his 'folk-song' *Land of Hope and Glory* at the first Wembley Cup Final in 1923. Daily newspapers such as the *News Chronicle* and the *Daily Express* caught the mood, and issued community song books, which sold in many thousands. Composers such as Sir George Dyson wrote new unison songs, but none took the public imagination in the same way as Elgar's tune, or Parry's *Jerusalem* had. Holst came nearest to them in achieving a national song when the central tune of *Jupiter* (*The Planets*) – which had always seemed to fit uneasily into that movement – was given words.

A host of composers whose instrumental and orchestral music has languished are still remembered by amateur choralists, who continue to defy fashion by singing their part-songs and light cantatas. Geoffrey Bush's (1920–98) *Twelfth Night* and *Christmas Cantata* are prime examples of such light choral music, as is *The Highwayman* cantata (Op. 72) and the many delightful part-songs of Cecil Armstrong Gibbs (1889–1960). Alec Rowley (1892–1958) and Eric Thiman (1900–75) are slipping out of the reference books, but their part-songs still find ready acceptance among amateurs.

The decline of the larger choral societies became even more marked in the second half of the twentieth century. The factors that resulted in this decline will be considered in Chapter 16 since, to an extent, they are those which have adversely affected light music generally. But the choral movement which flowered so spectacularly in the period covered by the first part of this study suffered in particular from the wholesale abandonment of class-singing in schools, which began to be noticeable in the late 1950s, hardly compensated for by the corresponding increase in instrumental music. Inevitably, the habit of singing was lost.

Note

1. Elgar knew his Wagner thoroughly. Is it possible he had in mind Siegfried's forging the sword Nothung when writing this chorus?

CHAPTER THIRTEEN

The 1930s

The 1930s are still within the memory of many people. The images and sounds of that age are still potent. An airship silently floating; the night sky lit up as the Crystal Palace burned; long days by an unpolluted sea at Brighton in an everlasting sunshine, a sunshine not yet perceived as malignant. The 1930s' voices too, remain, grey and impersonal: 'the king's life is drawing peacefully to its close'; grating and brittle: 'and now we have a new king'; disbelieving and almost defeated: 'I have to tell you now that no such message has been received'. But more than anything, the time are recalled by the recorded music of the period, in sounds almost too vivid to bear.

Memory tends to consign to oblivion anything unpleasant. And so, the last decade before the Second World War may, for many, be suffused in golden sunlight. But reality knows it was an age of uncertainty and of unspoken fear. It was increasingly apparent to politicians, if not yet to the populace, that the previous war had settled little, and was in fact unfinished. Worldwide, the weakness of the democracies had been exposed, as one by one they were supplanted by dictatorships. Whether in the name of Communism, Fascism or National Socialism, the various dictators – Stalin, Mussolini, Hitler and Franco, to mention only the most prominent – represented a threat from which the remaining democracies recoiled. The United States of America, the most powerful nation on earth, had withdrawn in isolation. 'The business of the USA,' intoned the somewhat grey president Coolidge, 'is business'. Quite so, but the rest of the world could not withdraw from the USA. When Wall Street failed, other economies failed with it. In Britain, as there, fortunes were lost, and slump brought in its train unemployment, for which there was in place no palliative in the form of adequate social security. In the USA, the new president Franklin D. Roosevelt attempted a 'New Deal' recovery programme. In Britain, nothing really recovered until the Second World War. For, as Arnold Wesker sagely remarked,[1] everyone makes money in war.

The American slump produced, in *Brother, Can You Spare a Dime?*, at least one song of intensity and immediacy, and in *Shoe-Shine Boy* (1936: Sammy Cahn and Saul Chaplin) another of compassion. The British national character reacted differently, producing songs of optimism and of exhortation. In the forefront of artists singing them were Gracie Fields, Jessie Matthews and Cicely Courtneidge. Gracie Fields (1898–1979) – an authentic Lancashire mill-girl – provided one of the enduring celluloid images of the 1930s, marching out at the head of her fellow workers, encouraging us to *Sing as We Go* (1934). Jessie Matthews (1907–81) was an equally authentic central Londoner whose struggles to overcome both the poverty into which she was born, and the self-inflicted bad publicity of her love-life, struck a similar chord with the public as she sang *Over My Shoulder Goes One Care* in the film version of *Evergreen* (1934).

As ever, the most successful composers were in tune with the needs and feelings of the times. In the case of Reginald Armitage, even his pseudonym seemed to reflect them. As Noel Gay (the word had none of today's resonances), he wrote *The Sun Has Got His Hat On* and *The Fleet's In Port Again* (sung by Bud Flanagan in *O.K. For Sound* at the London Palladium). If the former was an antidote to the bleak economic scene, the latter reflected the unreality of the response to the growing military menace on the continent. The fleet's homecoming is a pretext for a 'jolly good time'; similarly, in *There's Something About a Soldier* (sung by Cicely Courtneidge, dressed as one), or even in *The King's Horses*, we are aware that these soldiers are not yet prepared to face the gathering continental divisions.

Poverty itself was treated sympathetically by the leading comedy duo of the 1930s: Flanagan and Allen. Swaying gently to its rhythm on the variety stage, they would softly croon *Underneath the Arches*. It was a song for which Horatio Nicholls (alias song publisher Lawrence Wright) had written the music to Bud Flanagan's words. Where today the homeless congregate in and around the dark approaches to London's South Bank Centre, and other even less salubrious districts, sixty years ago they crept into the arches bearing the railway viaducts to the railway terminus stations. The doleful tale continued in a less successful sequel, *Where the Arches Used to Be*:

> They're building flats where the arches used to be
> There's somebody eating where we were once sleeping ...

Flanagan and Allen mined this seam further in Jimmy Kennedy's *Free* (1936), a song which pointed out that the hills and valleys were free and who needed to pay to hear a symphony when they could hear the songbirds for nothing? Twenty-seven years later, and a more materialistic response to poverty would be made:

> They say the best things in life are free.
> But I don't want what money can't buy.[2]

In the 1930s, a still relatively unsophisticated population could be enticed with visions of a bright future. Jimmy Kennedy (1902–84) – a still insufficiently acknowledged wordsmith of genius, whose lyrics include *Red Sails in the Sunset*, *South of the Border*, *The Isle of Capri* and *Under the Spreading Chestnut Tree* – wrote the words for Michael Carr's superbly syncopated *There's a New World* (1936).

In similar vein, Cicely Courtneidge – a performer of awesome energy – painted an even brighter vision in *We'll All Go Riding on a Rainbow*.

There were other possible responses to what were ominous times. One was to be found in the silly ditty or novelty song. Typical examples were *Flies Crawled up the Window*, sung by Jack Hulbert in the 1932 film *Jack's the Boy*, and *The Biggest*

Aspidistra in the World, sung by Gracie Fields in her other, gormless, persona. An offshoot of this response was the infantile archness of *The Teddy Bear's Picnic* (1932: Bratton and Kennedy. Performed by Henry Hall and the BBC Dance Band). This was an Edwardian-style lancers with words. The recording had huge sales.

Another response was to help the listener escape altogether for a while, by conjuring an imaginary alternative world, from which all aspects of the real one were excluded. The occasion found the conjuror in the person of the Cardiff-born Ivor Novello (1893–1951). We met him last as the young composer of *Keep The Home Fires Burning* (1914). On his discharge from military service after the 1914–18 war, he made a career in silent films, exploiting his soulful looks and classic profile. Throughout the 1920s, he had kept his contacts with the live theatre, and in 1935, in collaboration with Christopher Hassall, produced the first of a series of romantic musicals. *Glamorous Night* opened at Drury Lane on 2 May of that year. The story – a particularly daft one – concerned an inventor of television paid to go away by the head of a radio company. It was topical to the extent that the BBC's infant television service was only a few months from birth. But the real magic of Hassall and Novello was to erase dilapidated and shabby England and transport their audience for a few hours to Krasnia, a make-believe kingdom where there were still gypsy princesses to be found, to be loved and then to be renounced for the good of that happy country. *Careless Rapture*, which succeeded it, was less successful. It ran for only 295 performances – and it was reckoned that a show which made such a feature of its decor, costumes and music needed at least 400 performances to recoup its cost.

Further income could be expected from the publication of vocal scores and selections, which were usually in the hands of the publisher Chappell, whose still familiar blue 'curtains' wrappers were issued either for voice and piano, or for piano solo. But there was much extra expense involved in the production of a musical. After the composer had produced the tunes – sometimes harmonized, sometimes not – the technical processes of arrangement and orchestration would be sub-let to the real musicians.

Novello followed *Careless Rapture* with *Crest of the Wave* (1937) and *The Dancing Years* (1939). The latter finds him as a penniless composer working in an Alpine village and in love with both an opera diva and the daughter of the local innkeeper. It gave him a plausible reason for writing a fine waltz-song, *Waltz of My Heart*, and indeed, at least one striking and memorable waltz-song was an expected feature of every Novello musical. *The Dancing Years* ran throughout much of the Second World War, and achieved 969 performances.

Vivian Ellis and Noel Gay explored less obvious forms of escapism in their stage work, and never invaded the Ruritanian preserve of Novello. Ellis's *Mr Cinders* was an inversion of the Cinderella theme. It offered hope – the hope that, with the help of a fairy godmother (in the shape of Binnie Hale masquerading as a parlour maid), 'Mr Cinders' could escape the torments of his two wicked step-brothers. The escapism here, so crucial in 1929, was in the hope. It also suggested, in its hit song *Spread a Little Happiness*, a remedy for the encircling gloom. Eight years later, Noel Gay's *Me And My Girl* opened at the Victoria Palace (16 December 1937). It starred Lupino Lane as a cockney barrow-boy who resists the temptation of the wealthy flesh-pots to remain ultimately true to his cockney girl, Sally. The escapism here suggests that it is not necessary to leave your cage in order to find happiness. And a communal happiness was generated country-wide as thousands attempted *The Lambeth Walk*, a kind of 1930s' line dance.

For those who had jobs and money (still the majority), continuing improvements in transport and communications had speeded up life yet again. Scheduled air services were being established. Elgar took advantage of them in 1933 to fly from Croydon to Paris. Had he wished, he could have flown there and back for lunch, as some of the more adventurous did. If countries were not yet actually at war with one another again, they could and did compete for the biggest, largest and fastest. The Schneider Trophy for airspeed was one target; the Blue Riband for Atlantic liners was another. At the other end of the scale, Austin and Morris were bringing the motorcar down in size and price to within the grasp of thousands who, in the previous decade, would not have dreamed ownership to be possible.

The major factor influencing awareness, opinions and expectations was the dramatic effect of the communications revolution which had begun in the 1920s. The Harmsworth and Beaverbrook presses moved downmarket, with the result that a much bigger proportion of the population saw a newspaper. Cinemas, too, as they now came to be called, included a newsreel between features. But the biggest impact of all was made by radio broadcasting.

The British Broadcasting Company became the British Broadcasting Corporation and was given a monopoly, which would be financed by the sale of licences. In 1926, when the company was first incorporated, two million licences had been issued. By 1939, this had grown more than four-fold. With a market of this size, and no advertising permitted, the BBC programme planners found themselves early victims of the practice of song-plugging. But air-waves could not be switched off, and so in most parts of the country, the broadcasting monopoly was circumvented by commercial stations, beaming in their wares from Luxembourg, Hilversum or Normandy. So it was possible to hear Jack Hylton's band by courtesy of a washing powder (Rinso), or Carroll Gibbons's Savoy Orpheans by courtesy of a shoe-maker (Dolcis). A margarine (Stork) brought Gibbons's Rhythm Boys. To commercial radio, too, we owe the innovation of the commercial jingle:

Ex. 13.1 'We Are the Ovaltinies'

etc.

We   are   the   O-val-ti-nies,   Lit-tle girls and   boys.

There would be none of this frivolity for the BBC; the first Director General ensured that. John Reith (1889–1971) was a Messianic Scots civil engineer, possessed of purpose and vision. His purpose was quality, and his vision was of a service which would dispense not so much what was wanted as what ought to be wanted. He picked up the mood of self-improvement which was prevalent at a time of visible social distress; a mood represented by a still potent Fabianism, which manifested itself from such organizations as the Workers' Educational Association down to self-educating book systems such as the Home University Library.

The BBC, with Reith as its prophet, would educate its listeners, directing them always upwards towards the cultural heights. Musically, many of those listeners were entirely inexperienced in anything but the music they might make themselves, or might hear in the street or chapel. Walford Davies was accordingly enlisted to give illustrated talks on classical music.

The sheer quantity of music devoured by a broadcasting service, when both its central and regional stations were to be provided for, meant that a network of instrumental groups had to be created. At first, the BBC Wireless Symphony Orchestra, formed under the direction of Percy Pitt to play the light music repertoire, had sufficed; then, after abortive negotiations with Sir Thomas Beecham, Dr Adrian Boult was brought in to form the BBC Symphony Orchestra. Beecham, with Dr Malcolm Sargent in tow, formed his own London Philharmonic Orchestra instead.

The design of the BBC's new orchestra – very largely the work of Edward Clark – was conceived in sections which could operate separately, or be put together as a whole. Other specialist groups were also formed:

The BBC Theatre Orchestra (Leslie Woodgate)
The BBC Military Band (B. Walton O'Donnell)
The BBC Dance Band (Jack Payne)
The BBC National Chorus (Stanford Robinson) (giving place to the BBC Choral
    Society: Leslie Woodgate)
The BBC Variety Orchestra (Charles Shadwell)
The BBC Singers (Leslie Woodgate)

Each region then acquired its orchestra:

The BBC Northern Orchestra
The BBC Scottish Orchestra
The BBC Midland Light Orchestra
The BBC West of England Orchestra
The BBC Northern Ireland Orchestra

The Corporation even commissioned a theatre organ from John Compton. It was installed in St George's Hall and was presided over (1936–38) by Reginald Foort.

The BBC had thus become the largest employer of musicians in the world. It nevertheless found itself caught in a crossfire of criticism from various quarters. It was soon realized that performing musicians needed the stimulus of public performance to maintain their standards, and so public concerts were offered by the BBC Symphony Orchestra. But in the columns of *The Musical Times*, the profession voiced its opposition to what it saw as unfair competition. The Corporation was taken to task, too, for what it chose to play. Despite the fact that its programming departments censored the more vulgar manifestations of popular music, there were many letters complaining that programmes carried too high a proportion of both popular and light music.

Reith could not, ultimately, keep his BBC pure. But he could, and did, set standards. Because of the huge audience he commanded – for the first time in history an audience measured in many millions – his organization focused a cultural war. The war, that is, between popular and serious and, therefore, minority cultures. In the musical aspects of this war, light music found itself uncomfortably in the middle. With the ultimate triumph of popular culture, to come some thirty years later in the 1960s, it would perish along with serious music.

The reputations of light artists of the late 1920s and early 1930s were nevertheless made on radio. Singers such as Arthur Tracy (*The Street Singer*) and Cavan O'Connor (*The Strolling Vagabond*) could now reach far beyond the variety theatres; moreover, they attracted new audiences when they topped the bill in them. Reginald Foort attracted sufficient attention in his BBC residency to have a massive travelling organ constructed, with which he profitably toured the suburban and provincial variety theatres. Rawicz (Maryan Rawicz: 1898–1970) and Landauer (Walter Landauer: 1910–83), two favourite broadcasting piano duettists, toured with their two grand pianos, dispensing light classics and Johann Strauss medleys, which were drenched in cascades of demi-semi decoration. In some ways, the duo were in the tradition of the early music halls, which as we have seen occasionally found space for light classics.

Even with its own house musicians, the BBC still found it necessary to call on the services of the hotel, theatre and seaside ensembles. Many of these became household names. Among them were Leslie Jeffries and his Orchestra, relayed from the Grand Hotel, Eastbourne, Sidney Kyte with the Piccadilly Hotel Band and Sidney Lipton with his band from the Grosvenor House Hotel. Many of these hotel bands were violinist-led, rather than conducted. Lipton (1906–96) was a pupil of the great violin virtuoso Albert Sammons – who had himself started his career playing in tea-shops.

Some of these outside orchestras became recruiting grounds for the Corporation to fill its own staff vacancies. Charles Shadwell, for example, came from the Coventry Hippodrome orchestra to conduct the BBC Variety Orchestra. Richard Crean came from the London Palladium, via his own orchestra, to be founder of the BBC Midland Light Orchestra. Crean himself was followed there in 1942 by Rae Jenkins, known in the late 1930s for the 'Rae Jenkins Buskers'.

It was the bandleaders – as opposed to the more sedate ensemble or orchestra conductors – who received the most adulation, gaining for themselves the icon status enjoyed today by pop stars. 'Why Did She Fall For The Leader Of The

Band?' asked the 1935 Jack Hylton song (Jimmy Kennedy and Michael Carr). Rarely was it for artistic reasons. The hard-bitten professionals in the band neither needed nor got much help from the cavorting figure prancing in front of them.

The music style of the bands softened in impact under the influence of the new swing idioms spreading from the USA. Its Swing was smoother and was less raucous. There was less improvisation. The new music styles complemented those of fashion, which softened too; longer skirts, softer hairstyles and, of course, the return of the bosom.

It must be said that the British bands rarely achieved the stylistic polish of Benny Goodman or Glen Miller, but through the medium of radio still achieved great popularity. Of the 'outside' bands, one of the most acclaimed was that of the Savoy Hotel, The Savoy Orpheans. The leader most closely associated with them after Debroy Somers left was Carroll Gibbons. An American-born pianist who trained at the Boston Conservatoire of Music, Gibbons arrived in London in 1924. His early association with the Orpheans was intermittent. Taking them on in 1927, he left them the following year on his appointment as Director of Light Music to the HMV record company, for whom he revived the Mayfair Orchestra. He followed this with a period in the USA, working for Metro-Goldwyn-Mayer, returning in 1931 to the Orpheans. Because the Savoy hotel was just round the corner from the original headquarters of the old British Broadcasting Company, the Orpheans had been heard broadcasting more frequently than any other band in the 1920s. In the succeeding decade, they would for ever be associated with Gibbons's relaxed, reassuringly intimate tones as he introduced their radio programmes, with his lazy signature tune *On The Air* murmuring in the background.

Each bandleader now adopted a signature tune – and many a signing-off tune – in order to establish an individual identity. Beyond this, many BBC radio programmes had signature tunes, sometimes specially composed:

Ex. 13.2   (Composer and author unknown)

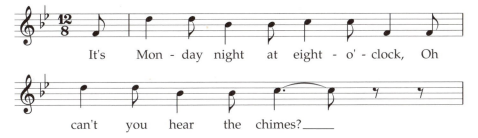

But often, a programme producer would use an existing piece and in the process would, almost as a by-product, bestow an unimagined popularity on it. This is what happened when the long-running Children's Hour picked as its ToyTown signature tune Leon Jessel's *The Parade of the Tin Soldiers*, written many years earlier, in

1911. For all who were children in the 1930s, this piece will not be associated with tin soldiers, but with Larry the Lamb, Dennis the Dachshund and all the other inhabitants of ToyTown.

Even more striking was the impact of radio on Eric Coates's *Knightsbridge* march. Coates had recorded it for Columbia in 1933, and its sales, if not outstanding, were satisfactory. But when the BBC's Director of Variety Planning (Eric Maschwitz) used it to introduce his topical new programme In Town Tonight in 1933, the results were spectacular. After only two transmissions, 20,000 listeners wrote in to ask the name of the piece. Within a year, the recording had sold 100,000 copies.

Even in the early days of broadcasting, publishers noted that, when the Orpheans played, for example, *Yes, We Have No Bananas*, or the novelty *Horsey, Keep Your Tail Up* (complete with trumpeter demeaning himself to produce an onomatopoeic neigh from his instrument), sales of sheet music copies would soar dramatically. The infant Broadcasting Corporation, too, noticed the popularity of its band broadcasts, and made provision for a dance band when structuring its house orchestras.

For this, the BBC called on the services of Jack Payne. Payne had hoped to be a farmer, but his ambitions were interrupted by the 1914–18 war, in which he served in the Royal Flying Corps. Needing immediate work on his discharge, he capitalized on his other talent. He was a useful pianist. Observing the post-war dance craze, he formed a trio to take hotel engagements. His business prospered, as he found himself providing bands for some of the bigger provincial hotels. Coming to London, he provided bands for the Hotel Cecil (the Cecil stood where Shell Mex House house now stands; not too far from Savoy Hill).

Payne may have founded the BBC Dance Orchestra, but it was to be indelibly associated with his successor Henry Hall, who took it over in 1932. The quietly-spoken and dignified Hall had come up the same way as Payne, playing in the provincial hotels. But he had an advantage in that he had held a scholarship at Trinity College of Music, and in addition had studied piano at the Guildhall School of Music. Over the 1930s and into the 1940s, his music was probably given more broadcasting time than that of anybody else, taking the pre-eminence previously held by the Savoy Orpheans.

There were many other bands of various sizes, constitutions and quality to be heard regularly broadcasting. Some, like those of Billy Cotton and of the master of 'scat' singing Harry Roy, specialized in novelty numbers. Others, such as Jack Hylton, Ambrose, Carroll Gibbons or Lew Stone, leaned towards a sweet style of playing. Yet others were masters of 'strict time'.

Most bands employed a singer, now more usually called a vocalist. The microphone had been in existence since 1877–78, when Edison and others first successfully mastered its principles. It became the vocalist's most useful tool. Few of them had what earlier years would have regarded as a powerful voice, but the microphone had rendered this unnecessary. But one thing they all shared: their diction was exemplary. Sometimes, as with Harry Roy or Jack Payne, the

13.1 Ambrose

bandleader would be his own vocalist. Occasionally, as in the case of the American vocalist Rudy Vallee, both bandleader and vocalist might become more famous as a cinema star.

Besides the standard dance bands, radio programmes of the 1930s reveal much use of European-style orchestras and what fifty years later might be termed ethnic ensembles. There were Montmartre Players and Bohemian Players. Ralph Elman, who directed the latter, also provided a Tzigane Orchestra. How many authentic continental players were in these is not known; the likelihood is that, as with the German bands of the previous century, the majority were free-lance Dean St Londoners. Falkman had his Apache Band, Troise his Mandoliers and – most exotic of all – Michaeloff his Bessarabian Orchestra.

Any eruptive movement such as the syncopated, pseudo-jazz craze of the 1920s was always likely to provoke a reaction. There wasn't much of one, it is true, but J.H. Squire and his Celeste Octet stood like a fortress against the onslaught. Squire made an enormous number of recordings – of waltzes, novelties and selections. He had formed the octet in 1913, and over the 1920s and 1930s made some five hundred broadcasts. No syncopation for him. The legendary De Groot, too, who held sway at the Piccadilly Hotel, was a traditionalist, and was generally reckoned to be the finest light violinist in the London of his time. His style would be adopted by the Palm Court violinist-leaders from Albert Sandler and Tom Jenkins to Max Jaffa.

The musician's life in this brave new world was a gruelling one, both physically and mentally. And it was an unhealthy one, in which the solace of alcohol was always lying in wait. Working in stuffy, smoke-filled rooms until three or four o'clock in the morning, musicians – as free-lances – would still have to take all other worked on offer, which might mean going on directly to a morning recording session. Jaffa, who knew the life only too well, pointed out the psychological strain:

> ... the partying on the one hand and the appalling poverty on the other. In a way, the band life created split personalities for us: by night, we watched the indulgence and excesses of the privileged and then went home to a life where we had to count every penny.[3]

As the orchestra pits of the silent picture-houses closed, another source of income opened up, to the very best, that is, of the free-lance orchestral professionals. Sound films needed not only words but music. It took a while before the implications were fully realized by the film makers, and before it was understood that a new medium was now in existence. Early sound films were wordy, and the words were gabbled. You had to get the words all in, even though the image had probably conveyed all the necessary information in a flash of time. As for the music, imagination at first went little beyond the transference of a stage musical success onto celluloid. A number of the musicals mentioned earlier were so treated. Subsequently, a film scene might be built around a song, as a complex studio set piece.

The power of music to enhance, or even to alter, the meaning of images and words had been known from Wagner. One has only to think, for example, of the scene in *Die Meistersinger* where Beckmesser, prowling around Sachs's workshop, alights on the Prize-Song poem. The orchestra at this point tells us all the thoughts going through his guilty mind. The studios were quick to learn, and soon called for specially written background music for all films – from thrillers to romances. At first, in-house studio professionals were used. The names of such experts as Louis Levy, Hyam Greenbaum, Ernest Irving and Muir Mathieson will be familiar still from the credits of British films of the period.[4] Gradually, however, composers from outside the industry were engaged for specific films, and the profile of this demanding branch of composition was raised. It was demanding because it had to meet three criteria:

1. It had to be written to precise, fractions of a second, timings, which might then have to be amended if there were late excisions in the cutting room.
2. The music must never obscure the words.
3. The music must not be too interesting, lest it divert attention from the film.

Among those composers who had already made a name for themselves were Hubert Bath, John Greenwood, Arthur Benjamin and Richard Addinsell. Bath worked on Alfred Hitchcock's first 'talkie' *Blackmail* (1929), but his work can be more readily sampled in a subsequent collaboration with Hitchcock, the splendid *The Thirty-Nine Steps* (1935). John Greenwood (1889–1975) wrote a host of film scores, of which *The Constant Nymph* (1933) and *Elephant Boy* (1937) are typical of their period. The nineteen film scores by Arthur Benjamin (1893–1960) represent a very large investment of time and energy. As Andrew Youdell has suggested,[5] it is time to rediscover the best of this work, if an enterprising company can be persuaded to assemble a representative CD. Benjamin's film scores started with Hitchcock's *The Man Who Knew Too Much* (1934). For the climax of this film – occurring at a concert in the Royal Albert Hall – Benjamin wrote a *Storm Clouds* cantata which, if still available, might stand on its own. The same year saw another major film score: that for the Merle Oberon/Leslie Howard period adventure *The Scarlet Pimpernel*. Over the next two years, he wrote a further eight film scores. Then a decade intervened before in 1948 he was commissioned for the full-length features *Master of Bankdam* and *An Ideal Husband*. Neither these, nor any of the remaining films on which he worked from 1948 to 1957 were as distinguished as those first two in 1934. But the music might well be another matter.

The early film music of Richard Addinsell (1904–77) included *Fire Over England* (1937) and *Goodbye Mr Chips* (1939). But there was a further blossoming of Bath and of Addinsell yet to come.

Over the 1930s, the film industry absorbed many European musicians. Most went to Hollywood, but some came to Britain first. Ernst Toch (1887–1964) arrived in 1933, and was immediately commissioned to write a score for Alexander Korda's *Catherine the Great* (1934). Mischa Spoliansky arrived in 1934, and produced music for the two Paul Robeson films *Sanders of the River* (1935) and *King Solomon's Mines* (1937), among many others.

These were distinguished musicians. But from the middle of the decade onwards, the possibilities of film music, not to speak of the financial rewards, began to attract the attention of composers in an altogether more exalted class. A defining point came in 1936, with Korda's *Things To Come*. For this, Arthur Bliss (1891–1975) was commissioned. In the film, there were sequences with little or no dialogue. Here, the composer could give free rein to his imagination. The set pieces from his work, which included a fine futuristic yet Elgarian march, subsequently were fashioned into an orchestral suite, and thus acquired an independent life of their own.

The young Benjamin Britten (1913–76) wrote the music for one feature film (*Love From A Stranger*: 1936), but his most remembered contributions to the screen are in the field of documentary. His most notable scores were for the director John Grierson (1898–1972): *Coal Face* (1935), and the influential and original *Night Mail* (1936).

Probably because as a young man he was not financially secure, Sir William Walton (1902–83) devoted a considerable amount of time to writing film music. He was, according to Spike Hughes,[6] the first of the real composers to turn his attention to it, and soon proved he had a flair for creating precise sounds to match imagery. In the 1930s, despite his painfully slow rate of composition, he was in constant demand, producing music for *Escape Me Never* (1935), *As You Like It* (1936: a substantial score), *Dreaming Lips* (1936) and *A Stolen Life* (1939).

In the succeeding decade, these three distinguished figures would be joined by Ralph Vaughan Williams, nearing seventy, but ever more adventurous the older he became. He, Walton and Bliss would produce some of their best work in their 1940s film scores.

*   *   *

In the 1930s, going to the pictures was cheap in relation to average earnings. Huge queues would form outside cinemas, some of which were similarly huge. Listening to the radio was even cheaper. Buying records was a little more demanding on the purse, but even so, the cheapest Zonophone or Brunswick ten-inch records were not unduly expensive. As a result, even if only as a by-product, music reached a wider audience, and a higher degree of popularity in this decade than anything seen hitherto. As Constant Lambert observed, it had attained 'appalling popularity'.[7]

But it was a passive response. Music had become professionalized, to an extent not previously experienced, and inevitably there were casualties in the amateur world. While Malcolm Sargent could still expect an army of Royal Choralists some seven to eight hundred strong, many other choral societies in the provinces were withering badly. Amateur orchestras, too, had fallen on their music stands. In the comfort of their own homes, music-lovers could now hear the very best choirs of the day – Sir Hugh Roberton's Glasgow Orpheus Choir, for example. They could hear how Beethoven's Violin Concerto sounded when Fritz Kreisler and a crack orchestra played it. Inevitably, audience support for the local choral society and amateur orchestra, with their many imperfections, fell away.

Concerning himself with trends of composition, Constant Lambert, in the influential book *Music Ho!* quoted above, saw little to delight him. Writing in 1934, he subtitled his book 'a study of music in decline'. Certainly, the decade was a turning point for British music. The major figures of the so-called musical renaissance mentioned or discussed in earlier chapters were mostly dead by 1936. With the outbreak of war three years later, the structures of musical society which had sustained light music, would begin to die also. But to some extent, recording and film work had taken their place and new opportunities were arising in advertising, mood music and, above all, in the new medium of television.

Notes

1. Wesker, Arnold (1959), *Chicken Soup With Barley*, Penguin Books.
2. The Marauders, *That's What I Want*, Decca, August 1963.
3. Jaffa, Max (1991), *A Life On The Fiddle*, Hodder and Stoughton, p. 142.
4. It did not necessarily mean that Levy, for instance, wrote all the music for which he was credited. A number of young composers of the period may have helped with the work – without a by-line. While Levy is credited, for example, as Music Director for the Will Hay film *Oh, Mr Porter*, the music was actually written by Clive Richardson (1904–1998).
5. Youdell, Andrew (1996), 'Storm Clouds: a survey of the film music of Arthur Benjamin', *British Music*, 18, p. 26, British Music Society.
6. Hughes, Spike (1946), *Opening Bars*, Pilot Press, p. 316.
7. Lambert, Constant (1934), *Music Ho!*, Faber & Faber, p. 233.

CHAPTER FOURTEEN

Instrumental Music (3):
the Post-World War 1 Generation

The composers discussed in this chapter were born in the new century. As such, while they missed the grim psychological legacies of the First World War (except where they suffered bereavement), some of them served in the Second, and some produced mature work during it.

For a number of these young composers, their coming to maturity coincided with the 1920s, the Jazz Age. They were therefore open to what was primarily an American influence. Where their predecessors had aspired to study in Germany, this was no longer seen as either necessary or appropriate. And even if it had been, with certain distinguished exceptions, of whom Kurt Weill was one, Germany was embarking on a period of musical mediocrity.

In Britain, the Royal College of Music and the Royal Academy of Music now met strong competition from other conservatoires both in London and in the provinces. There was no longer the major figure of Stanford at the RCM, although Corder was, for a little while longer, still at the RAM. Budding composers tended to use a wider variety of approaches to learning their craft. Some chose a British university. Others, still preferring Europe, chose Paris rather than Frankfurt or Leipzig. Yet others embarked on the more practical path of the instrumentalist, approaching their composition empirically.

With the exception of those who followed the Austro-German serialists, the Teutonic influence which had persisted throughout the previous century and into the early years of the new, now at last declined. From the 1920s onwards, the young composer could experience, through broadcast music and recordings, a vast variety of work, from which he could choose models at will.

These were factors in the fracturing of what had been a universal language, to be replaced by a number of dialects. With regard to light music, certain of these dialects would have little place. Serialism, for example, has stubbornly resisted attempts to be light (although a serialist such as Benjamin Frankel, when deliberately working in a tonal idiom, could achieve a light touch and the popularity to go with it).

If we return to the analogy, used earlier, of a musical spectrum ranging from the high seriousness of the right to the more populist left, the figures with which this chapter is concerned on the right will include Sir William Walton, Sir Lennox Berkeley, Constant Lambert, Alan Rawsthorne (1905–71), William Alwyn (1905–

85) and the above-mentioned Frankel (1906–73). While the main corpus of the work of these composers is serious, they each wrote some light music.

Walton, whose innate, grainy toughness was belied by his benign appearance, had been a chorister and then an undergraduate at Christchurch, Oxford. Here, he came under the influence of Henry Ley and Sir Hugh Allen, but he seems to have had a haphazard training. Its chief benefits seem to have been the access afforded him to the scores in the Ellis Library, and the widening of his circle of friends. One of the friends – the poet Siegfried Sassoon – introduced him to the Sitwell family. Walton needed financial support; they could supply it. They could also unlock for him the doors of London Society.

It was for this sophisticated society that Edith Sitwell and the twenty-year-old William Walton conceived their entertainment: *Façade*, for reciter and six instru-mentalists (in the revised score: flute/piccolo, clarinet/bass clarinet, saxophone, trumpet, percussion and cello). The façade was the decorated curtain through which, with megaphone, the words were declaimed at the first performance on 24 January 1922. It is arguable whether or not the experiment works. Some find the rhythmic poetry declamation obscures the music; others vice versa. But the music, especially in its versions for orchestra, piano duet and solo piano, has acquired a life of its own, through which we may savour the young Walton's wit as he apes the foxtrots, tangos and syncopations of the times; pokes fun at his fellow Lancastrians beside the sea at Blackpool, and at everything Swiss – from the cuckoo-clock and yodelling to William Tell.

One quality suppressed in Walton's major symphonic and concerted work but given full rein in his light music is a certain earthy – and indeed refreshing – vulgarity. Like Dame Gracie Fields, the other distinguished child of Oldham, he has twin personae, of which the second, more disreputable, one will peep out from time to time. The appearance of it in *Belshazzar's Feast* has already been mentioned. It is also to be heard in light works as disparate as *Portsmouth Point* (other nautical overtures such as Rowley's *Down Channel* or John Ansell's *Ply-mouth Hoe* are nowhere near as bracingly salty) and the Johannesburg Festival overtures. The finale, too, of the *Partita* (1957) has an element of banana-skin humour to it.

The common touch – quite distinct from vulgarity, and a phrase used here as a term of approval – can be heard in the two Coronation Marches (*Crown Imperial* and *Orb and Sceptre*), which take on the *Pomp and Circumstance* of Elgar, with whom Walton shared the ability to tune in, without loss of quality, to the needs of a people. These marches show Walton's public manner; a work such as *Siesta* reveals a little more of the reserved Walton. A wry, bitter-sweet waltz, it exploits major/minor contradictions shortly to be taken a stage further in the impending Viola Concerto.

It is in the light music miniature, too, that Constant Lambert (1905–51) reveals the sensitive soul behind the unnerving brilliance of his outward personality. As a teenager, he had heard the American Blues singer Florence Mills. Her impact on him was profound. A few years later, he paid eloquent tribute in the delicate, gentle *Elegiac Blues* for piano (1927). Walton much admired Lambert. He himself, he lamented to a friend, had achieved nothing so fine as *The Rio Grande*.

The son of an eminent portrait painter, and the father of Kit Lambert, the organizing genius behind The Who pop group, Constant Lambert was a latter-day polymath who, with Ninette De Valois and Frederick Ashton, virtually founded the Sadlers' Wells Ballet. As a conductor, he was one of the finest Walton interpreters. As a reciter, he had no peer in *Façade*. As a composer, his originality showed at the early age of twenty-two, when he chose to set Sacheverell Sitwell's poem *The Rio Grande* as a kind of choral piano concerto. The superficial attractions of the work may obscure the fact that it illuminates Lambert's understanding, expressed in *Music Ho!* and quoted in Chapter 1 of this book, that seriousness does not always have to mean solemnity.

Lambert's contemporary Alan Rawsthorne (1905–71) may not seem to be a likely source for light music, since his harmonic idiom, featuring as it does the ambiguities of augmented triads, tends to produce a somewhat gloomy ambience – well suited, as it happened, to the film *The Cruel Sea*, for which he wrote the music. But his work could smile when he wanted it to, as can be heard in the suite for piano duet *The Creel* (1940). The street in the overture *Street Corner* (1944: written in response to a commission from Walter Legge at Ensa, who also commissioned overtures from Moeran and Bax) is a murky Lancashire one, singing of times before the Clean Air Act, but it is lit by a sure gift for memorable melody.

Rawsthorne wrote the music for twenty-one other films, apart from *The Cruel Sea*. Both William Alwyn and Benjamin Frankel were also prolific film composers, Alwyn producing sixty and Frankel over one hundred film scores. Alwyn and Frankel were examples of composers coming to their art via an early career as instrumentalists, the former a flautist and the latter a café violinist. But both were 'on the right' in that they were major symphonists (Alwyn wrote three; Frankel eight). Alwyn's light music includes sets of Scottish and Elizabethan Dances, and a Festival March. Frankel achieved popularity for a while with *Carriage And Pair*; an excerpt from the music he wrote for the 1950 film *So Long At The Fair*.

Frankel had been a scholarship holder at the Guildhall School of Music And Drama, but he was also one of the few who did manage six months' study in Germany. Lennox Berkeley also studied abroad, in Paris, where he worked with Nadia Boulanger, whose pupils also included the Americans Aaron Copland, Roy Harris, Elliot Carter and Walter Piston. In the years Berkeley was there (1927–32), the Parisian musical scene was dominated by the French composers who had earlier comprised the group *Les Six*.[1] Their influence can be heard in much of his light music, particularly in the Serenade for Strings and the Divertimento, which both favour short, pert phrases in preference to the long, romantic melodic line. This was not, however, an exclusive influence. Berkeley was also open to the attractions of the Blues – perhaps more smokey London night club than authentic New Orleans:

Ex. 14.1   Lennox Berkeley: *Six Preludes for piano* (Prelude No. 6)

Berkeley wrote one work in collaboration with Benjamin Britten. This was the suite of Catalan Dances, *Mont Juic*.

Britten's own early work includes much light music, and when after the Second World War he became principally a composer for the theatre (using the church, too, as a theatre), he remained close to his audiences. Very often, the early light work involved a re-working of other people's tunes – and in the instance of *A Simple Symphony* (1933–34), even of his own. The *Soirées Musicales* (1936) and *Matinées Musicales* (1941) present some of Rossini's *Pêchés de Vieillesse* in attractively piquant orchestration. While he could be a superb interpreter of the Austrians in particular, Britten rejected the construction methods favoured by both them and the Germans (detesting in particular the work of their exemplar Brahms) in favour of variation techniques which had a true English pedigree. Such sets of variations as those on themes by his teacher Frank Bridge and Purcell (*The Young Person's Guide to the Orchestra*) are authentic light music. But even his most profound works, such as *Peter Grimes* or *Noyes Fludde*, employ an approachable idiom, compounded of instantly memorable diatonic tunes, commonplace waltzes and hymns which, through the example of Mahler and Shostakovich, he learned to invest with emotional significance out of all proportion to the simple means used.

If film music had become one of the more financially rewarding substitutes for theatrical incidental music, it had a not-too-distant relative in the music sometimes needed for radio productions of drama. Britten was one of the pioneers here, starting in 1937 with music for two BBC radio productions: *The Company of Heaven* and *King Arthur*. But his radio music – and, indeed, that for film – has proved to be ephemeral, and has not acquired an independent life of its own, since little of it was arranged into free-standing suites.

A more unlikely pioneer in this field was Gerald Finzi. Unlikely, because although an enthusiastic theatre-goer, until the early 1940s he had seemed to stand aloof from purely commercial considerations – the considerations that drive the professional world of commissioned music. But in 1946, Finzi accepted a commission to write music for a radio production of *Love's Labours Lost*. Normally a slow worker who revised constantly, he on this occasion finished his score in three weeks, and displayed a marked talent for dramatic work. The music was subsequently used for a theatre production (at Southend), but started its independent life in 1952 at the Cheltenham Festival. Never so protean in pouring out music as Britten, Finzi was not going to waste his work, and it reached its final suite form in 1955, when his friend John Russell conducted the London Symphony Orchestra in a broadcast. It is a rare example of incidental music for a radio play providing a small masterpiece of light music. The ten movements constitute an enchanting divertimento lasting nearly half-an-hour. While Shakespeare has set his play in Navarre, Finzi has remained firmly in England, taking Elgar and Walton as his models. He could hardly have failed to take note of Walton's *Henry V* music where ceremony was required, but Elgar's *Falstaff* – dreaming in Shallow's orchard – has suggested the more ruminative movements. But at least the scoring, in its wit and delicacy, reflects the Gallic setting.

One isolated figure – a contemporary of Britten – must be mentioned here. This is the Cornishman George Lloyd (born 1913), only in very recent years emerging from obscurity. Within the parameters set by this book, he is hardly a light composer. He is primarily a symphonist, whose brilliant orchestration (it is difficult to think of a superior exponent) may obscure the essential simplicity of his work. Since Haydn, there have not been too many light, uncomplicated symphonies, but one can be found in Lloyd's Symphony No. 6 where, using an approach quite different to Britten but similar in intent, the composer, working with the well-tried tools of melody, colour and thorough craftsmanship, entices his listener.

These were the major figures of the right. There remains a number of composers who are known by one or two light works each; an undeserved fate, perhaps, to be accounted for only by British philistinism.

Reginald King's one work is *Song of Paradise*, a tune known by many, although few could put a name to its composer. King (1904–91) studied at the Royal Academy of Music, where he wrote a Piano Concerto in F Minor. When in 1923 he wrote a Fantasy for piano and orchestra (revised 1946), he incorporated in it material from the earlier work. A fine pianist, he seemed set on a classical career, but this was brought to an untimely end when he was engaged by Swan and Edgar to play in their store restaurant. From there he became a radio artist – indeed in due course, a veteran – making over 1400 light music broadcasts, each of them introduced, of course, by *Song of Paradise*. Inevitably, his other work was neglected. At least in the case of the Fantasy, this has been a pity, for it is a finely crafted work in a late romantic idiom quite at odds with its 1920s background, except to the extent that the occasional phrase and harmony reminiscent of John Ireland is reflected. It foreshadows the film concertos that would achieve such popularity in the 1940s. King's dusting down of his work in 1946 may even reflect an understandable hope to get in on the act.

Howard Ferguson's *Four Diversions on Ulster Airs* (Op. 7) still receive occasional performances; Gilbert Vinter's fine *Hunter's Moon* is still given by intrepid horn players. Walter Leigh (1905–42) studied in Berlin with Paul Hindemith, but managed to avoid absorbing the more dour qualities of his teacher's work. Leigh's neo-classicism is attractively present in his one work: the short Concertino for Harpsichord and Strings (1936). Leigh, who held such thwarted promise, was killed in action near Tobruk in North Africa.

The South African Victor Hely-Hutchinson (1901–47) came to England to join the BBC in 1926. Subsequently he was appointed Professor of Music at Birmingham University, but returned to the BBC in 1944 as Director of Music. As with so many British musicians, his creative work was hampered by the demands of administration. He did, however, leave some chamber music and some settings of Edward Lear. The one work by which he is remembered is *A Carol Symphony*, in which the well-known carol-tunes are effectively subjected to a neo-baroque choral prelude treatment.

Eric Fenby (1906–97) – a superb and seriously underrated musician, conductor and accompanist – sacrificed much of his early manhood to heroic attendance on his stricken fellow Yorkshireman Frederick Delius. Later, he would assist Julius Harrison too with some of the orchestration drudgery of Harrison's *Requiem*. His own work, which includes a symphony and music for the Hitchcock film *Jamaica Inn* (1939) suffered in consequence, and has been overlooked; with the solitary exception of the entertaining overture *Rossini on Ilkla Moor* (1938).

Few, if any, of the composers discussed above would have made any distinction in quality between their light and their serious work. They saw themselves as musicians who from time to time relaxed, in a mood to entertain. With the single exception of the young Walton's dalliance in *Façade* with something approaching the constitution of a 1920s' jazz band, none of them seems to have seriously contemplated writing for anything other than the string-based symphony orchestra. Even Eric Coates – although he adopted some of the features of the jazz and dance bands – never used any other medium. Nor did his followers, who saw the standard orchestra as a basis to be adapted and moulded to their needs.

Coates had found that, once his use of syncopation and the various jazz mutes for brass had been noted, he was no longer accorded serious criticism by the respectable music periodicals; he was relegated to the gossip columns. This was an outcome that could have damaging and far-reaching consequences for the composers mentioned above. In the 1930s, there was a suspicion felt by composers of light music that their work neither needed nor merited performances of quality, and that it could be played effectively enough with reduced forces – particularly in the string departments. Coates resented this, for he usually conceived his work for the full symphonic sound with which he was so familiar from his days as a violist.

To cope with this problem, light music composers of the 1940s and succeeding years would often be selective in the woodwind and brass they specified. They would use strings, horns and perhaps a solo woodwind, strings and harp or just strings alone. But the suspicion remained that light music was, in some way, the child of a lesser God.

Note

1. Georges Auric (1899–1983), Louis Durey (1888–1979), Arthur Honegger (1892–1955), Darius Milhaud (1892–1974), Francis Poulenc (1899–1963) and Germaine Tailleferre (1892–1983).

CHAPTER FIFTEEN

Patriotism and War (2): 1938–1945

It had been apparent for most of the 1930s that a resumption of the European War was inevitable. The likely nature of that war, whenever it should come, was evident to those who read their newspapers, or saw cinema newsreels. The reports from the Japanese attacks on China, from those of the Italians on Abyssinia and of General Franco's forces on their own people showed that modern war was total, respecting neither soldier nor civilian. For those who preferred fiction to fact, Korda's film *Things to Come* was as graphic as it was prophetic. Fear of bombs dropped from aircraft was widespread. For, as the prime minister Stanley Baldwin had said, 'the bomber will always get through'.

As the war became imminent, audiences in the concert halls and theatres dropped off drastically. On 2 September 1939, the house for *The Dancing Years* was so thin that Ivor Novello invited the gallery patrons down into the stalls. War broke out the next day, and the dispersal of children, adults and moveable treasures gathered pace. Until they were torpedoed at sea, children were sent abroad. After that, evacuation into 'the country' seemed far enough. Except that 'the country' was often perilously near such cities as Cardiff or Bristol, which were themselves to be the target of bombing raids.

Music-making is essentially an urban activity which thrives on large reservoirs of people. A war in which the civilian population would be perceived as a target clearly posed a threat to those who earned their living performing to it. And at first, so it proved to be. The BBC evacuated its Symphony Orchestra to Bristol. This proved futile, since even apart from the danger there of bombing, a third of its younger members were soon called up into the forces, some of them to serve in such military organizations as the bands or, for a lucky few, the RAF Symphony Orchestra. For a while, the BBC fed its licence-holders a meagre diet of endless gramophone records.

Orchestras such as the Hallé were also reduced to a mere shadow of their former glory. The London Philharmonic was left high and dry, since its charismatic founder Sir Thomas Beecham was fulfilling engagements abroad. Seaside and pier orchestras closed down; in any case, the piers themselves were closed, in the phrase of the times, 'for the duration'. Sir Henry Wood's Promenade Concerts were terminated. The Sadlers Wells Ballet lost most of its male dancers to the forces. The Royal Opera House, Covent Garden, closed its doors – according to Dame Ninette de Valois, the only opera house in Europe to do so at that time. When it did re-open, it was as a dance hall. The end of the musical world seemed to have come in 1941 when the Queen's Hall, London, was destroyed by bombing. Players were out of work; composers' royalties dried up.

Gradually, the need for order and organization began to take this depressing scene in hand, driven by the British genius for creative improvisation. The Proms resumed in 1940, moving after the Queen's Hall bombing to the Royal Albert Hall (they closed again in 1944 when the flying bomb offensive began). The London Philharmonic Orchestra under the left-wing reforming zeal of its violist Thomas Russell, turned itself into a self-governing cooperative. With conductors as disparate as Malcolm Sargent and Eric Coates, and sponsored, in a fairy-godmother reincarnation, by band leader Jack Hylton, it toured northern and Midland industrial towns. Playing to packed audiences in cinemas and variety theatres, it assuaged a newly discovered thirst for Beethoven, Schubert and Tschaikowsky. And under the shelter of their coat-tails, a handful of British 'shorts' might find a place also.

The BBC brought its orchestra back, deeming Bedford safe enough. The Hallé determined to rise again, and summoned John Barbirolli back from the New York Philharmonic to be its architect. The many gaps in these and other orchestras were filled by women. The Sadlers Wells Ballet filled its depleted male ranks with teenage dancers, and found it could get by with an accompaniment of two pianos. It had lost its costumes and sets in a hurried departure from The Netherlands as German paratroopers were landing; but what did that matter when it had Margot Fonteyn, Frederick Ashton, Robert Helpmann, Ninette de Valois and Constant Lambert?

The RAF victory in the Battle of Britain banished German bombers from the city skies, at least during daylight. But at night, it was a different story. There was, therefore, an unassailable logic in Myra Hess's conception of lunch-time concerts. She put her idea to Sir Kenneth Clark, the Director of the National Gallery, who gave her enthusiastic support. It offered justification and point to his art gallery, which had sent many of its most priceless paintings to the safe haven of a Welsh slate quarry.

Much of the repertoire of these concerts was Austro-German, and the spread of audience went little beyond nearby civil servants and office workers. But this series of 1,698 concerts, running for eight years (1939–1946), symbolized the place of beauty in war-torn London. For an hour each day, civilized values prevailed.

In 1940, two organizations were created which were to dominate nationally the provision of music. One of them, metamorphosed, is still with us, for good or ill. The Council for the Encouragement of Music and the Arts – CEMA in acronym – was formed in June 1940 with Treasury help and grants from the Pilgrim Trust. In 1945, it became the Arts Council of Great Britain. CEMA promoted tours by performing artists, and organized concerts in factories, canteens and even air-raid shelters. On the credit side, it brought welcome employment to the many musicians who, for their various reasons, had not been consumed by the forces. But what they performed was not always to the taste of their culturally challenged audiences; they usually had on offer only what was in their existing repertoire. And the artists soon found that few venues were equipped even with the minimum requirement: an adequate piano.

The second organization was ENSA, formed in October 1940. The acronym stood for Entertainments National Service Association or, among its more sardonic beneficiaries, Every Night Something Awful. As with CEMA, ENSA's artists suffered the miseries of provincial tours – dingy lodgings, damp halls, squalid green rooms and overcrowded train services. But despite the jibes they endured, they found their way to every theatre of war from Libya to Burma.

ENSA's Director of Music was Walter Legge (1906–79), recruited from the recording firm of Columbia. His personal tastes in music were restricted almost exclusively to European, and in particular, Austro-German work. He nevertheless attempted to reach the audiences he found himself catering for by commissioning new music. But the fact that he commissioned from Bax, Moeran and Rawsthorne rather than from Coates, Haydn Wood or Richard Addinsell shows only too clearly how far he remained above his enforced market-place.

The musical establishment perceived symphony and chamber music concerts to be worthy of its attention, but light music, marketed as it was by individuals or small commercial groups, generally had to fend for itself. The BBC was its saviour, with its day-long consumption of records, its house orchestras and its hire of outside groups. The Second World War was the golden age of radio; you worked or relaxed to its music, listened to its news and were cheered by its comedy series.

It was primarily from broadcasts that war-songs were spread – even if they had started in a variety revue or on a band tour. As in previous wars, composers rapidly perceived a public mood and rushed to reflect it, so that the emotional graph of the conflict is quite faithfully reflected in its music. In retrospect, it is embarrassing to remember Neville Chamberlain, worthy though he was, commemorated by band leader Harry Roy at the Café Anglais:

> God Bless You, Mr Chamberlain,
> We're all mighty proud of you,
> You look swell holding your umbrella,
> All the world loves a wonderful feller – so
> God Bless You, Mr Chamberlain.

Mr Chamberlain and his umbrella had first made their musical mark in 1938 at the time of the Munich crisis, in the song *The Umbrella Man*. Before the war, references were covert and decorous. Despite its cradle-song style, Harry Leader's recording of *Little Man You've Had a Busy Day* (selling over 400,000 copies) was widely believed at the time to refer to Adolf Hitler.

In the early stages of the war, songs had an insouciant truculence. Noel Gay, whose *Me And My Girl* was still filling the theatre, contributed *Run, Rabbit, Run* to George Black's 1939 London Palladium revue *The Little Dog Laughed*. In case anyone should miss the symbolism, Gay himself later made it more explicit as *Run, Adolf, Run*. The war, at this stage, while real enough in the air and on the high seas, was dubbed 'phoney' on land. It seemed fair enough to deride the German border defences in *We're Going To Hang Out the Washing on the Siegfried Line* but the humour was soured when, a few months later, the enemy threatened the French Maginot Line, designed to be impregnable. So it probably was, but the Germans never put it to the test. They went round it.

As the war dragged on, the character of its songs changed, in the same manner if not in the same direction as they had in the previous war. They became assertively defensive, as in *There'll Always Be An England*. They rebuffed the nightly raids on the capital with *The King Is Still In London*, much as the Germans themselves would do with *Berlin Is Still Berlin*. Sagging morale was bolstered with renewed visions of what it was all about; of the idyllic England that had been, and would be again, when …

> There'll be bluebirds over
> The White Cliffs of Dover

(no matter that Noël Coward saw them as distinctly off-white, and that, within a few years, local seaside authorities would be begging visitors not to feed the scavenging birds).

Other 'when' songs included *When They Sound the Last All-Clear*, and *When the Lights Go On Again*. For some, the last-named still had resonances of Lord Grey's evocative words in 1914: 'the lights are going out all over Europe … '.

These songs, and others like them, were sung by girl-next-door icons, 'ordinary' young women. Ordinary, that is, in their projection; far from ordinary in charisma and talent. Anne Shelton was one; Joyce Grenfell (with Richard Addinsell's *I'm Going To See You Today*) another. Dominating them all was Vera Lynn. The fact that she was not of striking appearance mattered not. She symbolized every girl friend and fiancée at home, and when her records were relayed in the mess, a reverent silence was both expected and enforced. Her songs conveyed reassurance over faithfulness – a major worry, especially in the later stages of the war, when the country was flooded with hordes of virile young Americans in preparation for the Normandy landings.

The Americans had begun to arrive from late in 1942 onwards; American films were already dominant in our cinemas, and American music was familiar here from records and even from their broadcasting stations. The American forces brought their own entertainment and their own stars with them. We, too, could worship such icons as Artie Shaw, Tommy Dorsey and Glen Miller. Our vocalists now began to distort their vowels in an attempt to sound like the Andrews Sisters. (Crosby and Sinatra were, of course, inimitable.) American dances enlivened our otherwise staid dance halls. Sixty years before, such musicians as Sullivan, followed a little while later by Coleridge-Taylor and others, had exported British musical culture to the USA. The debt was now being repaid, as American style – rhythmic, melodic and especially vocal – made its influence felt.

The Second World War does not seem to have been so rich in major statements of eloquence such as characterized the First, in works by Elgar, Cyril Rootham,

Ernest Farrar and even (in his Requiem) Delius. But at its outset, Michael Tippett made his protest against oppressive, totalitarian régimes in his oratorio *A Child Of Our Time*. Towards its end, Vaughan Williams, in his Symphony No. 6, appeared to warn that another war would be annihilating (although he refused to endorse any such interpretation). Some years after it, Britten – like Tippett, a conscientious objector – attempted a unifying symbolism in his *War Requiem*, when he wrote specifically for soloists from three of the warring nations.

Popular music provided a vulgar wartime eloquence of its own, while light music reflected its victories and campaigns.

The Allied victory at El Alamein was generally perceived as a first ray of hope. As always, Winston Churchill found the right words: 'the end of the beginning'. The Church bells, silent since 1940, were allowed to be rung. Eric Coates produced an Eighth Army March. Various Special Days were held from time to time, with the object of raising money for specific war objects. For Red Army Day in February 1944, Bax and Walton produced works, and Moeran wrote the fanfare mentioned in Chapter 10 which he also used to serve as an introduction to his Overture for a Masque, for Walter Legge at ENSA; 'Legge's Overture', as he usually referred to it.

Coates wrote other war marches, such as *Over to You* (1941) and *Salute the Soldier* (1944). The former was for the Bristol Aeroplane Company, and performed there in December 1941 by the company works band. The latter was in response to a call from Sir Harold Mackintosh's War Savings Committee. Coates, a martyr to asthma and bronchitis, donned his overcoat to conduct it with the Band of the Scots Guards in Trafalgar Square on a cold March day (25 March 1944).

Many songs appeared to be purpose-made for encouraging work – reincarnations, perhaps, of the old capstan songs. Songs such as *Roll Out the Barrel* or *Yes, My Darling Daughter* were rhythmically simple, and invited singing along. They, and their like, would be the basic fodder of the long-running radio programme *Music While You Work*. Mass production of weapons of war depended on repetitive manual movements, the rate of which could be increased if performed to rhythmic music. For this programme, Eric Coates's recently completed march *Calling All Workers* (1940) was used. Written originally for his wife's Red Cross workers, it matched the rhythm of their sewing machines with a simple ostinato, against which its main tune is sharply contrasted (see Ex. 15.1).

Dedicated 'To All Workers', it was one of the unsung contributions to the war effort, and underlines the civilian involvement in it.

The characteristics of the musical rejuvenation which took place after the initial shock of the outbreak of the war suggest that, as in the previous one, there grew a craving for beauty: a neo-Romanticism channelled particularly into the cinema, and into music. It was, perhaps, a down-market romanticism, but when the two media were combined, their force was powerful indeed. Audiences packed concert halls, for anything from symphony concerts down to single recitals. A promoter such as Harold Fielding even found it practicable to add to the established orches-

Ex. 15.1   Eric Coates: *Calling All Workers*

tras with one of his own. It toured provincial towns, spending a week in each one, much as the touring opera companies had done. The programmes would often include a piano concerto. Soloists included relative newcomers such as Moura Lympany and Cyril Smith, established virtuosi such as Solomon and Benno Moiseiwitsch, and veterans such as Mark Hambourg. The pianos were variable. The author remembers Hambourg dismantling much of the elderly instrument in the Grand Theatre, Croydon, before assaulting Tschaikowsky in B flat minor.

The fascination with piano concertos was focused by the cinema (with its huge wartime audiences, far transcending those for music) and by one film in particular. This was the tragic romance, *Dangerous Moonlight* (1941) starring Anton Walbrook. For this story of a Polish pianist-composer who loses his memory after being injured as a fighter-pilot in the Battle of Britain, a piano concerto was needed. Rachmaninoff was said to have been asked to supply one, but declined. In the event, Richard Addinsell wrote a well-crafted one-movement rhapsody: *The Warsaw Concerto*. It was orchestrated by Roy Douglas (born 1907), who was also a noted composer and arranger. Walbrook was himself a reasonable pianist. While he did not play the work on the sound-track, it proved possible to use the actor's own hands for close-ups of the work being played. Addinsell's concerto, which achieved enormous popularity, paid due homage to Rachmaninoff, both in melodic style (and its melodies are very nearly as memorable as those of the master himself) and in harmonic language. Beyond that, Addinsell was writing not only for an aural, but also for a visual medium, and the appearance of his concerto in performance was therefore important. It featured much hand-over-hand arpeggio work and a fair helping of big chordal passages, all of which contributed to the image of one man –

the soloist – battling against the might of the full orchestra. The concerto, in its widely distributed film, made an impact on British audiences, viewed as it was in the months after the fall of France. It may even be that the image of man against orchestra suggested a subconscious metaphor: that of the island race defying the might of the Axis powers.

Addinsell's piece prompted imitations. Probably, too, it was a factor in the wartime popularity of concertos. Many listeners, some of them new to the world of music, now explored the authentic Rachmaninoff. The Second Piano Concerto, in C Minor, was over forty years old in 1945. It now reached wider audiences than it had ever done, especially after its use in two films of that year, *The Seventh Veil* and *Brief Encounter*. The latter film in particular provides a striking illustration of the redoubled power achieved when image and sound are used intelligently together.

Film makers and composers were quick to recognize the rich commercial seam opened up by Addinsell. Hubert Bath had already written a number of distinguished film scores by 1944, when he achieved the greatest success of his life with his *Cornish Rhapsody*, composed for the film *Love Story* of that year. Like *The Seventh Veil*, this was pseudo-psychological claptrap; as the critic Richard Winnington wrote, it was 'straight out of Mabel's Weekly'. But the film was tolerated for Bath's *Rhapsody*, even though in quality it hardly matched Addinsell's work.

Composers learnt that they didn't have to wait for a film commission in order to satisfy concerto-mania. Clive Richardson (1909–98) produced a *London Fantasia* for piano and orchestra (1944) – described in the printed score as 'a musical picture of The Battle of Britain'. Albert Arlen contributed *The Alamein Concerto* (1945). Both battles were fought musically under the banners of Rachmaninoff.

The 'concertos' of Addinsell, Bath, Richardson and Arlen were issued in various forms in original and simplified versions for piano and for organ, in versions of the 'theme' only and others. They were financially rewarding. Serious composers eyed the sales enviously, and tried their hand; E.J. Moeran (Rhapsody No. 3 in F sharp: 1943) and Arnold Bax (*Morning Song*: 1946) among them. Even as late as that year, the film 'concerto' had currency, when Arthur Bliss devised an African Dance *Baraza* for piano and orchestra, for the Thorold Dickinson semi-documentary *Men of Two Worlds*. Mention must also be made of the *Mediterranean Concerto* written by Alberto Semprini (1908–1990) for his radio series *Semprini Serenade*.

It was with films made in or just after the Second World War that film music came into its own, almost as a separate art-form. Addinsell's *Warsaw Concerto* may have overshadowed some of his other fine work in this field, of which that for the David Lean film of Coward's *Blithe Spirit* (1945) was outstanding, displaying as it did a remarkable capacity for matching image with sound. On the other hand, it also became apparent how a potentially great film might actually be marred by mediocre music. How much more enduring might Coward's near-masterpiece *In Which We Serve* (1942) have been, had the Master acknowledged the trite ideas of his own music, and commissioned a score from Walton or Bliss.

The veteran Vaughan Williams – sixty-seven years of age when the war broke out – demonstrated an extraordinary and perhaps unexpected ability to master the techniques of film. His contribution to *The Forty-Ninth Parallel* (1940) yielded some splendid title music, which three years later, and married to Harold Child's words, became a unison song beloved by schoolchildren and their music teachers: *The New Commonwealth*. Bax's major creativity was largely over by 1939, but he, too, turned his attention to film. His music for the film *Malta G.C.* (1942) yielded a march, while that for *Oliver Twist* (1948) survives in a six-movement suite.

Walton, having cut his film teeth on the run-of-the-mill features mentioned in Chapter 12, finally came into his own with a magnificent score for the Leslie Howard film on the subject of R.J. Mitchell, the designer of the Spitfire fighter, *The First of the Few* (1942). He confirmed his dominance in this field with his music for *The Next of Kin* (1942), and for the Laurence Olivier version of Shakespeare's *Henry V* (1944). For *Henry V*, Walton demonstrated an astonishing range, from Elizabethan pastiche to match exactly the artificiality of the opening Globe Theatre shots, to the grave passacaglia as the dying Falstaff 'babbled of green fields'; from the orchestral brilliance with which he treats the traditional Agincourt Song, as that battle rages before us, to the sensuous music to cushion Henry's wooing of Katherine.

CHAPTER SIXTEEN

The Post-War Years: 1945–1960

For the second time in thirty years, young people had fought, seen their friends die and died themselves in war. Those who survived were now returning home. They and their wives determined on social revolution. Nor were they ever likely to be so docile and submissive as their fathers had been. A Labour government was elected. It held long-cherished ideals, and had plans for 'the commanding heights' of industry, for health, social security and education. But the overseas investment portfolio had been sold off to pay for the war, and there was a dollar famine. 'We Work or Want', said the government posters. To earn precious dollars, whatever was made was exported.

The results of the collision between abstract ideals and the all-too-real shortage of funds were the austerity and greyness which were the most marked characteristics of post-war Britain. Bomb-sites were cleared, but for some years remained just wastelands. Housing shortages were universal; hard-to-get licences were needed before you could build. Young couples lived with their parents, with whom in winter they could all freeze together, since there was an almost permanent shortage of fuel. New cars had long waiting lists. Most went for export. Holiday makers attempting to go abroad to escape this gloomy scene found that the amount of money they could take out of the country severely cramped their style. Looming over all was the threat of possible nuclear annihilation.

Compared with the later years of the century, it was nevertheless a period of full employment. In consequence, young people in particular had more spare cash than their parents had ever enjoyed. The problem for them was what to spend it on. The answer was to be found in the entertainments industry, which flourished as never before. There were dance halls, records, radio, theatres and, after 1947, television. These would be the principal outlets for, and occupations of post-war light musicians.

In the late 1940s and in the 1950s, light music was dominated by the big bands and the light orchestras such as those of George Melachrino and Mantovani. These latter groups were often of near-symphonic proportions. Those who directed them or wrote for them were coming from a wider spectrum of musical background than their predecessors had done. Some, however, were still conservatoire-trained. In light music, Trinity College of Music was favoured. Peter Yorke (1902–66) and George Melachrino (1909–65) both trained there. They aspired to their own orchestras, as did Annunzio Mantovani (1905–80), who had himself come up, as so many had done, via the hotels and theatres.

Yet others started as arrangers, usually working for one of these three orchestras – Yorke, Melachrino and Mantovani. Each of these orchestras aspired to an individual sound which would be its characteristic. Melachrino evolved an instantly recognizable close-harmony string style, while Mantovani used what became known as 'cascading strings'. This can be heard in the slow waltz *Charmaine*, where the melodic notes drip downwards, each one overlapping the note before. This style was the work of his arranger Ronald Binge (1910–79), who subsequently followed a successful career as a composer in his own right.

Binge, like his near-contemporary Sidney Torch (1908–90), was one of a number of composers who started their careers in the rapidly growing profession of cinema organist. Like Torch, Binge served in the RAF during the Second World War, and it was the famous fighter-plane of that war which suggested his orchestral piece *Spitfire* (1940). The parallels with Torch continued when he wrote a *Duel for Conductors* (brass band and orchestra) while Torch produced a *Duel for Drummers*. Binge is remembered chiefly for his *Elizabethan Serenade* (1952), the effectiveness of which demonstrates just how much remains to be extracted from a memorable tune, a few triads and the simplest of modulations.

Binge had written the *Elizabethan Serenade* for Mantovani. He turned increasingly to conducting, and made his own recording of it. In his later years, he wrote for films and television, but also produced more novelties for orchestra. If any one of them is picked out here, it should, perhaps, be the exquisite miniature for oboe and small orchestra, *The Water Mill*.

Torch had become a conductor much earlier, directing an RAF Orchestra during the Second World War. From 1953 to 1972, he directed the BBC Concert Orchestra on the popular radio programme *Friday Night Is Music Night*. Both Binge and Torch were commissioned to write works for the annual BBC Light Music Festivals held in the 1950s. So, too, was Geoffrey Bush, for the festival held in 1958. Bush, from a more academic background than Binge or Torch, wrote for it his *Concerto for Light Orchestra*.

From the 1930s onwards, the BBC had become by far the most powerful force for music in the country. Despite the continental commercial stations, the corporation held a monopoly in both radio and television. Its power was consolidated in the post-war years before Independent Television and the pirate and other commercial radio stations opened. This power was nationwide, and for some composers provided a good and regular income. Apart from the musicians mentioned above, other figures such as Charles Shadwell, Stanley Black (BBC Dance Orchestra: 1944–53) Eric and Stanford Robinson (BBC TV and Theatre Orchestras respectively) worked for it. While not primarily composers, they were experienced arrangers, and could and did compose their own light music when called upon to do so. But the BBC could be a fickle organization. It had, of course, to reflect public taste – especially after the competition arrived. But inevitably, it concentrated its commissioning power into a few hands, which meant that a composer could be discarded as rapidly as he had been previously favoured.

The orchestras of Yorke, Mantovani and Melachrino were soon joined by that of Geraldo. As a pianist, Gerald Bright had been much in demand between the wars. Adopting the name Geraldo, he created a musical organization in the post-1945 years which could supply orchestras for most situations, and which was crowned by his own Geraldo Orchestra of up to seventy-five musicians. This ensemble had an associated choir, and nurtured its supporters through a Geraldo Music Club. Geraldo was thus an early model for the music business promoters whose methods would characterize the music scene in the closing years of the century. His music was marked by its polished presentation, a trait which endeared itself to the BBC.

The Corporation itself commissioned Cyril Stapleton to create an ensemble which would represent the very best of its kind: the BBC Showband. This, and others, took part in band and orchestra shows. The divisions – barriers almost – between the various areas of entertainment were beginning to crumble, so that a bandleader such as Billy Cotton could present his band and its vocalists in broadly comic roles. It was no longer enough to play the trombone well; a virtuoso such as George Chisholm had to be something of a comedian as well. Conversely, the comedian Vic Oliver was a useful conductor. Oliver was in fact more than he seemed. To his thousands of variety stage and broadcasting fans, he was a droll comic. But he claimed to have graduated in medicine at Vienna University, to have worked as a conductor under Mahler, and to have conducted Wagner and Verdi at the Graz Opera. In the United Kingdom, he formed and conducted his own British Concert Orchestra, which specialized in light classics. With it, he toured and broadcast, in a regular series for which he wrote his own signature tune: *Prelude to the Stars*.

These bands and orchestras were recruited from the pool of British free-lance players, whose standard – particularly in sight-reading – had, and still has, no superior in the world. This quality was essential to perform, with minimum re-hearsal, the quantities of 'mood music' composed to meet commercial demands during the post-war years. Just as, in the 1920s, publishers had commissioned music which might be used to accompany silent film, so now they did again; this time to create recorded libraries of 'off-the-peg' music to meet the requirements of virtually any film, radio, and eventually television change of scene or mood-establishing sequence.

Torch's own work illustrates well the rise in standards of instrumental virtuosity. His *Shooting Star* exposes the violins and the trombones. The former need to play rapid spiccato passages with precision; the latter some spectacular syncopated solo work with little cover. Composers and arrangers now felt such confidence in those who were to play their work that they could relinquish the 'fail-safe' orchestration of earlier times, when prudence had suggested much doubling in the orchestra of passages which might present difficulties.

Shooting Star is typical mood-music. The most consummate master of this art was not British, but must be mentioned because much of his work has been written during long-term residence here. Robert Farnon (born 1917) was born in Toronto. After an early career as a trumpeter doubling on percussion, he approached composition via arrangement, working for such distinguished figures as Paul Whiteman and André Kostelanetz. Despite this, it seemed likely at first that he would make his mark in serious music. His first two symphonies, No. 1 in D flat (1938) and No. 2 in B (1942), were written for Sir Ernest Macmillan and the Toronto Symphony Orchestra. That the First Symphony was then performed by Eugene Ormandy and the Philadelphia Orchestra must have given the work some kind of accolade.

Farnon came to the United Kingdom as conductor of the Canadian Band of the Allied Expeditionary Forces, and stayed on after the war, working initially as an arranger for such big bands as those of Geraldo and Ted Heath. But he soon showed something approaching genius in his ability to conjure orchestral sounds and harmonies that somehow precisely delineated a character, a scene or a mood.

An early example can be found in *Portrait of a Flirt* (1947). With its gleaming surface-polish, brisk rhythm and sunny optimism, it proved to be a model much imitated. It was transatlantic music, injecting a new element into the jaded British music scene. In his mood music, Farnon showed an ability to match repeatedly the success of *Portrait of a Flirt*, in miniatures such as *Pictures in the Fire* (1947), *Little Miss Molly* (1959) and *A Star Is Born* (1947). *Jumping Bean* also appeared in 1947. Not only did it serve as an introduction to innumerable broadcasts, but in its quirky humour prompted many imitations. Farnon's work had glamour, a quality much lacking in the Britain of the late 1940s. It matched the fashion world of its time – the world of the 'New Look'. It fed the aching need for some kind of escape. The film maker Herbert Wilcox recognized this hungering in what are now period pieces: *Spring in Park Lane* (1948) and *Maytime in Mayfair* (1949). It was, perhaps, inevitable that he should commission Farnon for their music. Although it appeared a few years later, the opulent waltz *Westminster* exactly met the needs of the times. For it was nothing to do with the Houses of Parliament, but a lot to do with expensive shopping at Harvey Nichols.

Like Torch and Farnon, Charles Williams (1893–1978) was also a conductor – associated primarily with the Queen's Hall Light Orchestra, with whom he made many recordings. In the 1930s, he had worked for the Gaumont British Film Company, although most of his work for it was enshrouded in anonymity behind the general credit to Gaumont's director of music: Louis Levy. But in the 1940s, he emerged in his own right. Some of his best work was enshrined in *Kipps* (1941), *Young Mr Pitt* (1942) and *While I Live* (1947). The last-named suffered from a particularly inane story about a Cornishman (why are they always Cornish?) who believes a young girl suffering from memory loss to be the reincarnation of her dead sister. The popularity of the film derived in part from the appeal of Williams's theme for it: *The Dream of Olwen*. Apart from film scores, he too wrote much mood-music for his publisher's library, but his name is chiefly associated with one work, *The Devil's Galop*. It provides an interesting instance where the composer gave his work a title, but a radio producer (in this case seeking introductory music for the series *Dick Barton, Special Agent*) heard in the sounds other resonances. Something similar happened with another radio series: that chronicling the activities of the sleuth Paul Temple. This series had at first used music from Rimsky-Korsakov's *Sheherazade*, which never worked satisfactorily. It was replaced by music from the pen of the song-writer Vivian Ellis. Ellis had written a piece of railway-train mood-music, inspired by the LMS express Coronation Scot. This, of course, had nothing in common with the idea of the detective, but it fitted better, and its fortunes were made by the association with Temple. In this instance, the music seemed to adopt the persona of its new host happily enough. But it was soon perceived that music was sufficiently powerful, when used to back a given sequence of words or dialogue, to qualify or even to alter totally the meaning of those words.

A large proportion of the mood-music written over the decade 1947–57 pandered to the psychological need of the times to escape. It is brightly coloured and optimistic; it sings of a rural arcadia, which it views (from behind city and suburban magic casements) through rose-tinted spectacles. It reflects the West End of London and prefers to ignore the East, at that time still un-gentrified. And it seems always to be travelling away – by shooting star, by train, and even if necessary by old jalopy.

Such escapism was taken further by the current crop of stage musicals, which could transport their audiences to a new world, even if only for a few hours. Ivor Novello and Vivian Ellis were still the chief dream-mongers. Novello's *The Dancing Years* finished at the Adelphi Theatre in July 1944. Less than a year later in April 1945, his *Perchance to Dream* opened at the Hippodrome Theatre. This essay in nostalgia traced a family chronicle from Regency times onwards. Its score provided two enormous hits, the waltz-song *Love Is My Reason* and the ballad-like *We'll Gather Lilacs*. Along the Strand at the Adelphi, C.B. Cochran, a veteran producer from the 1920s and even earlier, brought out *Bless the Bride* (1947). While it had no star of the magnitude of Ivor Novello, it did have the benefit of a book by the expert wordsmith Sir Alan Herbert, and of music by Vivian Ellis. *Bless the Bride* was to crown Ellis's distinguished career. A story of elopement and separation in the France of the time of the Franco-Prussian War, its songs dominated the radio programmes of the times. Such examples as *Ma Belle Marguerite* and *This Is My Lovely Day* still have currency, and indeed potency, today.

Bless the Bride ran for 886 performances. *Perchance to Dream* did even better with 1022. When the time came to replace it, Novello and his librettist Christopher Hassall went back to their well-tried formula of Ruritania and Renunciation. The result was *King's Rhapsody*, the theme of which still had some topical currency. A number of royal houses had fallen since the war, and the British abdication crisis took place only thirteen years earlier. The work, which opened at the Palace Theatre in September 1949, was appropriately Viennese in style. It did not impress the critics, but by this time Novello had such a huge personal following that their verdict hardly mattered. But its success depended on him personally. He died on 5 March 1951, and its closure a few weeks later was inevitable.

Despite these successes, the British musical was again under threat. The menace was the reception which was being given to the American imports, in the vanguard of which were Irving Berlin's *Annie Get Your Gun*, and the Richard Rodgers and Oscar Hammerstein II collaboration, *Oklahoma*. Both reached London in 1947. This was a second invasion by American musicals. Shows like Youmans's *No No Nanette* and Gershwin's *Funny Face* among others, had been seen here in the 1920s, but they had been countered by efficient British products. *Annie* and *Oklahoma* heralded a period of American dominance which in the succeeding years British composers and librettists found difficult to break. Apart from their sheer energy and power, these two musicals in particular offered a far more generous number of hit-songs than their British counterparts. The American musicals were as romantic as those of Novello and, to British audiences, their settings were unusual and even exotic. These imports brought with them a bracing realism. Annie Oakley and Frank Butler had been real enough sharp-shooters in Buffalo Bill's Wild West Show, even if now somewhat glamorized. There really had been an Oklahoma land stampede, and murder was rife in that newly born state. Even so, the killing of the sordid Jud Fry by the show's hero Curly was strong stuff for a musical. Above all, where the British (and indeed Viennese) musical had usually been an indoors affair, these newcomers were refreshing in their open-air exhilaration.

The invasion continued with the arrival in London of *Carousel* (1950) and *South Pacific* (1951), both by Rodgers and Hammerstein. It was to be many years before this American stranglehold was finally broken.

* * *

By 1950, the post-war Labour Government, with its associated austerity, was in terminal decline. Aware of its electoral unpopularity, in 1951 it seized on the fortunate chance of the centenary of the 1851 Great Exhibition to promote a Festival of Britain. The brain-child of Herbert Morrison – the government's most politically astute minister – the Festival was intended not only to provide a shop-window for British culture and material products, but also to offer a public, oppressed for too long by home shortages and general drabness, some colour and spectacle: what the Romans had called *panem et circusae*. The permanent legacy of the Festival is the Royal Festival Hall, a sorry replacement acoustically and architecturally for the Queen's Hall.

Despite this, and other, efforts, the government lost the 1951 election and the Tories were returned for an unbroken thirteen years of power. A paradox ensued. Britain declined as a world power, dismantling its empire and finding no alternative role to its imperialism – as Dean Acheson (US Secretary of State) was to point out with painful realism. Yet within the country itself there was a growing affluence, and an ever-expanding range of ways of spending it. As prime minister Harold

MacMillan – ever the master of the telling, if vulgar, phrase – put it: 'You've never had it so good'.

The results of having it so good were to have a profound effect on the light music industry.

CHAPTER SEVENTEEN

The 1960s to the Present Day

The gradual relaxation of the overseas travel allowance limits combined with the growth of international airlines to promote a massive increase in holidays taken abroad. Cliff Richard and his friends seemed to symbolize a new mood when, on film, they took a London bus to tour Europe; 'We're All Going On A Summer Holiday', he sang from the convenient platform it provided. This new adventurousness created problems for the struggling British resorts and the spas. Piers had re-opened, but housed only slot machines. Seaside orchestras dwindled in numbers, usually to be replaced by an electronic organ. At best, a spa might rise to a dispirited (and dispiriting) trio of piano, violin and cello.

A parallel relaxation of credit regulations led to a vast expansion of hire purchase, which facilitated the acquisition of material goods for home use. These, of course, included television sets, radios and record-players.

Television had made hardly any real impact when the service took its first faltering steps before the war; when transmissions were resumed after it, TV progressed and expanded rapidly. By common consent, it had 'arrived' with its coverage of the Coronation of Queen Elizabeth II in 1953. Television provided work for light musicians. But with each advance the service made, attendances at cinemas declined, so that home viewing replaced public viewing. With the introduction of commercial television and such technical innovations as colour, the trend intensified. Film appeared for the moment to have no effective answer. Radio, however, was able to respond to the challenge of TV with the newly available portable transistor, and with the establishment of pirate offshore radio stations – which led inevitably to the legalizing of commercial broadcasting.

In the recording industry, the invention of the long-playing record made an impact. But of far greater significance for light music was the introduction of the extended-play record, and of the 'single'; not so much in themselves as in their formidable partnership with the portable Dansette and other record-players of this type.

All these structural and technical developments presaged a huge increase in the sheer quantity of 'mechanical' music. It now became a question of some concern as to who, or what, controlled this output.

A tradition of benevolent dictatorship in radio and recording had dominated the early years of what now came to be called the media. Sir John (later Lord) Reith at the BBC had laid down guidelines and had set standards for his corporation. So had Fred Gaisberg and Walter Legge at HMV and Columbia. They and their staff held sway not only over what music was promoted, but also over who was commissioned to produce it. This concentration of commissioning power continued in the post-war years at least in the BBC. It was joined now by the major arts-dispensing organization: the Arts Council of Great Britain. But the introduction of independent television, and subsequently of commercial radio, led to ratings wars and, more particularly, to a serious consideration of who the audiences – or consumers – really were.

It rapidly became apparent that a fundamental shift in the markets for music was taking place; from the middle-aged and elderly to the teenagers and young twenties, and from the so-called middle classes to the lower, or so-called working classes. For the first few years after the ending of the war, young people had not really perceived the power over the music world conveyed to them by that slot of comparative solvency between leaving school, and marrying and starting a family. When, at the beginning of the 1960s, they finally did so, a musical revolution ensued as the music media responded to their enormous spending potential.

Youth now flexed its new-found muscle. Bob Dylan – one of the icons of the late 1950s – commented: 'Your sons and your daughters are beyond your command'.[1] Previous societies had at least respected their elders as the repositories of standards, both moral and cultural. But now, there seemed little point in respecting those who had not, as it seemed, had the wisdom to avoid two world wars, who had not solved the problems of inequality, colour, disease and poverty, and had created an Age of Anxiety under the shadow of nuclear weapons.

Even as late as the 1940s and 1950s, standards of culture were still being passed on in schools by teachers – expert in their specialisms – who indicated what was, and what was not, worthwhile in our cultural legacy. But from the 1960s onwards, the new educational orthodoxies laid down (in state schools at least) that didacticism must give way to questioning. That expounding of the qualities of a work of art by an expert must give way to the child's own exploration of it. Or not.

Inevitably, for the vast majority of young people, concepts of quality, which had until then been passed on from generation to generation, were effectively discounted. Worse – they became weapons in the battle between the generations. The new consumers rejected the music offered by the professionals: the big bands of Cyril Stapleton and the symphonic-style orchestras of Mantovani and Melachrino. Rejected, too, were the older generation of singers, Frankie Vaughan, Denis Lotis, Matt Monro and many others, whose appeal now shifted to parents.

From the United States came the first manifestations of new styles, ranging from Elvis Presley and Bill Haley's rock styles, from Dolly Parton's country and western style to Bob Dylan's pseudo-folk protest songs. From the early 1960s onwards, these fed into and influenced a British 'pop' phenomenon, led by such groups as the Beatles and the Rolling Stones.

The chronicling of this major movement, however, has no place in this study except to describe the extent – which was considerable – to which it contributed to the decline in the provision of British light music. But within the movement, major talents were to be found. Rick Wakeman, Eric Clapton and the group Pink Floyd are mentioned as examples. Paul McCartney and John Lennon, once past the earliest Beatles' songs, demonstrated a marked capacity to explore and develop, and in McCartney's case, a wistful lyricism of melody which is firmly in an English tradition of centuries' duration.

As the groups matured, the more adventurous looked for a significance beyond mere expression of basic emotion. Emerson, Lake and Palmer endeavoured to reinterpret Mussorgsky and Tschaikowsky in terms of the pop trio, Jon Lord enlisted Malcolm Arnold and a symphony orchestra in an attempt to marry classical and pop styles, while Pink Floyd (in *Dark Side of the Moon*) used elements of *Musique Concréte* ranging from the sounds of aircraft to those of cash registers to make comment on aspects of contemporary materialism.

Most influential of all were the Beatles. Exploring human isolation and loneliness, their *Sergeant Pepper's Lonely Hearts Club Band* was in its time a landmark. Its instrumentation went far beyond guitars and drum-kit. There were french horns, recorders and the sitar, on which George Harrison exercised his newly acquired skills. The subjects ranged from the young girl leaving home to meet her man from the motor-trade ('What did we do that was wrong?', wail her parents) to the couple looking forward only to a pointless holiday on the Isle of Wight – 'if it's not too dear'. The heartless jollity of the tune seems to emphasize their non-communicating misery: 'send me a postcard, drop me a line … '. The Beatles have no solution to offer, except the philosophy of their Maharishi – expounded by George Harrison in his song *Within You, Without You*:

Try to realise you are really very small …

They attempted to give simple utterance to universal human hopes. The intention behind Beethoven's D major melody which sets the opening of Schiller's *Ode to Joy* as a great universal song is not so far in intention from John Lennon's *Give Peace a Chance* – one easily memorable phrase, repeated mantra-like to create a hypnotic effect:

Ex. 17.1   John Lennon and Yoko Ono: *Give Peace a Chance*

The talents of the pop artists were usually musically untrained, and this was to prove a disadvantage when they ventured beyond the confines of their basic art. Thus, when McCartney attempted his *Liverpool Oratorio*, the technical problems involved made it necessary for him to employ the services of the highly respected professional composer and arranger Carl Davis (1936–). Nothing to be ashamed of here; Gershwin had Ferde Grofé (1892–1972) to supervise the orchestration of *Rhapsody in Blue*; but Gershwin learned fast, and thereafter mastered the art.

Professional music-making, to an extent hardly paralleled in other arts, with the exception of live theatre, cinema and TV, relies on an infrastructure of interrelated techniques. For these, training is usually necessary. Rarely can a composer present his work directly to his audience. He needs numerous instrumentalists and singers, for whom he must provide an elaborate code (notation) which they must under-stand, read, and then perform (since in British professional music organizations at least, there is no time for learning – as, for example, a young pianist learns a piece or an actor learns a role). Since the composer cannot have the instrumentalists permanently at his command in his studio, he must imagine and actually hear in his mind the combination of sounds, harmonies and instrumental timbres that he wishes to produce. This, and the way the music is to be performed, must be worked out and then precisely notated. Such were the skills possessed by Sullivan, German, Haydn Wood, Eric Coates, Robert Farnon and many of the other giants of light music. The music those skills had produced had no appeal to the youth of the 1960s, who called for 'madder music' – and had the financial muscle to command it. They would provide their own music.

A musical Do-It-Yourself movement began, whose practitioners disdained skills they could never hope to master. Their new music was basic, raw and and direct. It was built around the guitar, whose electric counterparts made it highly suitable for solo or group playing. It was a matter of a few hours to master three simple chords, armed with which it was possible to harmonize any diatonic tune. This repertoire of basic chords could then be gradually enlarged to include more exotic ones. Rhythm would then be added by drums (not including timpani, which require an acutely sensitive ear for tuning). To the basic drum-kit could be added various oriental and West Indian percussion instruments.

To the new performers, the trained voice was anathema; even the sophisticated tones of a Frank Sinatra, or the subtle phrasing of a Tony Bennett had no place. Clarity of diction – so marked a feature of the vocalists of the 1920s and the 1930s – was abhorred. Regional accents were preferred, distortion of vowels prized. The hoarse, untrained teenage voice was something with which the new teenage audi-ences could readily identify. But even then, some performing groups allowed the machinery of the amplified instruments to obliterate the vocal sounds, so that the resulting noise might almost seem to offer a potent metaphor for the twentieth century: Man crushed by the machinery of his own invention. A mere trio consist-ing of percussion, electric guitar and keyboards could, and usually did, achieve more sheer volume than a full symphony orchestra.

In the 1970s, the keyboards began to include the synthesizer, which in itself could achieve a variety of sound previously available only from the use of a number of different instrumentalists. The electric guitar, in the hands of a player of genius such as Eric Clapton, was capable of both expressive power and an astonishing range of tone colour. But the overwhelming characteristic of the 'New Music' was the relentless, motoric pulse of its percussion.

Huge numbers flocked to hear the most popular groups, which eventually found even the biggest halls inadequate and moved outdoors, to open-air pop festivals at places such as the Isle of Wight, Woodstock or Glastonbury. There was in this a strong element of rejection of the Establishment, and of one of its tools – parental control. Mud, drugs, dress as you please or not at all. Such 'festivals' tended to be sordid and insanitary.

The impact of the pop revolution on all aspects of music was immense. It actually benefited serious music, when recording companies could divert some of the profits from best-selling pop records to subsidizing discs of the less popular serious works. But its impact was greatest on that which it replaced. That is to say, on the gamut of light music from the crooner derivatives and latter-day ballad singers, from the jazz and close harmony groups to the big bands and orchestras, and from the cinema organists to the Charlie Kunz and Billy Mayerl-style pianists. Cash-rich young people, often replete in the 1960s with maintenance grants, wanted their own music, and their purses could dictate to the established record companies and to the media. Youth created the market for the new record companies being set up. Youth could dictate to commercial radio and to the newly organized Independent Television. In the process, viewing and listening audiences were pulled from the licence-financed BBC, whose response was inevitably to follow its competitors down into the market place.

Light music of quality was under siege. The new electronically amplified instruments and synthesizers seemed to render traditionally trained musicians redundant. Sir Thomas Beecham had once remarked that the English do not like music, only the noise it makes. By the late 1960s, a bigger noise could be made by amplifying a few electric guitars and drums than by a whole symphony orchestras. In due course, the synthesizer could be programmed to do that, and much more, by itself. In the 1980s, in the race to prove that anybody could do anything, schools eagerly lapped up the new technology, which made the 'creation' of 'music' so easy that anybody probably could do it. But if anybody could do it, was it worth doing? For, as Kingsley Amis wrote so perceptively and cryptically:

More means Worse.

The highly professional sessions men now found themselves reduced in the recording studio to a simple framing of the pop group, playing everlasting long notes to provide a bland backwash.

The platform, or shop window, for light music had been taken over. The various circumstances discussed in the foregoing had unintentionally, but unerringly, conspired to starve it of the essential oxygen of need. British light music had entered a Dark Age.

In previous Dark Ages, the medieval church, through its priests and monks, provided some thread of cultural continuity. Not this time. A kind of me-too-ism afflicted a supine Church as it hung on to the sweatshirts of the rampant pop musicians. The Evangelic wing, in particular, rejected traditional hymns and organ-accompanied services in a bid to attract young members. 'Hymns Ancient and Modern' on the organ retreated before the onslaught of 'Mission Praise' on guitars and drums. But church pop was insipid in comparison with real pop, and self-conscious in execution.

But light music has never been completely extinguished, and its enthusiasts have fought back. As an endangered species, British music, and British light music in particular, attracted the attention of a number of preservation societies. These range from general 'umbrella' societies such as the British Music Society, the British Light Music Society and the late, lamented Vintage Light Music Society, to groups promoting and researching a particular composer, such as the Percy Whitlock Society or the London Billy Mayerl Society. The BBC maintained a light music presence, most notably through its Concert Orchestra. The showcase for this splendidly versatile orchestra remained the regular weekly radio programme, *Friday Night Is Music Night* – still with us at the time of writing.

The preservation societies helped in a practical way by promoting recordings of especially neglected composers. The big recording companies tended to be loath to explore, preferring the security of the thirtieth recording of *The Planets* to something untried and untested. But some of the smaller labels such as Lyrita, Chandos, Hyperion and Marco Polo were prepared to explore. In the 1990s, for example, Marco Polo issued admirable compact discs of representative works by Sir Frederick Cowen, Ronald Binge, Frederick Curzon, Haydn Wood and many others. The admirable orchestras involved were rarely British, but were from Slovakia, Eire, and even South Africa.

Against all the economic odds, fine light music continued to be written. From the 1950s onwards, a new generation of composers, born after the 1914–18 war, joined the veterans. This generation, many of whom are still active at the time of writing, displays as much talent – and in at least two instances genius – as its predecessors. But it has had to seek different markets for its wares. Radio broadcasts have shrunk in quantity and symphony orchestras have been reluctant to mix symphonies and concertos with light music suites and intermezzi. Moreover, the overture, once a natural spot for light music, now rarely finds a place. Major festivals such as the annual Promenade Concerts, still emulate their founder Sir Henry Wood in featuring much contemporary serious music, and are beginning to find a place – if somewhat gingerly – for some of the better quality pop music. But Wood's policy of offering light music after the interval did not long survive him. With fewer professional orchestras and ensembles performing light music, fewer recordings of it, and with the broadcasting and concert-giving authorities no longer championing it, new outlets were needed.

There was television; no longer TV concerts of light music such as had been a feature of the early days of the medium, but incidental and 'titles' music were still needed. TV advertising needed music, from 'jingles' upwards. There was the residual film industry, which in recent years has shown signs of recovery. And there was also à rapidly growing educational market, needing not-too-demanding music for tuned percussion and the ubiquitous family of recorders.

In this educational field, the breakdown of subject barriers created, as a by-product almost, a need for musical/dramatic works in which children of all ages could take part, works which were yet not so elaborate in their demands as those pioneer examples by Benjamin Britten. In the wake of the expanding teams of locally employed peripatetic instrumental teachers, an ever-increasing number of youth and amateur orchestras and wind-bands arose. And there were choirs – both secular and sacred; not of a size such as Elgar and Parry wrote for, and no longer able, therefore, to afford a full orchestra to play for them, but still providing opportunities for those who could write tunefully and needed only small instrumental forces. There was, too, still a place for those who had the vision to find a striking or unusual subject. The composers now discussed have made their mark in one or more of these markets.

One of the earliest of the post-First World War generation was John Addison (1920–98). A graduate and subsequently a member of staff of the Royal College of Music, he had hoped to become a concert pianist. This was not to be, and he found instead a ready demand for his music, achieving success with his ballet score *Carte Blanche* and his *Trumpet Concerto*. But it is for his film scores that he is primarily known. There are over sixty of these. They include the film about the legless war pilot Douglas Bader (his brother-in-law), *Reach for the Skies* (1956), the historical fantasia *The Charge of the Light Brigade* (1968) and the film chronicling the 1944 Battle of Arnhem, *A Bridge Too Far* (1977). His work for the John Osborne film *The Entertainer*, starring Lord Olivier as the seedy comedian Archie Rice, demonstrates his versatility, with the insight it shows into the appalling standards of the last variety theatre orchestras.

Sir Malcolm Arnold was born a year later, in 1921. Like Addison, he studied with Gordon Jacob at the Royal College of Music, but he also studied the trumpet. Arnold's career at the College was, to say the least, chequered. Such incidents, described by Piers Burton-Page,[2] as stuffing fish down the pipes of the organ in the Great Hall offer pointers to the man who would in 1956 be an accomplice of Gerard Hoffnung in the Hoffnung Music Festivals. For the first one, he wrote the Grand Grand Overture, Op. 57. It was scored for full orchestra, organ, three vacuum cleaners, one floor polisher and four rifles. The rifles were needed by an execution squad, whose job it was to silence the vacuum cleaners. Messrs Hoover Ltd had provided a programme note. The humour went on even after Hoffnung's death from leukaemia in 1959. For the 1961 Hoffnung Astronautical Musical Festival, he contributed not only a Beethoven satire, the Leonora No. 4 overture – a merry melange of all three Leonoras together with Fidelio – but also a Grand Concerto Gastronomique, Op. 76.

The humour, and the insouciance of some of the melodies, together with their occasional brashness and vulgarity, may blind us to a perception of Arnold as a major composer of his times. He is a rigorous symphonic thinker, capable of great profundity. But within his huge output are to be found many examples of purely light music. Typical are the English, Scottish, Cornish, Irish and Welsh Dances for orchestra. The tunes are his own and the orchestration, as befits an ex-trumpeter who heard the orchestra from the inside, is brilliant. For a few years in the mid-1960s, Arnold lived in Cornwall. Here he demonstrated the extraordinary litmus quality of his creative imagination, which responded intensely to both Cornish landscape and to Cornish folk. While in no sense the 'artist-in-residence' that Britten became in Aldeburgh, Arnold in Cornwall easily and naturally took what he found and transmuted it into musical gold. Since Cornwall is strong in brass bands, it was natural that, as a brass man, he should write a march for his local band. This was the march *The Padstow Lifeboat*, Op. 94. He found, too, that Cornish folk are natural singers, and that many Cornish towns had their own repertoire of carols. These had been written by humble nineteenth- and early twentieth-century organists, and are hardly known outside the Duchy, except in Cornish communities. For the simple, yet sturdy, work of one of them – Thomas Merritt (1863–1908) – Arnold conceived an admiration. He lavished loving care on the orchestration of some of Merritt's work, including the Coronation March Merritt had entered (with no success) for the competition to celebrate the crowning of King Edward VII in 1901. All this work on Arnold's part was for a concert which he conducted in Truro Cathedral in 1968 to mark the sixtieth anniversary of Merritt's death. For it, he wrote a Salute to Thomas Merritt, for two brass bands and combined amateur orchestras of the Duchy. Strong Cornishmen wept under the emotional force of the occasion.

If this aspect of Arnold's work has been dwelt on here, it is because work with and for amateurs has been one of the avenues which have assumed great importance in recent years for composers of light music. But amateurs do not like to admit they are playing music specifically designed for them. Arnold never falls into the trap of writing down to them. His *Little Suite* No. 1, Op. 53, is brilliant in effect when played by professionals, but is yet well within the capacity of a reasonably competent amateur orchestra.

The apparent high spirits and real ebullience and energy of much of Arnold's light music is, perhaps, a façade behind which shelters a tragic and fragile man. Even in such transparently light work as the Concertos for harmonica and orchestra, Op. 46, and for guitar and chamber orchestra, Op. 67, the wistful, longing spirit is not far from the surface. The rhythmic quirks and tear-jerking sentimental tunes, when set starkly against darker thoughts as they often are in the symphonies, face us with some of the most disturbing music of the century. But in the purely light works, the humour is robust enough. As a brass player, Arnold will have endured enough the long periods of counting rests while the strings play countless rapid semi-quavers, only to be given a simple fanfare when finally allowed to break silence. It is, therefore, a funny inside joke when in the English Dances (1951) the strings as usual play their passage-work, only to be obliterated by the spectacular, and very loud, brass writing. The humour, too, of the third of the Cornish Dances

(1966) – a very tubby slow march of hilariously banal harmony and non-existent melody – will not be lost on anyone familiar with Cornish male voice choirs and their partiality to loud 'amen' cadences. But this gentle teasing apart, no one has penetrated the elusive Cornish magic so profoundly as Arnold. He has seen the desolate, haunted mine workings, and has experienced the trembling anticipation of distant approaching dances to welcome Spring, and has transmuted these into evocative sound.

It is this capacity which for many years led film directors to make him their first choice for background music of all kinds. Even for such a fluent writer, the sheer number of film scores – over one hundred – represents a staggering quantity of notes on manuscript paper. These scores range from a school song for the girls of St Trinians to the haunting melody written for *Whistle Down the Wind* (1961). Here we must touch on a problem with Arnold's film music. It is axiomatic that background music must be just that. The trouble, sometimes, with Arnold's work is that it is too good as music. It finds difficulty with being anonymous, and thus draws attention to itself. And when, rarely, inspiration does fail him, some of the devices on which he will fall back – such as a rather threadbare chromatically rising crescendo – can be tiresome. But against this must be set such masterly scores as those for *The Inn of the Sixth Happiness* (1958) and for the David Lean film *Bridge on the River Kwai* (1957). For the latter, Arnold won an Academy Award.

Less well known than Malcolm Arnold are Madeleine Dring (1923–77) and Trevor Duncan (1924–). Like Arnold, Dring was a product of the Royal College of Music. She specialized in songs and miniatures. Her deft craftsmanship can be heard in *Lady Luck*, an orchestral miniature for strings, woodwind and touches of xylophone, somewhat reminiscent of Robert Farnon's *Flirt*. Her eye was always firmly fixed on the enjoyment of those performing her work; a trait to be admired in such a piece for two pianos as her *Tarantella*.

Like Dring, Trevor Duncan (pseudonym for Leonard Trebilco, a Cornish name, although he was born in the South London district of Camberwell) is one of those composers whose music is well known – but anonymously. He has written many single-movement pieces such as *High Heels* or *Tomboy*, together with orchestral suites, film and TV scores. His best-known music is the first movement (*March*) from his *Little Suite* for orchestra. Just as Coates's *By the Sleepy Lagoon* achieved fame after its association with the radio programme Desert Island Discs, so Duncan's march is known as the titles music for the BBC television series *Dr Finlay's Casebook*. Why did it work so perfectly on the audience's psyche? Perhaps because of its clean lines and bracing tunes, which suggested resonances of the perceived Scottish landscape and the well-scrubbed Scots characters.

Contemporary with Dring and Duncan is Ernest Tomlinson (1924–). Tomlinson studied at the erstwhile Royal Manchester College of Music, and made an early reputation as an arranger and organist. He has devoted much time and energy to promoting the cause of British light music, through such agencies as the Composers' Guild of Great Britain and the Light Music Society. Perhaps because of this, his own music has not had the exposure it deserves. His *Little Serenade* and the two suites of English Folk Dances are good examples of his gentle, fastidious style.

Ron Goodwin (1929–) has written many orchestral miniatures but his career has been spent mainly in film work, where, as a 'safe pair of hands', his skills have made him into a film-score doctor. The score of the luckless film *Battle of Britain* (1969: net loss ten million dollars worldwide) was started by Sir William Walton, and then expanded into Walton-style pastiche by Malcolm Arnold when Walton – a painstaking but slow composer – got 'stuck'. According to Piers Burton-Page,[3] the last third of the 'Battle in the Air' sequence is by Arnold, but most of what Walton had written was replaced by Goodwin's music. Goodwin does seem to have a particular aptitude for stirring war films; among his best are those scores for *633 Squadron* (1964) and *Where Eagles Dare* (1969).

Like Ernest Tomlinson, Peter Hope (1930–) studied in Manchester, and also like him began his career as a staff musician, arranging for a music publisher. His light orchestral suite *Ring of Kerry* won him an Ivor Novello Award in 1969. Its three movements (*Jaunting Car*, *Lough Leane* and *Killorgin Fair*) celebrate that part of South West Ireland which had also held such fascination for both Moeran and Bax. In *Ring of Kerry* we can hear Hope's talent – one which he shared with the two elder men – for projecting an open-air ambience. Of his other works, one of the most substantial is a trumpet concerto.

Richard Rodney Bennett (1936–) studied at the Royal Academy of Music under Sir Lennox Berkeley and Howard Ferguson, following this with a spell of tuition from Pierre Boulez. An impressive pedigree, yet it seems likely that he learned most from thorough acquaintance with the work of Walton. A composer of infinite versatility and resource, his output ranges from songs and arrangements for artists as diverse as Eartha Kitt and the King's Singers to string quartets and concertos. He is the son of the poet Royden Barrie, whose lyrics, set with such popular success by Eric Coates, included *I Heard You Singing* and *Birdsongs at Eventide*. While Bennett's work in no way resembles that of Coates (it does occasionally echo Walton), it cannot escape one Coates characteristic. For like Coates, Bennett seems to be a man-about-town. In Coates's music, this appears as the sumptuousness of the ballroom or the busy-ness of the streets. Bennett's music has the slightly smoke-infused feel of the night-club. He has appeared in cabaret with Marian Montgomery for whom he has written songs, but he is perfectly capable of singing them himself, to his own accompaniment. The wry, ironic wit of *Let's Go and Live in the Country* parallels the attitude of Coates, who would if necessary make the occasional excursion to the home counties but otherwise saw 'ruraltania' as fit only for the production of turnips.

Bennett, a splendid pianist, is adept at most styles from avant-garde classical to ragtime. In his Four-Piece Suite for two pianos (1974), the movements are clever pastiches of American pop styles: Caribbean, blues, ragtime and rock. Bennett puts his personal stamp on each movement. The ragtime, for example, is in waltz time, while the blues are country and western blues. And is not Bennett teasing his listeners in his first movement – *Samba Triste*– which threatens at any moment to turn into Cole Porter's song *Just One of Those Things*?

Among his latest works is the *Partita for Orchestra* (1995), the commissioning of which by a public company (British Telecom) illustrates a promising trend for new music as traditional commissioning funds dwindle away. Bennett stated that he hoped he had written a 'lively and accessible' piece. The idiom owes something to that of late Walton, but so eclectic is Bennett that the first movement finds echoes also of Richard Rodgers in South Pacific mode and (in the last movement) of Benjamin Britten at church on Sunday morning. There is, overall, a sheer sensuous beauty of sound; and in the central movement, a certain misty, twilight quality which had occasionally come over Bennett's work from as far back as the 1960s, when he wrote his superb, understated work for the film of Thomas Hardy's *Far from the Madding Crowd* (1967). For this score he was nominated for an Academy Award. He was nominated, too, for his work for the film of Agatha Christie's *Murder on the Orient Express* (1974). Bennett's solution to the problems posed by this film was not an obvious one. It was, nevertheless, one which worked triumphantly. The express itself is the constant backdrop, but there had also to be luxury and opulence. Ordinary 'Coronation Scot' music would not suggest the distinctiveness of this particular train. For the opulence, Bennett conceived a waltz; the cross-rhythms set up within it suggested the complex engine mechanisms. Connoisseurs may not sit through the film these days, but many will savour over and over again the moment the express, buoyed up by Bennett's waltz, first gets under way.

Some composers looked again to the needs of religion as a market for their wares. With the pop revolution in full spate, the churches themselves felt the need to prod their musicians into a response. John Rutter (1945–) was one who needed no prodding. Rutter's carols, while in no sense pop, shedded any inhibiting churchiness, and were an immediate success. He first came to notice with his early *Nativity Carol*, which achieved great popularity with singers, and appeared in the second volume of *Carols for Choirs* (1967). Rutter has many choral arrangements to his credit, but was to write as many original carols, in which, like the *Nativity Carol*, he wrote both words and music. His work includes *Shepherd's Pipe Carol*, *Donkey Carol* and *Jesus Child*, while his arrangements of *The Twelve Days of Christmas* and *The Sans Day Carol* are now established repertoire pieces. These all typify a trend in the last four decades of the century for church music to approach the condition of light music.

Rutter's versatility embraces the secular pop cantata with narrator. A good example is *The Reluctant Dragon*. It is structured around amusing pastiches of Victorian ballad, 1950s Bop and a particularly wicked apeing of Britten/Pears, whose own sense of humour was notoriously limited. Space is even found for a droll quotation from *Tristan and Isolde*. Rutter's more substantial work includes settings of the *Magnificat* and of the *Requiem*.

Why include them in light music? The point is arguable, but the one constant quality to be found throughout his work is fluent, memorable melody, while much of it features also syncopated rhythms and piquant, even exotic, harmony. These had been the qualities of popular light music, and light music had for many years kept itself to the secular field. This had not always been the case, for late medieval composers had occasionally based their masses on popular songs of the day, and, as was noted in Chapter 1, in a later age Haydn saw no reason to adopt a different style when writing his sacred work.

But Rutter's work does not venture far beyond the gratification of the performer and listener. It makes no pretence of offering a spiritual experience akin to that of Bach's *Magnificat*, Stravinsky's *Symphony of Psalms* or, in our own day the work of Tavener. In a word, there is no mysticism. The philosophy – such as it is – appears therefore to complement, at admittedly a high level of skill and artistry, the pop pseudo-religious work beloved of the evangelical wing of the Church, and as such achieves its purpose well.

From his position as a leading musician of the Methodist Church, Dr W.S. Lloyd Webber (1914–82) had seen a similar need, and catered for it with such cantatas as *The Saviour*. His cantata is in the tradition of Stainer's *The Crucifixion*, eminently practical and beautifully written, but in an idiom deriving from an earlier age, and therefore limited in appeal.

William Lloyd Webber also wrote chamber music, many songs, some works for organ and an orchestral tone poem: *Aurora* (1951). His son Andrew (now Lord Lloyd Webber; 1948–) dedicated to his memory a Requiem (1984), and also wrote for his brother the cellist Julian Lloyd Webber a set of Variations (1978). But with the exception of these, he has so far eschewed the standard musical forms in favour of the stage musical. The first of them appeared in 1968, at a time when publishers identified a need for new musical material suitable for production by schools looking for an alternative to Gilbert and Sullivan. In its original pop cantata version, *Joseph and the Amazing Technicolour Dreamcoat* made little impact. It took adaptation with many additions and alterations before its success in 1973 at the Albery Theatre, and subsequently in 1991 at the London Palladium.

By then, other Lloyd Webber stage musicals had established their credentials, beginning with *Jesus Christ Superstar* (1971). Critics found it banal. Religious leaders took exception to the portrayal of Christ as a pop star. But the public flocked to it, as they would to its successors: *Evita* (1976), *Cats* (1981), *Starlight Express* (1984), *Phantom of the Opera* (1986), *Aspects of Love* (1989) and *Sunset Boulevard* (1993).

There is in Lloyd Webber's work a certain short-windedness in the melodies, and an uncertainty in the creation of contrasting themes. The hit melodies, too, are spread somewhat thinly. Where he has scored is in finding subjects with which the public find an affinity. Eva Peron, T.S. Eliot's felines, Gaston Leroux's disfigured anti-hero, a passé Hollywood star and even roller-skaters imitating trains; all have been grist to his mill, and powerful magnets to the coach-parties and tourists who support him year after year. As with Ivor Novello, the appeal has been at least as much for theatrical effect as for musical qualities. But Novello did not translate well from London, his spiritual home. Lloyd Webber, to his credit, has been at least as successful in the United States as in London, and has virtually stemmed the tide of American musicals which for some thirty years after the 1939–45 war threatened to submerge the British product.

By the1980s, Lloyd Webber's domination of the musical stage was as complete as Sullivan's had been a century before. D'Oyly Carte had built his Palace Theatre from his share of the profits of the Gilbert/Sullivan/D'Oyly Carte triumvirate. Though at least as successful, Lloyd Webber's work can bear no comparison in quality with that of Sullivan. But there is a certain symmetry in the fact that D'Oyly Carte's Palace Theatre – which brought him no luck – is now the hub of the Lloyd Webber empire. For the musical wheel has turned full circle and we are back at our starting point.

When Gilbert and Sullivan were at the height of their powers, their success and that of their imitators and successors was based on the living musical theatre. But Sullivan stood on the threshold of a vast expansion in light music which would derive from the needs of the ballad singer, the rapidly proliferating light orchestras and the ensembles of the holiday resorts. Their age passed, to be replaced in part by the needs of on the one hand the media, and on the other the needs of the amateur and education-based groups.

Musicians of talent and adaptability can still make a good living from the media. But dependence on the world of the amateur, of music in schools and of youth orchestras looks increasingly precarious. For the virtual elimination of grant aid to amateur choirs and orchestras has reduced many of them to a pale reflection of their former glory, and has withered their grass roots. It is, in fact, remarkable how little the general public realizes just how much expense is incurred in mounting even an amateur orchestral concert, let alone an amateur-staged musical comedy or operetta. In education, schools in the public sector in particular have tended in recent years to constrict music as the other demands of the National Curriculum have taken priority. The youth orchestras which have been the musical glory of this country find their standards and even their very existence under attack. They had come into being as a direct result first of Mary Ibberson's Rural Music School movement, and then of the peripatetic music teaching service organized through the agency of the local education authorities. Through the philistinism of successive governments, funds have dried up. Music has been an obvious target for economy. Light music has taken its share of attrition.

But insecurity and struggle to obtain a hearing have always been the partners of British musicians. And from Handel onwards, musicians have usually found a way of overcoming indifference to their wares.

Notes

1. Bob Dylan, *The Times They Are A-Changing*.
2. Burton-Page, Piers (1994), *Philharmonic Concerto*, Methuen, p. 15.
3. Ibid., p. 104.

Bibliography

This bibliography is divided into two sections: (1) major sources of information, and (2) equally important sources, but ones in which light music is not a prime concern of the author.

1. Major sources

Bailey, Leslie (1952), *The Gilbert and Sullivan Book*, Cassell.
Baker, Richard Anthony (1990), *Marie Lloyd: Queen of the Music Halls*, Robert Hale.
Berry, Patricia Dee (1995), *Theatrical London*, Alan Sutton Publishing.
Blom, Eric (1942), *Music in England*, Penguin.
Coates, Eric (1953), *Suite in Four Movements*, Heinemann.
Cole, Lesley (1979), *Noël Coward and his Friends*, Weidenfeld and Nicholson.
Collins, José (1932), *The Maid of the Mountains. Her Story*, Hutchinson.
Courtneidge, Cicely (1953), *Cicely*, Hutchinson.
Darewski, Herman (1937), *Musical Memories*, London.
Dawson, Peter (1951), *Fifty Years of Song*, Hutchinson.
Delgado, Alan (1971), *Victorian Entertainment*, David & Charles.
Dickinson, Peter (1999), *Marigold, The Music of Billy Mayerl*, Oxford University Press.
Disher, Maurice Willson (1955), *Victorian Song*, Phoenix House.
Finck, Herman (1937), *My Musical Memories*, Hutchinson.
Foreman, Lewis (1994), *Music in England. 1885–1920*, Thames.
Foreman, Lewis (ed.) (1981), *The Percy Grainger Companion*, Thames.
Foreman, Lewis (ed.) (1987), *From Parry to Britten: British Music in Letters: 1900–1945*, Batsford.
Freeman, Michael (1993), 'Josef Holbrooke and the Music Hall', *British Music*, vol. 15, British Music Society.
Hancock-Child, Ro (1993), *A Ballad Maker (C. Armstrong Gibbs)*, Thames.
Hindmarch, Alan (1996), *Leslie Stuart*, Issue 44, Vintage Light Music Society.
Hudson, Derek (1945), *Norman O'Neill: A Life of Music*, Quality Press.
Huntley, John (1947), *British Film Music*, Shelton Robinson.
Hyman, Alan (1978), *Sullivan and His Satellites*, Chappell & Co.
Irving, Ernest (1959), *Cue for Music*, Dennis Dobson.

Jacobs, Arthur (1986), *Arthur Sullivan*, Oxford University Press.

Jaffa, Max (1981), *A Life on the Fiddle*, Hodder & Stoughton.

Kent, Greta (1983), *A View from the Bandstand*, Sheba.

Kington, Beryl (1993), *Rowley Rediscovered*, Thames.

Lambert, Constant (1934), *Music Ho!*, Faber.

Larkin, Colin (ed.) (1994), *The Guinness Who's Who of Stage Musicals*, Guinness Publishing.

Lee, Edward (1982), *Folksong and Music Hall*, Routledge.

Lloyd, Stephen (1995), *Sir Dan Godfrey*, Thames.

Mackerness, E.D. (1964), *A Social History of English Music*, Routledge and Kegan Paul.

Morley, Sheridan (1987), *Spread a Little Happiness (The First Hundred Years of the British Musical)*, Thames and Hudson.

Nettel, Reginald (1946), *The Orchestra in England*, Jonathan Cape.

Pearsall, Ronald (1973), *Victorian Popular Music*, David & Charles.

Pearsall, Ronald (1975), *Edwardian Popular Music*, David & Charles.

Pearsall, Ronald (1976), *Popular Music of the Twenties*, David & Charles.

Pearson, Hesketh (1935), *Gilbert and Sullivan*, Hamish Hamilton.

Russell, Dave (1987), *Popular Music in England 1840–1914*, Manchester University Press.

Sayers, W. Berwick (1915), *Samuel Coleridge-Taylor: Musician*, Cassell.

Scholes, Percy (1947), *The Mirror of Music. 1844–1944*, London.

Scott, William Herbert (1932), *Edward German: An Intimate Biography*, Cecil Palmer.

Scowcroft, Philip L. (1997), *British Light Music*, Thames.

Seidenberg, Steven, Sellar, Maurice, and Jones, Lou (1995), *You Must Remember This*, Boxtree.

Self, Geoffrey (1986), *In Town Tonight (Eric Coates)*, Thames.

Self, Geoffrey (1995), *The Hiawatha Man*, Ashgate.

Shenton, Kenneth (1995), 'From A to B. Kenneth Alford and Hubert Bath', *British Music*, vol. 17, British Music Society.

Turner, Michael and Miall, Anthony (1982), *The Edwardian Song Book*, Methuen.

Upton, Stuart (1980), *Eric Coates: A Biographical Discography*, Vintage Light Music Society.

Upton, Stuart (1996), 'J.H. Squire – Musician and Adventurer', *Vintage Light Music*, issue 88, Vintage Light Music Society.

Vedey, Julian (1950), *Band Leaders*, Rockliff.

Venton, Alasdair (1996), 'Vivian Ellis – an Appreciation', *Vintage Light Music*, issue 88, Vintage Light Music Society.

Weightman, Gavin (1992), *Bright Lights, Big City (London Entertainment: 1830–1950)*, Collins & Brown.

Wetherell, Eric (1995), 'Gordon Jacob', *British Music*, vol. 17, British Music Society.

Wetherell, Eric (1995), *Gordon Jacob: A Centenary Biography*, Thames.
Young, Kenneth (1968), *Music's Great Days in the Spas and Watering Places*, Macmillan.

2. Subsidiary sources

Banfield, Stephen (1997), *Gerald Finzi*, Faber & Faber.
Bird, John (1976), *Percy Grainger*, Paul Elek.
Burton-Page, Piers (1994), *Philharmonic Concerto: the Life and Music of Sir Malcolm Arnold*, Methuen.
Celia, Mike (1992), 'Dorothy Howell (1898–1982)', *British Music*, vol. 14, British Music Society.
Cowen, Sir Frederick (1913), *My Art and My Friends*, London.
Cox, David (1980), *The Henry Wood Proms*, BBC.
Daubney, Brian Blyth (ed.) (1992), *Aspects of British Song*, British Music Society.
Gaisberg, Fred (1946), *Music on Record*, London.
Godfrey, Sir Dan (1924), *Memories and Music*, Hutchinson.
Grainger Society (1982), *Percy Grainger*, Schott & Co. Ltd.
Hughes, Spike (1946), *Opening Bars*, Pilot Press.
Kenyon, Nicholas (1981), *The BBC Symphony Orchestra. 1930–1980*, BBC.
Lebrecht, Norman (1992), *Music In London*, Aurum Press.
Lloyd, Stephen (1984), *H. Balfour Gardiner*, Cambridge.
Morrison, Angus (1993), 'Anyhow, about Walton and Lambert' (ed. Stan Meares), *British Music*, vol. 15, British Music Society.
Motion, Andrew (1986), *The Lamberts*, Chatto & Windus.
Shead, Richard (1973), *Constant Lambert*, Simon.
Thornton, Michael (1975), *Jessie Matthews*, Granada Publishing Ltd.
Wordsworth, David (1990), 'Sir Lennox Berkeley: A Tribute', *British Music*, vol. 12, British Music Society.

Societies and Relevant Organizations

Billy Mayerl Society
   Shellwood, St Leonard's Rd, Thames Ditton, Surrey KT7 0RN.
British Music Hall Society
   Wendy Lunn, 74 Turnpike Drive, Luton, Beds LU3 3RF.
British Music Society
   David Burkett, 30 Chester Rd, Watford WD1 7DQ.
Cinema Organ Society
   Andrew Paterson, 80 Merrylee Rd, Newlands, Glasgow G4 2QZ.
City of London Phonograph and Gramophone Society
   Suzanne Lewis, 51 Brockhurst Rd, Chesham, Bucks HP5 3JB.
Light Music Society
   Lancaster Farm, Chipping Lane, Longridge, Preston, Lancs, PR3 2NB.
London Billy Mayerl Society
   John Playle, 120 Ashcroft Square, London W6 0YN.
Percy Grainger Society
   Fairfax Crescent, Aylesbury, Bucks.
Percy Whitlock Trust
   32 Butcher Close, Staplehurst, Tonbridge, Kent TN12 0TJ.
Robert Farnon Society
   David Ades, Stone Gables, Upton Lane, Seavington St Michael, Ilminster, Somerset TA19 0PZ.
Sir Arthur Sullivan Society
   S.H. Turnbull, Cockfield House, 48 Front St, Bishop Auckland, Co. Durham DL1 5DS.
William Alwyn Society
   51 Bailey St, Old Basford, Nottingham, NG6 0HD.

General Index

Index of Music, Films and Literature Mentioned in the Text